21世纪商务英语系列教材

English Practical and Commercial
WRITING AND TRANSLATION
(Second Edition)

商务英语应用文写作与翻译
（第二版）

林　静　◎编著

北京大学出版社
PEKING UNIVERSITY PRESS

图书在版编目(CIP)数据

商务英语应用文写作与翻译/林静编著. —2版. —北京：北京大学出版社，2022.8
21世纪商务英语系列教材
ISBN 978-7-301-33315-0

Ⅰ.①商… Ⅱ.①林… Ⅲ.①商务–英语–应用文–写作–高等学校–教材②商务–英语–翻译–高等学校–教材 Ⅳ.①F7

中国版本图书馆CIP数据核字(2022)第160207号

书　　名	商务英语应用文写作与翻译(第二版)
	SHANGWU YINGYU YINGYONGWEN XIEZUO YU FANYI（DI-ER BAN）
著作责任者	林　静　编著
责任编辑	郝妮娜
标准书号	ISBN 978-7-301-33315-0
出版发行	北京大学出版社
地　　址	北京市海淀区成府路205号　100871
网　　址	http://www.pup.cn　　新浪微博:@北京大学出版社
电子信箱	bdhnn2011@126.com
电　　话	邮购部010-62752015　发行部010-62750672　编辑部010-62759634
印刷者	北京溢漾印刷有限公司
经销者	新华书店
	787毫米×1092毫米　16开本　15.25印张　490千字
	2007年10月第1版
	2022年8月第2版　2023年7月第2次印刷
定　　价	58.00元

未经许可，不得以任何方式复制或抄袭本书之部分或全部内容。
版权所有，侵权必究
举报电话: 010-62752024　电子信箱: fd@pup.pku.edu.cn
图书如有印装质量问题，请与出版部联系，电话: 010-62756370

第二版前言

当今社会，复合型人才炙手可热，尤其是我国成为世界贸易组织成员国之后，对外贸易必将迎来新的发展机遇，各行各业都需要大量的对外贸易人才。因此，许多非外贸金融专业的学生毕业后也很可能从事与外贸有关的工作或与外商打交道。在走出校门之前，在大学英语基础上，进一步学习外贸和金融英语，掌握常见的英语应用文写作，了解并学习有关的基础外贸金融知识，如国际上进出口商之间的支付方式和具体做法、常见英语外贸单证基本知识、英语合同写作与翻译等就成为绝大多数在校生及准毕业生们的实用的首选。

本书根据国内外大环境的需要，针对目前许多学生的现状而编写，内容包括（1）请假条、启事、推荐信、备忘录、简历、海报等常见并且实用的英语应用文写作要点及范例；（2）具有代表性的外贸信函的写作，如促销、订单、催改信用证及抱怨、争议、索赔等及其范例；（3）外贸合同的结构、文体特征及语言特点；（4）外贸合同的翻译原则及条款翻译；（5）信用证及信用证项下要求提交的装船文件介绍等。本书编写目的：本着快而有效的宗旨，普及外贸英语，拓宽学生的英语知识面，扩展英语词汇量，传授基础外贸金融知识，使学习者在一至两个学期内基本掌握英语外贸知识，熟悉常见的英语外贸单证；正确地理解并翻译英语外贸合同等，从而为他们今后顺利地进行外贸工作打下良好的专业基础。

本书自出版发行以来受到持续的好评和欢迎。因此，应北京大学出版社的要求，本书推出第二版。在第一版的基础上，作者对个别内容进行了更新与修改，增加了简历的写作技巧、范例及注意事项；"外贸合同的写作特点及翻译"部分增加了常用的商务英语词汇及其用法。此次再版最大的亮点是增加了一个对在校生很重要的部分：学术论文的英语写作。衷心地希望新版的问世能为在校生以及其他想了解、学习英语应用文写作及外贸商务英语的人士提供帮助和参考。

本书的作者林静老师是厦门大学外文学院副教授。长期教授非英语专业研究生的英语精读必修课及商务英语选修课课程。并有在美国圣地亚哥州立大学孔子学院任教两年的经历。也曾在英国威斯敏斯特大学进修过高级商务英语。在进修过程中，不仅在商务外贸专业知识上得到提高，也在应用文及商务合同所体现的英语文化方面有所领悟，并把它们编进《商务英语应用文写作与翻译》一书中。

本书在编写过程中，参考了国内外许多相关资料，也得到北京大学出版社外语编辑部的倾力相助，在此，一并向他们表示敬意和感谢。

CONTENTS

Part One   Secretarial Writings

Chapter 1   Note 3
    1. Definition 3
    2. Kinds of Notes 3
    3. Examples of Notes/Signs 3
    4. Writing Assignment 9

Chapter 2   Notice 10
    1. General Information 10
    2. The Writing Guide 10
    3. Model Expressions 10
    4. Examples of Various Notice 11
    5. Writing Assignment 16

Chapter 3   Poster 17
    1. What's a Poster ? 17
    2. The Writing Instruction 17
    3. Examples of Posters 17
    4. Writing Assignment 18

Chapter 4   Announcement 19
    1. General Information 19
    2. Model Expressions 19
    3. Examples of Various Announcements 19
    4. Writing Assignment 23

Chapter 5   Report 24
    1. General Information 24
    2. Model Expressions 24
    3. Examples of Business Reports 24
    4. Writing Assignment 27

Chapter 6　Memorandum (Memo) ································· 28

   1. Memo and the Structure ································· 28

   2. About the Writing ································· 28

   3. Examples of Memos ································· 28

   4. Writing Assignment ································· 30

Chapter 7　Agenda ································· 31

   1. Introduction of Agenda ································· 31

   2. Examples of Agendas ································· 31

   3. Some Expressions (of Amendments) ································· 33

Chapter 8　Minutes ································· 34

   1. Introduction of Minutes ································· 34

   2. The Written Form of Minutes ································· 34

   3. Examples of Minutes ································· 34

   4. Writing Assignment ································· 36

Chapter 9　Application ································· 37

   1. Tips of Writing a Job Application ································· 37

   2. How to Write an Application Effectively ································· 37

   3. Examples of Applications ································· 38

   4. Writing Assignment ································· 41

Chapter 10　Résumé ································· 43

   1. Introduction of Résumé ································· 43

   2. Examples of Résumés ································· 44

   3. Writing Assignment ································· 46

Chapter 11　Recommendation ································· 47

   1. The Contents Involved ································· 47

   2. The Usual Sentences in the Letter ································· 47

   3. Letter of Self-Recommendation ································· 47

   4. Examples of Recommendations ································· 47

Chapter 12　Letter of Introduction ································· 50

   1. Two Kinds of Introduction Letters ································· 50

   2. The Beginning Words of the Letter ································· 50

CONTENTS

    3. Examples of Official Letters ········· 51
    4. Examples of Personal Letters ········· 52
    5. Writing Assignment ········· 52

Chapter 13   Certificate ········· 53
    1. Introduction of Certificate ········· 53
    2. The Usual Expressions ········· 53
    3. Examples of Certificates ········· 53
    4. About Notarial Certificates ········· 55
    5. Commercial Certificates ········· 56
    6. Writing Assignment ········· 58

Chapter 14   Letter of Resignation ········· 59
    1. About the Writing ········· 59
    2. Example of a Letter of Resignation ········· 59
    3. Writing Assignment ········· 59

Chapter 15   Advertisement ········· 60
    1. Language Characteristics ········· 60
    2. Ads. in Purchases and Sales (with Chinese Translation) ········· 64
    3. Ads. for Vacancy ········· 65
    4. Usual Abbreviations in Ads. ········· 66
    5. Writing Assignment ········· 66

Chapter 16   Letter of Invitation ········· 67
    1. The Writing Skill ········· 67
    2. Expressions in Different Situation ········· 67
    3. Examples of Exhibition Invitations and Acknowledgements ········· 68
    4. Invitation Cards ········· 69
    5. Writing Assignment ········· 70

Chapter 17   Letter of Congratulation ········· 71
    1. The Writing of the Letter ········· 71
    2. Patterns and Expressions ········· 71
    3. Examples of Letters of Congratulation ········· 71
    4. Writing Assignment ········· 72
    5. Greeting Card ········· 72

Chapter 18　Others ·· 73
    1. University Codes of Behavior—More Information ··· 73
    2. Course Work ·· 74
    3. Tips to Keep Your Instructors Happy ·· 74

Part Two　Academic Paper Writing

Chapter 1　Ways of Preparation ·· 77

Chapter 2 ·· 79
    1. Learning Objectives ··· 79
    2. General Features ·· 79
    3. Major Sections ·· 79
    4. Acknowledgement ·· 90
    5. Reference/Bibliography ·· 91

Part Three　Business Letters

Chapter 1　Sales Promotion ·· 97
    1. The Purpose of Writing "Sales Letters" ··· 97
    2. How to Write a Good Sales Letter? ·· 97
    3. Examples of Sales Letters ··· 97
    4. Useful Sentences on Sales Promotion ··· 99

Chapter 2　Ordering ··· 100
    1. What's an Order? ··· 100
    2. The Quality of an Order/an Order-Letter ··· 100
    3. Examples of Ordering ··· 100
    4. Useful Sentences on Ordering ·· 102

Chapter 3　Urging, Examining and Amending L/C ······································· 103
    1. Urging the Establishment of L/C ·· 103
    2. Examining and Amending L/C ·· 105

Chapter 4　Complaints, Disputes and Claims ·· 108
    1. Why Do the Complaints Arise? ·· 108
    2. How to Write a Complaint or Claim Letter? ·· 108

3. How to Write Letters Concerning Disputes? ·· 108
4. Examples of Correspondence（Letters of Complaints, Disputes and Claims）··········· 108
5. Useful Sentences on Complaints, Disputes and Claims ······································ 111
6. Some Terms Used in Complaints, Disputes and Claims ···································· 112
7. Exercises ·· 113

Part Four   Contractual Writing and Translation

Chapter 1   What's a Contract？ ·· 117

Chapter 2   The Structure of a Contract ·· 118
1. Preamble of a Contract ·· 118
2. Body of a Contract ·· 118
3. Witness/Final Clause of a Contract ·· 120
4. The General Clauses Involved in a Contract Summed Up ································ 121

Chapter 3   Letter of Credit ·· 122
1. The Definition of L/C ··· 122
2. Kinds of L/Cs ·· 122
3. The Contents Involved in an L/C ·· 125
4. Useful Sentences on L/C ·· 129
5. Examples of 9 Kinds of L/Cs ·· 131
6. Shipping Documents Required under L/C ·· 143

Chapter 4   Stylistic Features of Contractual Writing ·· 164
1. Using Archaic Words ··· 164
2. Using Capitalization ·· 166
3. "Shall" in Legal English ··· 167
4. "Should" in Legal English ·· 167
5. Using Formal Words and Phrases ··· 167
6. Using Pairs of Synonyms ··· 169
7. Using "Include" and the Like ··· 169
8. Using "ONLY" ·· 169

Chapter 5   About Contractual Translation ··· 170
1. Specific Criteria for Contractual Translation ·· 170
2. Confusing Synonyms ··· 170

3. More Examples of Words with Multi-interpretations ················ 171
4. Exercises ················ 176

Chapter 6 Translation of the Frequent Clauses in a Contract ················ 177
1—16. Clauses and Their Translations ················ 177
17. Exercises ················ 186

Chapter 7 Contracts and Agreements ················ 189
1. Sales and Purchase Contracts ················ 189
2. Sales Agency Agreement ················ 199
3. Consignment Agreement ················ 204
4. Compensation Trade Contract ················ 206

Appendices

Ⅰ. Reference Key to Writing Assignments ················ 213
Ⅱ. Reference Key to Part Four, Chapter 6 ················ 218
Ⅲ. Reference Translation of Some Contracts (Part Four, Chapter 7) ················ 220
Ⅳ. A List of Abbreviations and Simplified Words Commonly Used in Trading Documents ················ 223
Ⅴ. Frequent Words and Phrases in Foreign Trade ················ 228
Ⅵ. References ················ 234

PART ONE

SECRETARIAL WRITINGS

CHAPTER 1 Note

1. Definition

(1) A note is a short *letter*;

(2) A note is a short *comment*;

(3) A note is a *notice/sign* or *attention*.

2. Kinds of Notes

(1) Message

(2) Leave or Absent Permits

√ Sick Leave

√ Private Affair Leave

(3) Notice as Public Signs/Signs and Notes

√ Notes in Buses/Coaches

√ Notes in Tubes/Trains

√ Notes in Airport

√ Safety Instructions in Airplane

√ Notes in Public Places

√ Notes of Telephones

√ Notes in Shops

3. Examples of Notes / Signs

(1) **Message**留言/便条

留言/便条是一种简单的书信形式,内容简要、文字紧凑、形式不拘。多数为本人留言或托人转交,很少用信封。

Example 1

8:30 A. M.

Dear Peter,

　　I have done all my things here. I sincerely thank you for the trouble you have taken for my sake. I am leaving for home by train at two this afternoon. This is to say good-bye to you.

Please kindly remember me to your wife.

Yours ever,
Jack

Example 2

Thursday

Dear William,

　　Mr. White of the ABC Company has rung up saying that he will call on you tomorrow afternoon.

Mike

　　(2) **Leave or Absent Permits** 请假条

请假条是便条的一种，相当于一种便条或短信，无论在学校或在职场都难免要用到。请假条主要有Sick Leave（病假条），Private Affair Leave（事假条）等。格式通常包括日期、称呼、正文和署名等内容。

√ **Sick Leave**

Example 1

March 2, 2021

Dear Sir,

　　Owing to a bad cold, I'm unable to attend classes today. I now submit a medical certificate issued by the doctor.

　　Hoping you can excuse my non-attendance.

Yours respectfully,
Liu Kun

Example 2

May 17, 2021

Dear Mr. Pike,

　　I very much regret I was unable to attend school this morning owing to a severe attack of illness. I am enclosing here with a certificate from the doctor who is attending me, as he fears it will be several days before I shall be able to resume my study. I trust my enforced absence will not give you any serious inconvenience.

Yours Sincerely,
Jack

√ Private Affair Leave

Example 1

Machinery Engineering Department
Class 5
Sep.15, 2021

Dear Mr. Wang,

  As my Canadian friend is flying home tomorrow, I have to see her off. I shall be very obliged if you will grant me my application for one day's leave tomorrow.

Yours respectfully,
Chen Hua

Example 2

To: John Smith, Supervisor
From: George Chen, Accounting Department
Date: March 11, 2021
Subject: Casual Leave of Absence

  John, I would like to know if I could ask for a casual leave of absence from March 22 to 26.

  Yesterday I received a letter from my parents, who are both over 70, telling me that a big flood took place at my home village, causing serious damage to my house. As the only son of my parents, I should be back to assess the situation, and help them to get over these difficulties.

  Though I cannot stay at home for too long a time, I should at least make arrangements for repair work. I believe my relatives in the village and my neighbors will also come to help. Financially I have no difficulties.

  I will call you at 1:30 p.m. or you can call me at any time.

（3）**Notice as Public Signs / Signs and Notes** 标示/提示语

标示/提示语的写作特征是简洁，采用祈使、命令语气，起着提醒、指示的作用。

◆ The simplicity is most appreciated for public signs when acting as warning.

◆ Tips:

  Impersonal tone and positive tone may be preferable as those sound more friendly and

pleasant.
- ◆ Signs make people be aware of something.
- ◆ There are three types of signs: signs for forbidden or obligation, signs for warning and signs for indication or direction.

√ Notes/Signs in Buses/Coaches

In emergency, break glass. (on the bus window)

In case of fire, stay in vehicle.

Keep your belongings with you at all times.

The light indicates the door is not secured.

These seats are meant for elderly and handicapped persons & women with child.

This coach is for holders of full fare.

When the bus is moving, do not speak to the driver.

With permission, but at owner's risk.

√ Notes/Signs in Tubes/Trains

Please keep feet off seats.

Help us to keep the tube litter free.

Luggage must not be put in the gateway.

Please keep gateways clear.

Stand clear of the door.

To ensure punctuality, this barrier may be closed up to one minute prior to departure of each train.

√ Notes/Signs in Airport

Airport lounges

Airports shuttle

Check in area (zone)

Departure airport

Departure times on reverse

Exit to all routes

Flight connections

Help point (desk) / Inquiries

Left baggage

Lost property

Luggage from flights

Luggage pick up / Luggage reclaim

Nothing / Something to declare

Passport control

Reclaim belt

No smoking! No photographing!

No water! No perfume! No fruit! No liquid!

√ Safety Instructions in Airplane

When the plane is taking off and landing, return seat back and tray table to the upright position. Fasten the seat belt.

When the oxygen mask falls down, pull it toward you. Cover your nose and mouth. Adult first then children. No open flames.

Brace position and lights located on the floor will guide you to the exists if an emergency arises.

Life vest is under your seat. Slip it over your head and fasten the buckle.

Do not touch any emergency equipment with red marks except in emergency.

Please refrain from smoking during the whole flight Mobile phones, AM/FM radios, televisions and remote control equipment must not be used on board at any time. Life vest under your seat. Fasten seat belt while seated.

√ Notes / Signs in Shops

Open for business as usual.

Opening soon.

Hours of opening.

Computers in stock.

For more information, contact our customer service desk.

Please ask for assistance.

Please check your change before leaving the checkout area.

Please retain this receipt as proof of your purchase and your guarantee.

Please leave bags at the counter.

Services as usual.

Fill in your selection here and take to a pay point.

Thank you for your custom.

√ Notes / Signs of Telephones

London currently has three phone codes: 020 3, 020 7 and 020 8.

Last Number Recall

If you want to find out the number of the last person who called you, dial 1471.

Directory Enquiries

Dial 118 5000. Using the Directory Enquiry service is free if you call from a phone box. If you're using a private phone the charges are high.

Operator Services

Always dial direct if possible as call connections by an operator are very expensive. Call 100 to speak to an operator if you're having difficulty getting through, for an early morning alarm call, and to make credit card calls. Dial 155 if you need to reverse the charges (so the person who receives the call pays!)

Phonecards

Prepaid phonecards, which use a scratch-card to reveal your PIN (Personal Identification Number) are often the cheapest way of making international calls. They are available from newsagents.

Public Phones

Public pay phones take coins, credit cards or prepaid phonecards (and sometimes all three). The minimum cost is 20p.

EMERGENCY PHONE NUMBER
For Fire, Police or Ambulance

Phone 999

√ Notes / Signs in Other Public Places

No Entry!

No Way Out.

No Parking!

Not to Be Laid Flat!

Not for Sale.

Cycling Prohibited!

Automatic Cleaning.

Danger!Keep Out!

Hands Off!

Admission By Ticket Only.

Caution: Not A Weight Bearing On Surface.

All Bags Must Be Checked.

Keep Off the Grass.

Commit No Nuisance!

Dangerous When Wet.

VIP Lounge.

Private Park.

No Thoroughfare.

Keep Right.

Road Ahead Closed.

School Ahead, Use No Horn.

Sorry! No Fishing Here.

Wet Paint.

Not Available For Loan.

Buckle Up. It's Law.

We Accept No Responsibility for the Loss of Any Article the Customers Leave Here.

Queue Up here for Tickets.

This Side Up.

Positively No Admittance.

√ Notes in Magdalen College of Oxford University

Please:

Do Not walk on the grass or picnic in the grounds.

Do Not leave any litter.

Do Not enter any rooms or staircases or areas marked Private.

Be as quiet as possible, remembering that people are working here throughout the year.

Obey all notices.

Do not smoke.

Take care some paths and steps are uneven.

4. Writing Assignment***

Write a short note to Mr. Max Remington, the Public Relation's manager.

Ask for an advertisement for two translators.

Explain the reason.

Mention your urgency.

Write 30—40 words.

CHAPTER 2 Notice

1. General Information

通知就是用书信(letter)或布告(bulletin)的形式把要做的事或已发生的事告知给一定的对象。如会议通知、讲座通知、内部装修通知等。

通知大致分为三种：第一种是布告牌上的通知；第二种是写给目的读者看的通知；第三种是发表在刊物上的通知。

2. The Writing Guide

通知是要放在引人注目的地方，这样人们就很容易天天看到它(们)。字体应该写得大些，形式及内容都要有吸引力并且保持时新。它的写作特点是尽可能简洁、清楚地写明通知的事情及与该通知有关的人物、地点和时间等。

对于写在布告牌上的通知，要采用尽可能简单的词汇，因为此类通知的读者群文化水平不一，并且此类通知的措词要尽可能简洁，因为读者可能没有很多时间停留下来看你的通知。

另外，高分贝的电视商业广告，以及报刊杂志的大幅标题已使现代的人们不太可能去注意写得不起眼的通知了。因此，想使你的通知能吸引人们的眼球，使人们愿驻足观看，要特别注意标题或开头句的写法。

3. Model Expressions

We / I inform you that...

We have the honor to inform you that...

We announce you that...

We acquaint you that...

Please take note that...

PART ONE SECRETARIAL WRITINGS

4. Examples of Various Notice

Example 1

NOTICE OF STAFF MEETING

Sep. 10, 2021

All the staffs are required to be ready to attend the meeting in the conference hall on Wednesday, at 3:00 pm, Sep. 13, 2021, to discuss the teaching plans in the new semester and welcome the new teachers.

Office of Foreign Languages Department

Example 2

NOTICE OF SALES MEETING

To: all salesmen
Subject: the year-end sales meeting
From: Li Hua, secretary
The first sales meeting for 2021 will be held on Friday, April 9th 9:00 a. m. at the head office.
Lunch will be provided.
The agenda will be mailed by the end of March.
If you have any items to be present, please call 87654321 not later than March 29th.
Thank you.

Example 3

Notice of a Newly Established Branch

Dear Sirs,

We are pleased to inform you that on account of rapid increase in the volume of our trade with the United States, we have decided to open a new branch at 222 Broadway, New York City, with Mr. Zhang Xiaodong in charge.

We wish to take this opportunity to express our appreciation for your custom in the past and hope the establishment of the new branch will lead to higher standards in the service we provide.

Yours faithfully,
× × × Company

Example 4

Notice of Changing Address

On and after the 6th January, 2021—the office of Messrs. Mackinnon, Mackenzie & Co., Ltd., at 8, Nichome, Marunouchi, Tokyo will be closed and all communications addressed to this firm in future should be made to No.1—C, Yamashitacho, Yokohama.

Example 5*

Notice of Rememberance Service

Dear University of Westminster Staff and Students,

To mark the anniversary of the bombings, 7 July 2006, 12:30 pm, St. Pancras Church, an Euston Road near Euston Station, will be holding a multifaith remembrance service, with music and readings from all of the major religions. This is a public event, lasting for about one hour. All are welcome.

(注：这是一则纪念2005年夏天伦敦地铁爆炸案一周年的通知。英国是一个多信仰的国家，不同信仰的人可以在同一个教堂里举行纪念仪式，朗读各自所信仰宗教的经文并播放圣乐。)

Example 6*

Lunchtime Lectures
In the Wood Lecture Theatre at 1pm

Wednesday, 11 August

An Introduction to London

This first talk is to welcome you to London our capital city, how it is made up, a brief history, and to introduce you to some of the people that have influenced the make-up of London that we see today.

Reg Parks *Visiting Lecturer and Blue Badge Guide*

Example 7*

Lunchtime Lectures

In the Wood Lecture Theatre at 1pm

Friday, 13 August

The British University System

Hear about the differences between the universities of Oxbridge (Oxford and Cambridge), the red-brick and the new universities like Westminster. The talk will give you a basic understanding of the British education system and an introduction to the visit to Oxford University.

Edward Lee *Visiting Lecturer and City of London guide*

Example 8*

Lunchtime Lectures

In the Wood Lecture Theatre at 1pm

Tuesday, 17 August

The History of the Mystery

Kiki Olson explains why Bloody England is still the best place for a bloody murder. We will trace the history of the mystery from Edgar Allen Poe to Agatha Christie's Golden Age, and to the 1950s hardboiled PIs (private investigators). We look into the future of international mysteries and everyone attending will be able to take a book home.

Kiki Olson *Visiting Lecturer and Book Reviewer*

(注：以上三个都是关于"午餐演讲"的通知，表达形式特别。)

Example 9*

April 2, 2021

Dear Miss Chen,

 Thank you for coming in for an interview last Monday. Today I'm writing to inform you that we have decided to offer you employment with us as an assistant sales manager, as of May 1 this year. Congratulations!

 To confirm your acceptance of this employment offer, will you please forward the following documents to us by separate mail by April 15? Please be reminded that failure to forward these documents by this date could result in the cancellation of this employment offer.

　　√ Your letter of acceptance of this employment offer;

　　√ One copy of your birth certificate;

　　√ Two copies of your full resume.

　　As soon as we receive the above documents from you, I'll write to you again to let you know when you are to come to the office for further details.

　　Best Regards,

Wu Jun

Director, Personnel Department

(注：这是一则书信形式的聘用通知)

Example 10

Temporary Suspension of Television Broadcasting

23 July, 2021

Dear Guests,

　　Kindly be advised that for regular maintenance of our Hotel equipment, television broadcasting for all guest rooms will be suspended on 26 July 2021 from 2:30 pm to 3:30 pm.

　　Should you have any queries, please feel free to contact our Assistant Manager at Ext. 3003.

　　We apologize for any inconvenience that may be caused and we wish you a pleasant stay with us.

The Management

Panda Hotel

Example 11

Ongoing Renovation

Dear Guest,

A warm welcome to the New Century Hotel—We do hope that you have a pleasant stay with us.

In order to provide you a higher standard service, the Hotel is undertaking renovation work from 10 am to 8 pm daily to upgrade the facilities. We have given strict guideline to our contractors. So as to create least inconvenience to our guests.

PART ONE SECRETARIAL WRITINGS

We sincerely apologize for any inconvenience that may cause and your kind indulgence is much appreciated. Should you have any queries, please do not hesitate to contact our Assistant Manager at Extension 3.

Best regards,
The Hotel Management

Example 12*

Health and Safety Notice

In the interest of Health and Safety, this window has been set to tilt open, horizontally only.

It is an offence to:

(1) Tamper with the lock of this window

(2) Open the window at right angles

(3) Throw any objects out of this window

(4) Tamper with this notice Penalties

Penalties for non-compliance of this notice include

(a) Disciplinary action being taken

(b) Changes for any damage and lock replacement

(c) Eviction proceedings being instigated

(注：这是一则贴在英国Westminster大学学生公寓窗旁的通知/告示。英国许多窗子都是水平斜开[set to tilt open, horizontally only]，不能以直角[at right angles]开。)

Example 13*

The University of Westminster's Library Notice

Even if you don't read other library notice, please read this one about Library Sanctions and how to avoid them.

Return or renew your books on time

Risk: A ban on any further loans

Don't break the rules on behavior.

Risk: A 3-week computing library ban

Make sure you have everything properly issued to you before you leave the Library.

> Risk: A disciplinary hearing
>
> Check your record is clear at the end of your course.
>
> No degree certificate or invitation to graduation
>
> We want you to find out about rules the easy way, not the hard way.

(注：以上是两则典型的西方式的告示，它们更多地是告知人们不要做什么以及违反规定的后果，如Sample 12的"It is an offence to..."和Sample 13的"Don't"和"Risk"。)

5. Writing Assignment

Write a notice for display on your company's notice board announcing the forthcoming visit of a VIP (you may decide who the person is to be) to the company and appealing for the cooperation of all staff to make his visit a successful one.

CHAPTER 3 Poster

1. What's a Poster?

海报是贴在人来人往的地方，大多是告知广大群众喜闻乐见的消息，如电影、戏剧消息、球讯、文体活动、学术活动、商品报道等的招贴，其性质类似广告，有时配上各种画面来增加吸引力。

2. The Writing Instruction

海报可以说也是一种通知，介于通知与广告之间，因此标题或主题句的选择十分重要，另外，用词要求简洁、有新意。

写海报时，往往在正中写海报标题内容，如："Film News"，"English Evening"，"Recital"等，正文部分说明活动内容、时间、地点和活动的参加办法，主办单位等。出海报的单位署名要求放在右下角。

3. Examples of Posters

Example 1

GOOD NEWS
Summer Clearance Sales

All the goods on show are sold at twenty percent discount. Please examine and choose them carefully before you pay. There will be no replacement or refunding. You have been warned in advance. You are welcome to make your choice.

Personal Shopping Service

Example 2

Poster of Performance

　　The Foreign Language Department takes pleasure in announcing its foreign literacy and artist report performance, to be held in Jiannan Auditorium on Sep.18, 2021, at 3 p.m. The programme includes chorus, solo, dance, recitation and skit. All the teachers and students are warmly welcome.

Sep. 15, 2021

Example 3

STAMP-COLLECTORS MEET

In Miss Zhang's Office

ON TUESDAY, 24 AUGUST AT 5:00 P.M.

August 22, 2021

Example 4

THE OPERA

HOURS

A

PRODUCTION

OF

"MADAM BUTTERFLY"

Tues., Jan. 5, 7:15 p.m.

4. Writing Assignment

(1) Write a poster about a lecture.

(2) Write an English Poster on a Football Match according to the following message.***

足 球 赛

　　由本校学生会主办的足球友谊赛将于2021年2月28日(星期日)下午4时在足球场举行，参赛队为我校队与化工学院队。欢迎届时观战。

校学生会
2月25日(星期四)

CHAPTER 4 Announcement

1. General Information

启事是一种公告性的应用文。机关、团体或个人向他人公开说明某事或请求帮助，或对群众有什么要求，可把要说的意思简要地写成启事。启事有多种，如寻人/物启事、招领启事、征婚启事、订婚启事、开业启事、换址启事、招聘启事等等。

2. Model Expressions

- √ We / I inform you that...
- √ We have the honor to inform you that...
- √ We announce you that...
- √ We wish to notify you that
- √ We acquaint you that...
- √ Please take note that...
- √ Notice is hereby given that...

3. Examples of Various Announcements

(1) 寻物启事

Example

A Jacket Lost

In the playground, May 12, a jacket, red in color and with a zipper in the collar lost, please return it to the owner, Lin Li, Room 203, Dormitory 9. Thanks

Owner, Lin Li

---

(2) 招领启事

Example

> **Found**
>
> I happened to find a purse, inside which there are banknotes, credit cards and some cash... Loser is expected to come to classroom 201 to claim it.
>
> Finder, Li Nan

(3) 新的任命

Example

> Dear Mr./Ms...,
>
> We wish to notify you that Mr. Robert Smart, who has been our representative in Southwest England for the past seven years has left our service and therefore no longer has authority to take orders or collect accounts on our behalf.
>
> We have appointed Mr. Fred Harmer in his place. Mr. Harmer has for many years been on our sales force and is thoroughly familiar with the needs of customers in your area. We trust you will have good cooperation from him.

(4) 征婚启事

Example

> **SEEKING A SPOUSE**
>
> Robert Blake, a young bachelor of 30, graduate of Northern Illinois University, lecturer of New York Teachers College, nonsmoker, nondrinker, own home with pool, interested in sports, literature, music and outdoor life, seeks honest, quiet, warm and sincere female for long-term relationship. Photo appreciated. All letters and calls are to be answered. Visits unnecessary. If interested, please contact:
>
> Tel: 8719357
>
> P.O. Box: 793, local

(5) 订婚启事

Example

> **NOTICE/ANNOUNCEMENT OF ENGAGEMENT**
>
> Mr. and Mrs. Holand Walshman have the honor to announce the engagement of their daughter, Miss Lucy Walshman, to Mr. Samual Russell on Saturday, August 21, 2021.

(荷兰德·沃尔什曼先生及夫人荣幸地宣布，他们的小女露西·沃尔什曼与塞穆尔·罗素先生于2021年8月21日订婚，兹特敬告亲友。)

(6) 结婚启事

Example

WEDDING ANNOUNCEMENT

Miss Lucy Brown

And

Mr. John Stephen

Announce their wedding

On Sunday, September 19, 2021

At St. John's Cathedral, Hong Kong

---

(7) 招聘启事

Example

POSITION VACANT

Experienced Bank Accountant—with good knowledge of Western financial accounting (fluent English as added asset). Application in detail with photo taken within this year to China Merchants Bank, Chengdu Branch at 31 College Road.

(注: fluent English as added asset 英语流利者优先录取)

(8) 开业启事

Example

Announcement of a Newly Established Branch

Dear Sirs,

　　We are pleased to inform you that on account of rapid increase in the volume of our trade with the United States, we have decided to open a new branch at 222 Broadway, New York City, with Mr. Zhang Xiaodong in charge.

　　We wish to take this opportunity to express our appreciation for your custom in the past and hope the establishment of the new branch will lead to higher standards in the service we provide.

Yours faithfully,

×××Company

(9) 换址启事

Example

Announcement of Changing Address

On and after the 6th January, 2021—the office of Messrs. Mackinnon, Mackenzie & Co., Ltd., at 8, Nichome, Marunouchi, Tokyo will be closed and all communications addressed to this firm in future should be made to No.1—C, Yamashitacho, Yokohama.

(10) 歇业启事

Example

Dear Mr./Ms...

With the demolition of our premises at the above address under a redevelopment scheme, the part of our business carried on there will be discontinued after the end of October.

On Friday, 1st October, we are holding a closing-out sale. Stock on hand will be cleared regardless of cost. There will be substantial reductions in all departments and in some cases, prices will be marked down by as much as one half.

Stock to be cleared is unrivaled in both variety and quality. As the sale is likely to be well attended, we hope you make a point of visiting the store as early as possible during the opening days.

Yours faithfully,
James Harmer

(注: demolition 破坏; closing-out 抛售; stock on hand 现存货; marked down 标低价格)

公司解散与停业的多种表达:

√ We <u>inform</u> you that the partnership existing between us in the business of wool has this day been <u>dissolved</u> by mutual consent.

√ <u>Notice</u> is hereby given that the copartnership which has existed between Mr. Black and Mr. Brown under the style of Black, Brown & Co., has been <u>dissolved</u> by agreement.

√ We <u>announce</u> that on and after the 1st March the partnership existing between Mr. Black & Mr. Brown, trading as Balck, Brown & Co., will be <u>dissolved</u>.

√ We <u>advise</u> you that we have by mutual agreement decided to <u>dissolve</u> partnership.

√ The partnership hitherto existing between us under the style of B. & Co., having been <u>dissolved</u> by mutual consent, the business in future will be carried on by Mr. J. S.

√ We <u>advise</u> you that we have, by mutual agreement, decided <u>not to continue</u> our partnership.

PART ONE   SECRETARIAL WRITINGS

√ In consequence of the <u>dissolution</u> of partnership, the undersigned gives notice that he has taken over the interests and responsibility of the late firm of R.S. & Co.

√ We <u>inform</u> you that our partnership is this day <u>dissolved</u>, and that in future, our firm and our branch in Yokohama, will be used in <u>liquidation</u> only.

√ The term of our copartnership with Messrs. Shiba & Co., of Kobe, having expired on the 30th April, it was decided that the same should <u>not be renewed</u>.

√ The partnership will be <u>discontinued</u> owing to the retirement of Mr. Yokoi.

√ On account of the death of our partner, Mr. Gotoh, our business carried on under the name of Gotoh & Co., <u>will be discontinued</u> from the 1st March.

√ <u>Notice</u> is hereby given that the copartnership which has for some time existed between J.G. and T.C. under the style and title of G.C. & Co., has been <u>discontinued</u> by agreement.

√ The term of our copartnership with Messrs. M. & Co., of O. having <u>expired</u> on the 31st December last, it was decided by consent of all the parties concerned, that the same should <u>not be renewed</u>.

4. Writing Assignment

(1) Write an announcement about the Removal of a Company.

(2) Write an announcement about Looking for the Lost Mobile. ***

(3) Write an announcement about the Dissolution & Discontinuation of Business.

CHAPTER 5 Report

1. General Information

报告是一种对某事件或形势所做的描述；是就某一专题向一定的目标听众做系统的讲述。报告多用无人称主语，开头多用This report is to (aims to) ...，中间多用It is suggested that...; It is felt that...等等。注意不用缩略语。

2. Model Expressions

√ Here is the report about...

√ Following is the annual report...

√ The objective / purpose of this report is to...

√ This report includes...

√ Work in progress is as follows:

√ Accordingly, the following recommendations are offered:

√ I'd like to submit this report to you for your reference.

√ The progress that has been reported up to this point includes the following:

3. Examples of Business Reports

Example 1

Proposal Report

From: Public Relations Manager

To: General Manager

Date: 20th August, 2021

PART ONE   SECRETARIAL WRITINGS

Report on the English Standard of Our Promotional Materials

1. Terms of Reference

According to your instructions of 25th July 2021, to report on the English standard of our promotional materials, including brochures, leaflets, speeches and advertisements and to make recommendation.

2. Procedures

150 pieces of promotional materials were examined. They include 50 brochures, 40 leaflets, 30 speeches and 30 advertisements.

Each piece of material was assigned a grade according to their content, language readability and grammatical accuracy.

3. Findings

Only 20 pieces of articles were classified as excellent, 40 pieces as good and 60 as acceptable, the rest, 30, were regarded as below standard and unclassified.

4. Conclusion

It is clear that the English proficiency of our marketing staff is far from satisfactory.

5. Recommendation

Based on the above findings, I recommended that we should:

Set up a special course designed to develop writing skills for all marketing staff. Special emphasis should be placed on promotional materials subscribe to an English editing house with experienced editors to do English polishing and basic edits on the above mentioned materials.

If you think these ideas are feasible, I would be glad to assist in implementing the programme.

（注：brochure 小册子；subscribe to 预订）

Example 2

Directors' Report

April 30, 2021

Dear Sir or Madam,

During the year, although we met with many difficulties, we were still able to maintain the steady increase in our profits. The following is the account for the year under review:

Net Profit	￥6,000,000
Amount brought forward from last year	￥800,00
Total Profit	￥6,800,000
Interim Dividend	￥100,000

25

Balance	￥6,700,000

The Directors recommend to appropriate this balance as follows:

General Reserves	￥2,000,000
Final Dividend	￥3,700,000
Amount be carried forward	￥1,000,000
Total	￥6,700,000

　　The Directors retiring by rotation are Mr. Wu Dashan and Ms. Jiang Xiaoli, both of whom take part in re-election.

　　The auditors of the Company, Jiang Fang and Zhao Chuan want to serve us in the coming year and the resolution as to their remuneration will be made at the meeting.

By Order of the Board
Wang Jun

　　(注: fiscal year 财政年度; amount brought forward from 余额; interim dividend 中期分红; balance 余额; appropriate 分配; retiring by rotation 任期已满; auditors 审计员; remuneration 报酬)

Example 3

A Report of Customer Service (in the form of email)

Diane,

　　We have some serious customer service problems that need to be addressed. Below are the three most critical problems and my suggested solutions:

　　Problem 1: fifteen percent rise in the number of shipping mistakes in the past six months.

　　Solution: expand training to 20 hours a month for the next three months.

　　Problem 2: twenty five percent rise in absenteeism (缺席) among customer service representatives in the past six months.

　　Solution: meet with each employee who has missed five or more workdays in a single month.

　　Problem 3: antiquated (过时的) customer management software.

　　Solution: invest $75,000 in CMX, the latest customer management package.

Sincerely,
Moises

4. Writing Assignment

Your department has recently introduced some new equipment. Your manager has asked you to write a report analyzing the effects this equipment has had on the department.

Write your report, including the following information:

(1) a brief description of the new equipment;

(2) the reason(s) it was introduced;

(3) the benefits it has brought to the department;

(4) any problems it has caused;

(5) write 200—250 words.

CHAPTER 6 Memorandum (Memo)

1. Memo and the Structure

备忘录是用于各部门之间,以提醒、督促对方做某事。与报告不同的是,备忘录一般由六部分组成:

(1) Memo或Memorandum, 或内部备忘录(Internal Memorandum), 办公室间备忘录 (Inter-office Memorandum) 字样位于页首正中。

(2) 接受人 (To)

(3) 发文人 (From)

(4) 日期 (Date)

(5) 主题 (Subject)

(6) 正文 (Message)

通过阅读备忘录的标题栏,我们就可以清楚该备忘录的主要内容和相关信息。

2. About the Writing

备忘录写作应简洁明确地写明备忘录的目的、事由、原因、期限等。备忘录正文后面不再需要结束语和落款。

3. Examples of Memos

Example 1

MEMO

To: Department Managers

From: Juan Stevenson

Date: Nov. 30th

Subject: Answers to the Questions about Use of Temporary Help

1. Please answer the questions below about the use of temporary help in your department. With your ideas we plan to develop a policy that will help us improve the process of budgeting, selecting, and hiring temporaries. What is the average number of temporary

office workers you employ each year?

2. What specific job skills are you generally seeking in your temporaries?
3. What temporary agencies are you now using?

   Just write your answers on this sheet, and return it to me before March 20. By the end of the month, we plan to have an improved policy that will fill your temporary employment needs as efficiently as possible.

Example 2

MEMORANDUM

From: A.C. Bleakly, General Manager
To: J. Mackay, Deputy General Manager
　　B. Willis, Chief Accountant
　　F.G. Brown, Staff Manager
　　X. Gonzalez, Factory Manager
Ref. OG./3/7
Date: 3rd May, 2021

VISIT OF MR. CARL G. SCHULZ

1. Mr. Carl G. Schulz, President of World Business Machines Inc., will visit the Company on 3rd and 4th February, 2021. As previously discussed with you, the following arrangements have been made for his visit.
2. He will arrive at the Company's premises at 10:00 a.m. on 3rd February and be met by me and Mr. Mackay. After discussions, he will have lunch with me, Mr. Mackay and Mr. Willis in the Executive Mess.
3. After lunch Mr. Willis will take him to the Accounts Section and discuss our accounting procedure with him. It is expected that he will be in the Accounts Section till about 4:30 p.m. Mr. Willis should take the opportunity to introduce him to those of his staff he considers appropriate.
4. He will return to the Company's premises at 1:00 a.m. on 4th February and be met by Mr. Brown who will conduct him around the Company Training Unit and introduce him to the staff there.
5. He will have lunch in the Executive Mess with me, Mr. Brown and Mr. Gonzalez.
6. Mr. Gonzalez will company him on a visit to the Factory after lunch and introduce him to those of his staff he considers appropriate. He will then ring him back to the Company premises by 5:00 p.m., when I shall take him back to his hotel.

7. Will you all please attend the dinner that the Company is giving Mr. and Mrs. Schulz with your wives at 7:00 p.m. on 4th February in the Criterion Restaurant.

8. I will be grateful if you all do your utmost to make Mr. Schulz's visit a pleasant and informative one.

4. Writing Assignment

1) 请就以下情况写篇120字左右的备忘录(Management Development): ***

 (1) 备忘录是由董事长Carl Johnson写给副董事长Jim Hillman.

 (2) 我们需要培训自己的管理人员，请拟好公司内部管理培训计划。

 (3) 假设课程持续10周，每周4小时；同时假设受训人员没有任何管理经验。

 (4) 培训应达到一流水平。

2) A memo (note) writing

Directions:

 (1) You are the training manager of a company which has won a large-export order. You have been asked to organize a foreign language training for some of your staff.

 (2) Write a memo of 40—50 words to staff.

 (3) Explain why the courses are necessary.

 (4) Say which members of staff should attend.

 (5) Announce when the courses will start.

CHAPTER 7 Agenda

1. Introduction of Agenda

会议议程是指在会议上各项内容的安排。会议议程有助于与会者就要讨论的事务做好准备,有助于会议有条不紊的进行,提高开会效率。典型的大型会议议程主要有以下内容:

- √ 宣布会议开始　　　　　　Call to Order
- √ 点名　　　　　　　　　　Roll Call
- √ 宣布会议法定人数　　　　Announcement of Quorum
- √ 宣读上次会议记录　　　　Reading of Minutes from the Previous Meeting
- √ 通过上次会议记录　　　　Approval of Minutes from the Previous Meeting
- √ 会议主席发言　　　　　　Chairperson's Report
- √ 与会者发言　　　　　　　Subcommittee Report
- √ 讨论未完成事务　　　　　Unfinished Business
- √ 讨论新的事务　　　　　　New Business
- √ 宣布下次会议的日期　　　Announcement of the Date for Next Meeting
- √ 宣布会议结束　　　　　　Adjournment

2. Examples of Agendas

Example 1

Apologies for absence

Minutes of the meeting held on 25th June, 2021 (copies circulated)

Matters arising from the minutes:

　　　Minute 4 should be amended as follows: for "80%" read "85%"

　　　Minute 1—Mr. White's report on the market survey

Winter promotion plans

To review last month's sales record

Date of next meeting

Other business

Example 2

San Francisco Bay Area Chamber of Commerce
Agenda for Monthly Board Meeting

To be held on Monday, June 7, 2021 at 2:00 p.m.
At the Grand Hotel, Level 5, Conference Room,
516 Main Street, San Francisco Bay.

1. Attendance
2. Minutes of the May Board Meeting
3. Unfinished Business
4. New Business
   Chairman's Update Results of Fundraising Annual Luncheon
   Membership Report
5. General Business
6. Vote of Thanks and Adjournment

Example 3

Agenda

Management Training Center
Tuesday, March 9, 2021
Room 521
Kunlun Hotel
9:00 a.m.

1. Call to order: Mr. Han Xianhua, President
2. Consideration of the Minutes for February 7, 2004: Miss Ninglin, Secretary
3. President's report: Mr. Han Xianhua
4. Vice President's report: Mr. Duangang
5. Committee's reports:
   5.1 Mr. Yang Mingda, Financial Direactor
   5.2 Mr. Li Jiandong, Technical Director
   5.3 Ms. Wuli, Personnel Director
   5.4 Mr. Deng Zhihui, Director of Research and Development
   5.5 Mr. Guo Fengting, Director of Sales and Marketing

6. Unfinished business

7. New business

8. Adjournment

3. Some Expressions (of Amendments)

...for "80%" read "85%" (80%应改成85%)

Para.2, Line 3, should read...

Line 1 to read...

...should be amended to read...

...delete

...should be deleted to read...

...delete as irrelevant / inapplicable

...not applicable and should therefore be deleted

CHAPTER 8 Minutes

1. Introduction of Minutes

会议记录是记录会议的主要内容，会后分发给与会者(或应该出席的人)。缺席者也可以通过会议记录了解会上的决定。

2. The Written Form of Minutes

√ when and where 在报告会议当中，一般一开始就要明确日期、时间与地址。

√ who 注明谁出席了会议也很重要。

√ what 是记录的主体，应该记录下讨论的主要线索，记录在会上提出的建议及投票的结果。如果下次会议的时间地点做了安排，那么也应包括在内。

3. Examples of Minutes

Example 1

Ultradine Company

Minutes of a meeting held on Friday, 27 November 2020

Present:

Ben Walker	Head of the Manufacturing Division (Chairman)
Judy Carforth	Sales Representative
Lucy Leung	Marketing Manager
William Brown	Marketing Manager
Mike Manning	Production Manager

Judy reported that the purpose of the report was to present findings and conclusions from her visit to mainland China the previous week. She stressed that it had been a very small scale survey, and that her findings were tentative.

She stated that she had found a great deal of interest in Ultradine products when she had talked to senior staff at factories in Guangdong and Shanghai. She had discovered that there was a ready market for top quality products at reasonable prices, and that this might make

PART ONE SECRETARIAL WRITINGS

Ultradine products attractive.

Lucy asked whether people would be able to afford Ultradine products. Judy replied that, as the two areas visited comprised about 82 million people, many of whom were in the higher income brackets, it was quite likely that people could afford Ultradine products.

Judy then briefly outlined the options that were open to Ultradine: joint ventures, import-export arrangements, local sales and marketing and licensing arrangement. Mike suggested that each of these options should be investigated by undertaking another, longer, visit to China early next year, when contacts in mainland China could be extended.

Ben stated that he would recommend a further exploratory visit to the Senior Management Group when they next met in December.

Example 2

Minutes of the Marketing Department Meeting

Held on Monday, 26th July, 2021, at 10:00 a.m. in the meeting room.

Present: Mr. Bob Smith (Chairman)

Miss Mary Brown (Secretary)

…

1. Apologies for absence

    Apologies for Tom

2. Minutes of the meeting held on 25th June, 2021 were taken as read. The following amendments were made: Minute 4 for "80%" read "85%". The minutes were then approved as a corrected record and signed by the chairman.

3. Matters arising from the minutes

    Mr. White had prepared a preliminary report on the market survey. He would hand in the proposal by 10th August, 2021.

4. Winter promotion plans

    Two proposals were received from Jack Brown, who suggested a lucky draw programme, and Peter Green, who recommended free gifts. It was unanimously resolved that Peter Green's proposals be chosen. He would work out a detailed proposal for the next conference.

5. To review the sales record in June

    Lucy reported that the sales figure dropped 5% in June. The chairman urged the sales team to improve their performance.

6. Date of next meeting

    It was agreed that the next meeting will be held on 26th August, 2021, at 10:00 a.m. in the meeting room.

7. There being no further business, the Chairman closed the meeting.

4. Writing Assignment

Read the following notice and then write Minutes according to it.

NOTICE OF MEETING

A seminar on English language teaching will be held in Room 307 of the Main Building on 9th March, Tuesday, at 2:30 p.m. All the faculty are expected to attend the seminar. Students are also welcome.

Department Office
3rd March 2022

CHAPTER 9 Application

1. Tips of Writing a Job Application

(1) 写求职信重心应放在介绍写信者本人的最佳资历；

(2) 如果有必要，可以说明随函附上简历；

(3) 特别注意结尾，求职者可礼貌地请求答复或得到面谈的机会。

2. How to Write an Application Effectively

1) 如何写开头句

(1) 可以总结性地开头

√ This is to request your consideration of my qualification for a position in your company.

√ I'd like to apply for the job advertised in the *Times*.

(2) 可以从信息来源开头

√ Mr. Smith of your purchasing department has told me that you will soon need another secretary and I think that I am a qualified one.

√ I have read your advertisement in today's *China Daily* for a general manager and wish to be considered an applicant for the position.

(3) 可以以问句开头，以引起读信人注意

√ Can your stenographers write 120 words a minute? I can and I am eager to prove that such speed has no impact on my accuracy.

2) 中间段落写作示范

√ Because of my five years' experience as a salesman for P&G Ltd., I feel that I am qualified for the sales position which you advertised in *China Daily*.

√ My five years' experience in the Research Center of White Biomaterial Company makes me confident that I can contribute my effort successfully for your company.

√ Four-year-training at a Business College has given me some knowledge, which should be useful to you.

√ Mr. Smith has suggested that I might be well qualified for the sales work in your International Section for I master four languages and have worked as a salesman for four years.

√ My five years in the Finance Department of P&G Ltd. qualify me for a position as your accounting manager.

3) 结尾段可礼貌请求进一步面谈

√ May I have an interview?

√ Although there is the resume enclosed, I am ready to answer your further questions. I wonder if I may come in for an interview at your convenience.

√ Is it possible that you or some member of your staff will be kind enough to give me an interview at your convenience?

√ Hoping that my qualifications will meet your favorable consideration.

√ I look forward to your reply. I would be grateful if I have an opportunity to talk with you.

3. Examples of Applications

3.1 Application for a Position

Example 1

Application for a Position

April 12, 2021

Dear Sir/Madam,

I want to apply for the position advertised in *Times* this month. I feel that I am competent to meet the requirement specified.

I am 28 years old now. As you can see from my resume, I got a Master's Degree of Science and Engineering in 2018 and my major is Electric Engineering. I have worked in Great Wall Company for 2 years as a computer engineer. I am thoroughly experienced in computer maintenance and have published several papers in this field.

If you need more information regarding my experience, I am ready to provide details.

My email address is cp@hotmail.com. Looking forward to working in your company.

Sincerely yours,

Carol Paine

Example 2

Application for a Position

Shanghai

P.R. China

(Date)

Mr. Owens

Managing Director

IT Corporation

001 Zhongguancun Street

Beijing

P.R. China

Dear Mr. Owens,

    Having learnt from your advertisement in *China Daily* of January 15 that there is a vacancy in your company for a junior secretary, I would like to apply for the position.

    I am 26 years of age, a graduate of Beijing Languages University. Besides, I have had one year training at the South Secretary College. I have had three years' experience with the Bank as a clerk. The reason for leaving my present employment is that I am desirous of working as a secretary.

    In regard to my character and general ability, I refer you to Mr. Smith, the Managing Director of the Bank.

    I should welcome a personal interview.

    My mobile phone number is 13832647253.

Yours sincerely,
P. Tanner
Paula Tanner

Encls.:

    1. One copy of resume

    2. Two photographs

    3. One copy of ID card

3.2   Application for Studying Abroad

Example 1

Application for Admittance

Director

Graduate Admission and Enrollment Services

Graduate School of Maryland University

Baltimore, MD 21201

Dear Mr. Director,

    I'm interested in your graduate Program of International Management. I have just graduated from the Business School of Shanghai University, holding a bachelor degree and awarded the Title of Excellent Student.

I should be most obliged to you if you would send me your catalog and necessary application forms at your earliest convenience.

Enclosed please find my resume attesting to my outstanding academic performance at the Business School of Shanghai University.

Thank you for your time.

Yours sincerely,
Zhang Yang

Example 2

Application for Scholarship

Dear Sir,

I'm pleased to learn that my application for admission to graduate study at your University has been approved. From your recent information, I realize that I need to submit a Certified Sources of Support Form before an I—20 form can be issued. My problem now is that my financial resources are still somewhat short of the amount required.

Under this condition, I hope to obtain some additional financial assistance. Would you kindly advise me if there is such possibility?

I look forward to hearing from you soon.

Sincerely yours,
Zhang Yang

3.3 Application for Amendment to L/C

Example

Application for Amendment to L/C

TO: Bank of China, Shenzhen Branch

L/C No._____ amount_____

Amendment No._____

Please amend the above credit by fax as follows:

(   ) Shipment date is extended to

(   ) Expiry date is extended to

Others:

All other terms and conditions remain unchanged

Signature of the applicant

3.4 Application for Negotiation

Example

APPLICATION FOR NEGOTIATION

TO_____ Bank　　　　　No._____

Address_____　　Date_____

Dear Sirs,

　　We send you herewith for negotiation our drafts no. _____ for _____ Drawn under Letter of Credit no. _____ issued by _____ Accompanied by the following documents:

　　☐ Invoice_____　　　　　☐ Packing List_____

　　☐ Insurance Policy_____　☐ Consular Invoice_____

　　☐ Bill of Lading_____　　☐ Customs Invoice_____

　　☐ Certificate of Origin_____　☐ Import Licence_____

　　☐ Certificate of Inspection_____　☐ Letter of Transfer_____

　　Other documents_____

　　In consideration of your negotiation of the above mentioned documentary draft(s), we undertake to hold you harmless and indemnified against any discrepancy which may cause non-payment or non-acceptance of the said draft(s), and we shall refund you in original currency the whole or part of the draft(s) amount with interest or expenses that may be accrued or incurred in connection with the above upon receipt of your notice to that effect.

　　In consideration of your so doing we hereby agree to accept above mentioned terms and conditions.

In case of queries,　　　　　　　　　　　　　Authorized Signature and

Chop Please contact Mr.　　　　　　　　　　_____

_____　　　　　　　　　　　　Address_____

　　　　　　　　　　　　　　　　　　　　　　Telephone No._____

(注: negotiation 议讨; consular 领事的; indemnify 保证赔偿)

4. Writing Assignment***

4.1 请就下面的内容写一篇120字左右的求职信。

(1) 你看到昨天报纸上刊登的招聘公司部门经理广告。你本人认为自己符合要求。

(2) 你的年龄, 学习和工作经历。

(3) 你想应聘此职的原因。

(4) 你的联系方法。

  4.2　给纽约理工大学写一封留学申请信,内容是:你将于明年毕业于北京大学,希望毕业后能到贵校攻读电子工程硕士学位,请对方寄来简章以及申请入学及奖学金的表格。

CHAPTER 10 Résumé

1. Introduction of Résumé

Résumé is your first point of contact with potential employers, whether you are an experienced job seeker or fresh graduate, it is essential that you stand out from the crowd and get noticed by recruiters — make your Résumé more impressive and hopefully clinch a job interview — your goal.

简历包括的主要内容有：
个人信息：姓名(name)
联系地址，电话(address and telephone);
出生日期(date of birth);
婚姻状况(marital status);
国籍(nationality)
个人爱好，兴趣(hobbies)
联系方式（telephone, email)
工作经历(work experience)
教育经历(education experience)
证明人(reference)等.

Ten Tips for a Résumé
1) Design your résumé well: concise, well-organized, and relevant;
(1) emphasize the most important and relevant points about your accomplishment, skills and education etc., put them first
(2) keep information relevant to the goal of attaining an interview, concentrate on your contributions
2) no more than one page;
3) list your skill-set description, achievement and education etc. in reverse chronological order;
4) avoid first person like "I, me, my, mine" (in fact, no subject needed);

5) pay close attention to your use of tenses when describing past or present experience, ensure your tenses consistent;

6) use concrete figures, avoid the words like "many, all, few, some etc.";

7) use symbols like "880" (not "eight hundred and eighty");

8) avoid using too small, unconventional or unreadable fonts;

9) proofread properly;

10) target the job: adjust your résumé, write your résumé for one particular job— "re-package" yourself. Emphasizing that this is a job you truly wish to apply for.

2. Examples of Résumés

Example 1

Resume

Name:	Raymond Fields
Date of Birth:	July 11, 1996
Marital Status:	Married
Health:	Excellent
Telephone:	732-3324
Hobbies:	Traveling, Reading
Address:	376 Washington St., Somerville, MA 02143

Work Experience

Oct. 2014 to present	P&G Company, California Write advertising copy
June 2013—Aug.2014	The Mirror, George Town, New Jersey Sales clerk
June 2012—Aug.2013	Washing Publishing House, Washington D.C. Full-time proof reader

Education Experience

Sep.2011—June 2014	Washington State University Received MA in British Literature, June 2014
Sept. 2010—June 2011	Springfield College Received BA in English, June 2011
Sept.—June 2010	Holyoke High School

Scholastic Honors:	Nicholas Evans Scholarship in British Literature, 2013—2014

PART ONE　SECRETARIAL WRITINGS

	Washington State Scholarship, 2011—2014
Technical Training:	Attended a two-week seminar on Adverting

Reference

Dr. Carl Lindsay	Mr. David Lee
Prof. of English	Advertising Manager
Washington State University	682 Summer St.
Normal, IL 61762	Kafon, Washington
Phone No.: 401-3255	Phone No.: 443-0423

Example 2

Résumé

ERDONG HUA

　　　　No.2005 POBox%, TONGJIUNIVERSITY, Shanghai, 200092

　　　　+86-130-********

EDUCATION

Sep. 2017—present　TONGJI UNIVERSITY　　　　Shanghai

　　　　　　　　　　Dept. Of Business Administration

　　　　　　　　　　School of Economics and Management

Candidate for Bachelor in Business Administration degree(BBA), expected July,2020

Have a sound academic background, with overall GPA of 3.2/4.0 and GPA on specialized coursed of 3.6/4.0, top 10% academic ranking

Major academic courses highlight

Accounting, Engineering Economics, Enterprise Organization, International Finance

Human Resources Management, Marketing, Operations Management, Strategic Management

INTERNSHIP & EXPERIENCE

July2020—Sep.2020	ACNielsen CO.Ltd
Position held:	Intern, Client Service, Retail measurement Service
Key Account handled:	Coca-Cola(China) Beverages Ltd., (CCCBL)
Responsibility:	trace CCCBL's brand performance in retail channel by key indications
	cooperate with clients in coverage analysis to assess data quality
	prepare slide presentation documents for the clients
July 2019—Aug.2019	China Comforth Travel Service Co.Ltd. Wuxi, Jiangsu
Position held:	summer Assistant, International Dept.
Responsibility:	classy materials of hotels and scenic spots by location
	assistant in transaction of passport & Hong Kong-Macao Entry Permits
Mar.2019—July 2019	Management Association of Tongji University (MATU) Shanghai

Position held: Vice president
Responsibility: found MATU as a leading association in management
           build cross-department communication system to streamline efficiency
           integrate functional units for activities and arrange publicity
Activities involved: The 3rd Shanghai College Student Management Forum
           The 95th Anniversary Celebration of Tongji University

SCHOLASHIP & HONORS

2017—2018: Second class Scholarship for Excellennt Students of Tongji University

2017—2018: "Triple A" Student Award of Tongji University

2017—2019: Second class Scholarship for Excellennt Students of Tongji University

2017—2019: "Triple A" Student Award of Tongji University

2017—2020: Second class Scholarship for EPPERxcellennt Students of Tongji University

PERSONAL INFORMATION

English: a good command of both spoken and written English especially in business English
    CET-4 Excellent, CET-6 Certificate, TOEFL score 600

Computer: Master user of Microsoft Office software such as Word, Excel, Powerpoint
     Familiar with applied program including AutoCAD, Visual Basic, Photoshop etc.

                     THANK YOU FOR READING

3. Writing Assignment

Please write your own résumé dated from present to high school according to the tips above.

CHAPTER 11 Recommendation

1. The Contents Involved

推荐信的目的是向对方推荐某个人或某个产品,因此,推荐信应包括以下内容:
(1) 开头明确说明写信的目的。
(2) 说明自己与被推荐人认识的时间及场合,说明自己与被推荐的产品打交道的时间。
(3) 阐述自己对被推荐人或产品的印象: 优点(尽量多)及不足之处。
(4) 再次申明此信的目的。

2. The Usual Sentences in the Letter

√ I am glad to recommend ××× to you.
√ I am writing this letter to recommend ××× to you.
√ It's my pleasure to recommend ××× to you.
√ Therefore, I recommend ××× without any reservation/hesitation.
√ I do certify that...
√ From the reasons listed above, I don't hesitate to recommend ×××.
√ I strongly recommend ××× and hope you consider him/her favorably as a candidate for teaching assistantship.

3. Letter of Self-Recommendation

自荐信主要特点是强调自己的长处,给收信人留下较深刻的印象。

4. Examples of Recommendations

Example 1

The Department of Electronic Engineering
Peking University
Beijing , P.R.China
Oct.12, 2021

To whom it may concern,

  I do here with certify that Mr. Li Chiang named above, 27, graduated from the Electric Engineering Department of Peking University with excellent records in 2016 and is now in the service of Mob. Com Co. in Beijing. This time, he has been ordered to make a two-year study at an American university to brush up his technical knowledge, and he has selected your university best fit for the pursuit of his studies.

  I have known him for four years since he entered our university and assure you that he is diligent and earnest in the pursuit of learning. While in college, he was usually placed well among five from the top in his standing in the 40-member class.

  In particular, he is good at English reading, writing and hearing ability, though his speaking still leaves a little to be desired.

  Bright and sincere, he is most reliable and trustworthy though a little straight-forward and frank in his disposition. A sportsman in his college days, he is now at the best of his health, and you may rest assured that he is well qualified to continue his studies in your university.

Respectfully yours,
Xunfeng Xu

Example 2

Dear Mr. Manager,

  I am writing this letter to recommend my student Wang Gang who is seeking the position of marketing clerk of your company. He says you are satisfied with his presentation at the interview and require recommendation to be attached to his exceptional academic performance in the college. As his political instructor, I think Mr. Wang is well qualified for the position he seeks. He always ranks among the top five in his grade, he has passed cet-6 and obtains a certificate of intermediate computer skills. Mr. Wang is a studious, selfless and aspiring young man, and he is awarded the title of Three Good Activist by the college every year. I believe he is good candidate worthy of your consideration.

Yours sincerely,
× × ×

  (注: intermediate 中级; studious 勤学的; aspiring 热心的, 有抱负的; Three Good Activist 三好生)

Example 3

P.O. Box 36
BIIT University
Beijing, China 100000

Self Introduction

Dear Sir/Madam,

Now and then corporations send out feelers for just the right type of creative person. This person must fit very specific criteria. Usually, after all is said and done, the corporation wants a business person who can manage, create and communicate. A seasoned professional who's been around for a while.

If you've been looking for this rare combination of business savvy and design expertise, my background might interest you.

Ten years of working experience. Solid background in the management of creative up-and-comers.

Know new technologies that show instant profit, such as CAD/CAM.

This is but a brief summary of my abilities. And there is much, much more to share.

I feel I have strong marketable skills in which you would be interested. Please contact me if you would like to hear and see more.

With many thanks,

Huang Yan

Example 4

Exporter's Self Introduction

Dear Sirs,

Your firm has been recommended to us by John Morris & Co., with whom we have done business for many years.

We specialize in the exportation of Chemical and pharmaceuticals which have enjoyed great popularity in world market. We enclose a copy of our catalogue for your reference and hope that you would contact us if any item is interesting to you.

We hope you will give us an early reply.

Yours faithfully,

(注：exporter 出口商；chemical and pharmaceuticals 化学产品，药剂)

CHAPTER 12 Letter of Introduction

1. Two Kinds of Introduction Letters

介绍信通常有两类：一类是公函，另一类是私人介绍信。

(1) 公函(Official Letters)：是单位或机关派出工作人员对外联系，商谈事务时所持的书信凭证，属于正式介绍信。是写信人因公务把自己的同事或业务关系介绍给某单位或某个人。这种介绍信语言和格式比较规范、严谨，内容完整，文字明确简练。内容一般包括以下几个方面：

- √ 简单地介绍一下被介绍人的身份和情况。
- √ 说明事由，并要求对方给被介绍人提供某种帮助。
- √ 对对方的帮助预先表示感谢。
- √ 如果是熟悉的业务往来或已有的工作关系，也可以附带询问一下工作上的近况和向对方致以问候。
- √ 介绍信一般篇幅不长，前三个方面的内容常常可以放在一个段落里。

公函对收信人的称呼一般以To Whom It May Concern 或Dear Sir/Madam开头

(2) 私人介绍信(Personal Letters)：私人介绍信是写信人为持信人写给自己熟人或朋友，其语气随便，格式不大讲究；可以直接称呼收信人的名字。

2. The Beginning Words of the Letter

- √ I take pleasure in introducing...
- √ I am pleased to introduce...
- √ This will introduce...
- √ The bearer of this note, Mr. ×××, plans to be in Y city for about one week.

PART ONE SECRETARIAL WRITINGS

3. Examples of Official Letters

Example 1

Dear Mr./Ms....,

 This is to introduce Mr. Frank Johns, our new marketing specialist who will be in London from April 5 to mid April on business. We shall appreciate any help you can give Mr. Jones and will always be happy to reciprocate.

Yours faithfully,
James Black

Example 2

The Institute of High-Energy Physics
The Chinese Academy of Sciences
Beijing , China
July 9, 2021

To Manager
World Electronic Computer Company
Shanghai, China

Dear Mr. Manager,

 This is to certify that the bearer, Mr. Liu Dongming , an expert in our employ, is sent in the hope of making an investigation of the research work on the production of your newly-developed electronic computers. It is understood that this product is highly praised on the markets both at home and abroad for its fair price and good quality. We shall deem it a great help if Mr. Liu is provided with whatever information he may need to have.

Respectfully yours,
Li Yiweng
Secretary of the Director's Office

Example 3

To Whom It May Concern,

 We are pleased to introduce Mr. Wang Yue, our import manager of Textiles Department, Mr. Wang is spending three weeks in your city to develop our business with chief manufactures and to make purchases of decorative fabrics for the coming season. We shall be most grateful if you will introduce him to reliable manufacturers and give him any help or advice he may need.

Yours faithfully,
John Smith

4. Examples of Personal Letters

Example 1

Dear Smith,

    I have the pleasure of introducing Mr. Robert to you. I hope you will kindly show him attention which I shall consider as shown to myself.

Yours truly,
Black

Example 2

August 10, 2021

Dear Professor David,

    Allow me to introduce to you Mr. Lin, the bearer of this letter. He is one of my former students and is going to enter your institution after graduation here. Will you please give him some necessary guidance about the entrance examination? I shall be much obliged if you will show him any favor.

Yours,
Alice

5. Writing Assignment

(1) Write a Letter of Introduction:

写一封介绍信: 介绍张斌先生到某公司从事会计工作, 他办事认真, 值得信赖。

(2) Directions:***

Your friend Mary Brown will go to Washington D.C. next month.

Write a letter to Tony who is there and introduce Mary to him. You should write about 100 words and do not need to write the address.

这是一个向朋友介绍朋友的介绍信。Tony和Mary都是写信人的朋友, 在他看来, 他们志同道合, 有共同爱好, 所以希望他们相识。

CHAPTER 13 Certificate

1. Introduction of Certificate

证明信是以单位、团体或个人的名义凭确凿的证据,证明一个人的身份、经历或某件事情真相的信或文件。证明信种类很多,有工作经历证明、工作经验证明、病情证明、留学经济担保书、学业成绩证明书、离职证明等等。证明信的写法通常也采用一般信件格式,但多省掉收信人的姓名、地址及结束用语。称呼多用"To Whom It May Concern"或"Dear Sir (Sirs)",写证明信要求言简意赅。

2. The Usual Expressions

√ This certifies that...

√ This is to certify that...

√ It is hereby certified that...

√ I / We hereby certify that...

√ This is to confirm...

√ I have pleasure in certifying that...

3. Examples of Certificates

Example 1

DOCTOR'S CERTIFICATE

June 18, 2021

This is to certify that the patient, Mr. Harris, male, aged 40, was admitted into our hospital on June 9, 2021, for suffering from acute appendicitis. After immediate operation and ten days of treatment, he has got complete recovery and will be discharged on June 19, 2021. It is suggested that he rest for one week at home before resuming his work.

Jack Smith

Surgeon-in-charge

Example 2

CERTIFICATE OF LEAVING OFFICE

To Whom It May Concern,

    This is to certify that Miss Fang Li was employed in the General Manager's Office as English secretary for the period, from October, 2018 to November, 2021.

    During that time she proved herself to be industrious and capable. She left us of her own accord.

John Taylor

General Manager

Beijing Xinyue Hotel

Example 3

LU JIN

COLLEGE OF FOREIGN LANGUAGE AND CULTURES

XIAMEN UNIVERSITY

XIAMEN, FUJIAN

361005 CHINA

20th APRIL 2021

<u>TO WHOM IT MAY CONCERN</u>

<u>CERTIFICATE OF ENROLMENT</u>

TITLE OF COURSE: METHODOLOGY OF ENGLISH LANGUAGE TEACHING

DATES: 24th MAY—11th JUNE 2021

FEES: £×××.00

This is to certify: LU JIN, of the above address, is enrolled on the above course on the above dates at the University of ×××. The above named are full-time course from 9:00—12:15, Monday to Friday. Xiamen University will be invoiced for all tuition fees.

Should you require any further information, please do not hesitate to contact me.

Yours faithfully,

Laura Witt

EFL Administrator

Tel: 020 79153401

Fax: 020 79115201

Email: efl@wmin.ac.uk

4. About Notarial Certificates

公证信(Notarial Certificates)也是一种证明信，是由公证处开立的具有法律效力的信件，格式固定。

(1) A Marriage Certificate

(00) Xia Zi, No.20389

This is to certify that Huang Jun (male, born on September 18, 1992) and Wu Xia (female, born on July 24, 1994) registered a marriage on August 15, 2018 in Xiamen, Fujian, China.

Xiamen Notary Public Office

Fujian Province

The People's Republic of China

(sealed)

Notary Public: (sealed)

Dated this 3rd day of May, 2020

(2) Relative Certificate

(00) Xia Zi, No.18799

Applicant:

Wang Donghui, male, born on January 10, 1952, now residing in Room 301, Building 8, Lianhua Residential Quarter, Kaiyuan District, Xiamen, Fujian Province.

Tan Liying, female, born on November 25, 1958, now residing at the above said address.

Related persons:

Tan Kaimin, male, born on February 11, 1928, now residing in U.S.A.

Chen Weiwei, female, born on March 21, 1932, now residing in U.S.A.

This is to certify that the applicant Wang Donghui is the son-in-law of Tan Kaimin and Chen Weiwei, and the applicant Tan Liying is the daughter of Tan Kaimin and Chen Weiwei.

Xiamen Notary Public Office

Fujian Province

The People's Republic of China

(sealed)

Notary Public: (sealed)

Dated this 15th day of May, 2020

5. Commercial Certificates

5.1 The Kinds of Commercial Ceatificates

(1) Inspection Certificate of Quality (质检证明)

(2) Inspection Certificate of Weight/Measurement (重量检查证明)

(3) Inspection Certificate of Quantity (数量检查证明)

(4) Veterinary Certificate (兽医证明)

(5) Inspection Certificate of Sanitary or Certificate of Health (卫生健康证明)

(6) Inspection Certificate of Disinfection (消毒证明)

(7) Inspection Certificate of Origin (产地证明)

(8) Inspection Certificate of Temperature (温度检验证明)

(9) Inspection Certificate of Hold (验舱证明)

(10) Beneficiary's Certificate (受益人证明)

(11) Certificate of Shipment Sample (寄样证明)

(12) Certificate of Manufacturing Process and of the Ingredients (生产过程证明)

5.2 Illustrations

(1) Beneficiary's Certificate

JUN 23, 2021

INVOICE NO.: ELEOW2284 L/C NO. R7451G9C

WE HEREBY CERTIFY THAT SHIPPED GOODS HAS KEPT THE SIZE WITH 400×400×200MM TILES, DIMENSIONAL TOLERANCE+OR-1MM, DIAGONAL TOLERANCE+OR-1MM THICKNESS+OR-1MM.

CHINA NATIONAL METALS AND MINERALS

IMPORT AND EXPORT CORPORATION

GUANGDONG BRANCH

---

(2) Certificate of Shipment Sample

To whom it may concern,

<u>Re: Invoice No. 23546, L/C No.51089</u>

We hereby certify that in compliance with the terms of the relative Letter of Credit, we have requisite shipment samples by registered airmail to the nominees.

<u>(SIGNATURE)</u>

(3) Certificate of Manufacturing Process and of the Ingredient

---

TO MESSRS. SUMITOMO CORPORATION. OSAKA   RE: DATE: NOV. 18, 2021
                                          INVOICE NO.45 IN-C321
                                          L/C NO. LC-410-03234

DESCRIPTIONS OF GOODS: HALF DRIED PRUNE 2021CROP

	GRADE	SPFC	QNTY (CASE)
	A L: 700 CASE	M: 700 CASE	1 400
	B L: 700 CASE	M: 700 CASE	1 400

TOTAL QNIT: 2 800 CASE
PACKING: IN WOODEN CASE, 12 KGS PER CASE (N.W.)
MANUFACTURING PROCESS:

　　　　　　　　　　　　　　　　　　　　　　　　　　+SALT 28%—30%
MATUR MUME FRUITS—GRADING AND WASHING—SALTING POOL—
　　　　　　　　　　　　　　　　　　　　　　　　　　50—60 DAYS
　　　　　　　　　　　　　　　　　　　　　　　SUN DRY
MUME IN BRINE (SALT DEGREE 21—24° C BRIX) —HALF DRIED PRUNE
　　　　　　　　　　　　　　　　　　　　　　　　　　INSPECTING

INGREDIENTS: HALF DRIED PRUNE
　　　　　　　WATER CONTENT: 58%—60%
　　　　　　　SALT CONTENT: ABOUT 30%
　　　　　　　ORGANIC ACID CONTENT: 4.5%—4.9%

---

(4) Inspection Certificate of Quality

DATE: July. 19, 2021
RE: L/CNO. ILCT507553
　　INV.NO. 2021057WBS-5

DESCRIPT OF GOODS   MEN'S WOMEN'S SWEATERS

STYLE NO.	QUANTITY	NO. OF CTN.
22275	758 PCS	63 CTNS
22277	441 PCS	37 CTNS
22292	383 PCS	32 CTNS
22328	140 PCS	12 CTNS
22332	143 PCS	12 CTNS
52281	300 PCS	25 CTNS
52281BH	132 PCS	11 CTNS
TTL	2297 PCS	192 CTNS

THIS IS TO CERTIFICATE THAT WE HAVE INSPECTED OF CAPTIONED MERCHANDISES AND THE (CONTROL OF) QUALITY ARE IN CONFORMITY WITH S/C NO.2000CA44GMWBS11033

CERTIFIED BY:

(signature)

INSPECTOR

GUANGDONG TEXTILES IE WOOLEN KNITWEARS CO. LTD.
SIGNATURE:

(5) Inspection Certificate of Origin

HEBEI IMPORT & EXPORT COMPANY
INSPECTION AND QUARANTINE BUREAU OF THE (COPY)
PEOPLE'S REPUBLIC OF CHINA

Address:

No.

Cable: CERTIFICATE OF ORIGIN   Date

Tel:

Consignor (发货人)_____

Consignee (受货人)_____

Mark & N.	Commodity	Quantity	Gross Weight

THIS IS TO CERTIFY that the above mentioned commodities were produced or manufactured in the People's Republic of China.

Official

6. Writing Assignment

Write a certificate of leaving office for a staff member.

(为刘元先生出示一份离职证明：证明其自2017年7月至2020年10月在本公司任公关部经理，工作勤奋能干，现自愿离职。)

CHAPTER 14 Letter of Resignation

1. About the Writing

写辞职信时要选择有感情色彩的词语，以便给老板及同事们留下好的印象。语言要流畅、通顺、易懂。

2. Example of a Letter of Resignation

A Letter of Resignation

Dear Mr. Smith,

  It is with mixed feelings that I submit my resignation as your clerk. Because of the confidence you have shown in my ability to take on the job, my three years with the company have been a time of growth and challenge.

  But as you know, for some time I have wanted to gain experience in secretarial work. I now have that opportunity and will be leaving the company on March 15th.

  I appreciate the support and encouragement you have given me during the years we have worked together. And I believe I have gained valuable experience which will serve me well in the year to come.

  I will, of course, be happy to assist with training my replacement in the time remaining.

Sincerely,

Paula

3. Writing Assignment

Write a letter of resignation to the employer of the company where you are working as a clerk.

CHAPTER 15 Advertisement

英语广告是一种独特的语言形式，它遵循正规的英语语法规则，但是仍有许多独特的处理方式。下面举例分析英语广告的特色。

1. Language Characteristics

1) Wording

在用词方面，英语广告可以说是兼收并蓄、不拘一格、绚丽多姿。

(1) 在政府颁发公文、学校招生等广告中，用词极为严肃正统。

例：Our present Principal/Chief Executive has reached retirement age and the Governing Board wants to make the crucial appointment of his replacement in 2019. If you are a well-qualified and experienced individual and you think you have the vision, energy and enthusiasm to lead the college from the current solidly based state into the next decade, then please write for further information and post particulars to...

这是一篇招聘广告，用词是非常正规的，反映了广告的内容也是严肃认真的。

(2) 在许多情况下，广告为了产生一种幽默和诙谐的效果，故意使用一些不正式的语言。

例1：Each transfer weight advantage and power into real, all round performance at prices we know won't freak you out.

在这则广告中，freak out 是非正式词组，意思是精神恍惚、极度兴奋，它在此的意思是 frighten(使人害怕)，或是 scare 的意思。

例2：What's more, in our new appliance sale we've knocked up to 50% off top name brands.

knock在此的意思是defeat(击败)，但比起defeat来，却很不正式，但是表达效果比defeat要生动得多。

例3：Keep the frog out of your throat. 这是一篇咽喉片的广告中的最后一句话，广告策划者故意用这样一个非正式的短语取得一种幽默的效果。

(3) 在许多广告中，使用了大量的俚语和非正式的词汇，使广告显得通俗活泼，给人留下深刻的印象。如在一件外衣的广告中，为了强调该衣的特色、衣袋设计的不同凡响，甚至可以防盗，文字是这样的："pity the pickpocket"(可怜那些三只手吧)，其中pickpocket 就属于口语体，相当于汉语中的"三只手"或"扒手"。假如把它换成thief(贼)，效果就不如pickpocket 生动有趣。

(4) 专有名词的使用在广告中也很广泛，利用名人或名地等可以增加广告的说服力，引起读者的注意。如"This is one place Mick Doohan will never race."中, Mike Doohan就是一位著名的赛车手, 这是本田汽车公司的广告, 意思是"这是一块连Mike Doohan都不去比赛的地方"。又如"From the country that brought you Alain Delon. A new range of traditional cast-iron pots and pans, with smooth bottoms for use on all types of hob."广告中Alain Delon(阿兰·德龙)是一位著名影星。

(5) Use Compound Words(使用复合词): 广告中常用复合词, 这样容易制造许多新词, 这些新词能够给人留下生动深刻的印象。如: health-care(保健); color-fast(不退色); long-term(长期); shrink-proof(防缩); heat-resisting(抗热)等。例如:

√ Our newest design is made of rain-and-stain-resisting cloth. (我们的新款所用布料是防雨免洗的。)

√ It is user-friendly, pollution-free and easy-to-carry. (该产品方便使用, 无污染, 而且便于携带。)

√ We are a community-oriented store and provide a round-clock service. (本店面向社区服务, 全天营业。)

√ American Express—Do it right, first-rate, top-notch, without a hitch and absolutely flawless. (美国捷运——服务准确、质量一流、业内顶尖、交递准时、投送无误)

(6) Use Loan Words (使用外来词): 外来词能有助于加深消费者的印象, 增添广告的味道及色彩。

Loan words may help to impress consumers. If the copy is on food or restaurant, no wonder French words would be appearing here and there as French food and table manner are regarded the top.

√ We have the Chief *Chef* from Paris.

√ This is a real *la cuisine* from the sun-shone south part of French.

√ Bon appetite is your expectation and our promise.

2) Clauses

英语广告的句型也多种多样, 但最常用的句型有以下几类:

(1) <u>祈使句</u>　这是出现最多的句型。

例1: Ask any one who owns one. (汽车广告语)
　　　询问一下有这种车的人吧。

例2: Lay down your arms. (桌子广告语)
　　　放下您的胳膊吧。

例3: Please do not leave it too late.
　　　事不宜迟。

(2) <u>一般疑问句</u>　通常用在广告的前面。

例1: Have you ever dreamed of ascending the steps of great temple built to the Gods?
　　　(旅行社广告)您是否梦想过登上为众神修建的宏伟庙宇的台阶?

例2: Can a tired overworked voice command attention in class?

61

一个疲惫、过劳的声音能吸引全班的注意力吗?

又如下面这个广告全部由一般疑问句构成:

Ph. D. s should have acquiring minds. Considering this a simple test.

A) Do you want to work in world class research laboratories?

B) Do you want to apply your research skills to keep successful business at the leading edge of world technology?

C) Do you want to build your career with a major international company headquartered in Australia?

If your answers to these questions are positive, BHP would like to talk to you.

Your first challenge is to discover more by calling Theoni Parthimos, our Senior Personnel Officer.

(3) <u>省略句</u>　在英语广告中,省略句比比皆是,甚至整篇广告都由省略句构成。

例: Serviced greenfield sites aplenty. Ready for development. For sale. For manufacture. For business. For services. For leisure. A million square feet of ready-to-wear premise. Brand new business parks. Four-star conference facilities. Backed by 14 years' success in helping business to relocate, set-up, prosper, expand.

The hotel best facilitied and full entertainment service. (a hotel copy)

Bridging the distance. (Telecommunication service copy)

Born to run. (Car's copy)

Kissed by a whisper of mineral. (Cosmetic copy)

(4) <u>比较级</u>　比较级在广告中用得非常多,这是由于英语广告中有大量的形容词和副词作修饰语的缘故。

例1: Today in business fast is no longer fast enough, even faster is still too slow to keep pace with the incredible demands placed on people and the computers they work with. That's one reason why IBM developed P60/D. 60 MHz 64-bit Pentium Chip computers so fast, so powerful, it makes today's conventional computers like they are moving at a snail's space.

例2: These days succeeding in business means getting more competitive and making tougher decisions.

例3: The new Minolta Riva Zoom 105EX is the most compact camera in a very prestigious class.

例4: In short, the stronger your character, the brighter your future.

(5) <u>直接引语</u>　在英语广告中直接引语出现得很多,原因: 一是直接引语使得广告显得形式活泼、新颖;二是采用直接引语从心理学的角度看可以增强说服力。

例1: "It's like we're all in the same office. The office just happens to spread across 7000 miles of ocean," Tom Hughes MIS Director, Construction.

这是IBM公司的一则广告的开头语,通过该公司经理的话,使广告显得生动具体。

例2: "Through the NVQ initiative we have discovered talents and competencies we would never otherwise have known about." Says Ian McDermot of Philips Components in Blackburn.

这是用人单位对NVQ职业培训机构的赞扬。

3) Other Language Characteristics

(1) 语言简短精练

√ Let's make things better. (Philips电子公司)

√ Impossible made possible. (Canon打印机)

√ Take Toshiba, take the World. (Toshiba电子公司)

√ It's your life. It's your store. (Acme超市)

√ It's All inside. (JC Penny专卖店)

√ Got milk？(牛奶广告)

(2) 带有警句、格言的意味

√ Coke Adds Life.

√ To me, the past is black and white, but the future is always colorful. (轩尼诗酒)

(3) 多用并列结构

√ Easy to shoot. Easy to share. Share moments. Share life. (柯达数码相机)

√ To laugh. To love. To understand each other.

√ I click. I shop. I find the clothes I love.

√ No business too small, no problem too big. (IBM 公司)

(4) 利用谐音(partial tone)/拼写变异(abnormal spelling)使人回味

√ More reasons to shop at Morrisons.*

√ To laugh. To love.

√ Have a nice trip, buy-buy.

√ Quicktionary

(5) 使用双关语

√ A Deal with Us Means A Good Deal To You.

√ Spoil yourself and not your figure. (减肥冰淇淋广告)

√ Ask for More. (More: "摩尔"牌香烟)

√ From sharp mind, come Sharp products. (by Sharp)

(6) 押韵(rhyme)的使用能使广告词朗朗上口, 容易记忆

√ Talk global, pay local. (by a telecommunication company)

√ Cleans your breath while it cleans your teeth. (by P&G for Colgate, a toothpaste)

√ You can't Xerox a Xerox on a Xerox. (没人能用施乐复印机复制出施乐产品。)

√ In our garment, In trend. (穿本厂制衣, 领潮流之先。)

(7) 使用对照(antithesis)

√ Give a man a fish and you'll feed him for a day.

√ Teach him how to Yomp and he'll open up a restaurant.

√ It (Yomping) can't make you more beautiful.

- But it can make your future more attractive.
- Give people bread and they feel like beggar.
- Teach them to make their own and you give them their dignity.

(8) 使用第一人称语气("I" tone), 能使你的广告更具有说服力

- I've replaced 1,453 diapers, and 18 baby-sitters, but never the bulb since I became a dad two years ago. (a bulb manufacturer)
  身为人父两年来,我换过1453块尿布和18个保姆,却从没换过一次灯泡。
- I shaved myself every morning and I had tried scores of razors before I picked up XXX. Then it has been the only one I have kept in my bathroom. The only razor that senses and adjusts to the individual needs of my face. It's the best shave a man can get. (XXX, 某品牌剃须刀广告)

2. Ads. in Purchases and Sales (with Chinese Translation)

- 15% off with this flyer 凭此宣传品优惠15%
- 50% off on selected lines 部分商品降半价
- Big sale 大甩卖
- Brighter shopping, brighter prices 明智的购物, 透明的价格
- Buy any two together and save 10% off both products 满两件九折
- Buy one and get anyone free 买一赠一
- Buy two and get one free 买二赠一
- Closing sale 关门大甩卖
- Customer care is our top priority 顾客至上
- Easy to use and great value too. 好用实惠,物美价廉。
- Final clear out 清仓大甩卖
- Free delivery to your door 免费送货上门
- Furniture sale now on 家具现降价销售
- Half price sale 半价甩卖
- Massive stock, clear out 大量库存,清仓甩卖
- Offer is subject to availability. 现货优惠,卖完为止。
- We can provide the complete hospitality service. 我们提供热情周到的服务。
- Out of hours, delivery at... 下班时,送货到……
- Peace of mind from the minute you buy 买着放心
- Price crash 削价
- Sale 50% off original price 按原价的50%销售
- Sale at breakdown price 跳楼价甩卖
- Sale continues in store 商品继续削价
- Save up to 50% off 50%大降价

√ Save up to 40% 6折优惠

√ Save your money 贱卖

√ Savings and discounts all around the store 店内所有商品均削价处理

√ Special offer 特价

√ 50% discount on selected items 部分商品五折

√ Summer price cuts 夏季大削价

√ Try before you buy 先试后买

3. Ads. for Vacancy

Example 1

Beijing International Management Consultant Co. Ltd.

Seeking qualified candidates for the following vacancies for multi-national companies:

Sales Manager

- Excellent interpersonal and presentation skills
- Dynamic, easy-going, capable of being leader
- Fluency in English and Mandarin
- Good understanding and knowledge of above 2 years in the field of lighting preferred.

Human Resources Manager

- Bachelor degree and above, MBA preferred
- With about 5 years of relative work experience
- Good command of spoken and written English
- Familiar with computer skills

Minimum salary RMB 11,000 per month. Welfare package to be negotiated.

Interested applicant please forward resume to:

1201 West Tower, Blue Sky Commercial Mansion

19 Nantong Rd,

Beijing

100036

Example 2

Wanted

Whirlpool Corporation is a famous manufacturer and marketer of electrical home appliances with headquarters in Tianjin. It has more than 20 branches over the country. We are seeking for one sales manager now.

1. Chinese citizen, aged between 35—40
2. With college diploma in Marketing, Economics or related fields
3. Minimum of 5 years' experience in sales management
4. Proficiency in English speaking and writing
5. Willing to travel frequently
6. Good at using a computer

Those interested please contact Mr. John at 28476669.

4. Usual Abbreviations in Ads.

Pls.= please   exp'd.=experienced
mgr.=manager   P/ T=part time
Rd.=Road   Rm.=Room
Sal.=salary

5. Writing Assignment***

请根据下列中文信息登一则招聘广告。

招聘: 生产计划员

要求: (1) 大学毕业, 至少两年生产管理方面工作经验;

　　　(2) 数学好, 电脑操作熟练;

　　　(3) 通过大学英语四级考试者优先考虑。

有意应聘者请将英文简历、一张近照及工资意向邮寄到北京63214信箱。

CHAPTER 16 Letter of Invitation

1. The Writing Skill

邀请信是日常生活和工作中常用的一种信函，具有简洁、热情的特点。写邀请函时需注意：

(1) 礼貌友好地发出邀请

(2) 清楚地写明邀请的原因、活动的时间以及地点

(3) 结尾时表示希望对方接受邀请

(4) 如果要求被邀请人答复，应注明RSVP (意思是"请答复")

2. Expressions in Different Situation

(1) 提出邀请 Extending an Invitation

√ Would you like to...?

√ I'd like to invite you to...

√ I would like to know if you could come to...

√ May I invite you to...

√ Would it be possible to join us?

√ Would it be convenient to take part in the activity?

√ Would you be interested in...?

√ I sincerely invite you to visit our...

√ I was wondering if you would be interested in...?

(2) 接受邀请 Accepting an Invitation

√ Thank you. I'll be happy to come.

√ I'd love to go with you.

√ Thank you for invitation.

√ I'd be glad to come.

√ I accept your invitation.

3) 拒绝邀请 Declining an Invitation

√ I'd love to, but I can't come.

√ Thank you for your invitation, but I don't think I can make it.

√ Unfortunately, I'm already busy that day.

√ I'm sorry, but I have a prior engagement for that evening.

√ It's very kind of you to invite me, but I am not sure if I can...

√ Thank you for the invitation, but I am afraid I can't...

3. Examples of Exhibition Invitations and Acknowledgements

Example 1 Exhibition Invitation

Dear Sirs,

We are staging an important exhibition of our latest products accompanied by a series of technical lectures for our home and overseas customers at the Shanghai Exhibition Centre on May 16th, 17th and 18th.

The whole range of our products will be represented by eighty-eight companies in the Group. The exhibits which are of particular interest to you will be Teleprinter and View Finder.

It now gives us the greatest pleasure to invite you to visit this exhibition which we know will be of considerable interest to you and we would like to suggest such a visit on the afternoon of Monday, 16th May. The exhibition will be open until 5:00 p.m.

We hope you will be able to accept this invitation, and if you would kindly indicate the time of your arrival, we arrange to meet you.

Faithfully yours,

(注: stage 定于; teleprinter 电传打字机; view finder 取景器)

Example 2 Accepting the Invitation Above

Dear Sirs,

We have received your letter of invitation dated April 1st with thanks. Your exhibition is of great interest to us. We think it will benefit both of us a great deal, so we've decided to visit your exhibition to be held on May 16th, 17th and 18th. Since the exhibition is about a month ahead, we cannot decide specifically when we will arrive at Shanghai. However, once we make a specific decision, we will notify you by cable.

For your information, there is a heavy demand for teleprinters in the market here. We hope we can place large orders during this visit.

Faithfully yours,

(注: for your information 顺便奉告; a heavy demand 需求大)

PART ONE SECRETARIAL WRITINGS

Example 3   Declining the Invitation

Dear Sirs,

　　Thank you for your kind invitation. However, we cannot accept it since we are no longer dealing in light industrial products. Last June we shifted to handle the import and export of native produce.

　　We think you may be pleased to invite the largest dealer of teleprinters in this area and their address is as follows:

Messrs. Parson & Co.

37 Sunshine Ave.

Los Angeles, CA 90300

Faithfully yours,

(注: shift to 转向; dealer 经销商)

4. Invitation Cards

　　1. 请柬分为正式及非正式两种。正式请柬通常是印好的, 它有一定的格式, 习惯上邀请者及被邀请者均用第三人称。请柬必须将内容、时间、地点说清楚。被邀请人收到请柬后, 不管接受与否均应回复。

　　2. 英文请柬的格式, 范例:

Example 4

Mr. and Mrs. Oliver Barrett III

Request the pleasure of your company

At a dinner in celebration of

Mr. Barrett's sixtieth birthday

Saturday, the sixth of March

At seven o'clock

Dover House, Ipswich, Massachusetts

R.S. V.P.

(注: company 陪伴)

Example 5

> Mr. and Mrs. Robert Smith
> Request the pleasure of the company of
> Mr. and Mrs. George Mailer's
> At dinner at the Faculty Club
> On Friday
> March 26th, at seven o'clock p.m.
> 21 Show Lane
> March 20th, 2021
>
> R.S.V.P.

5. Writing Assignment***

(1) 假设你的老板Mr. Howard想邀请Mr. Smith以及他的雇员参加12月31日，星期五晚8点在假日饭店(Holiday Inn)二楼舞厅举行的化妆舞会(costume ball)。请你为他写一封邀请信。

(2) Try to write back to Example 5 above, one is to show acceptance while another is to decline the invitation.

CHAPTER 17 Letter of Congratulation

1. The Writing of the Letter

一般贺信的写法不必太长，往往以祝贺词开头，文中应具体提到对何事表示祝贺，结尾致以衷心的祝福。

2. Patterns and Expressions

√ Congratulations on one's promotion/marriage/success in.../graduation from.../excellent performance in...;

√ I am delighted but not surprised by your success;

√ Congratulate you on...; It is quite an accomplishment for...;

√ We look forward to the continuing growth/future success/later promotion.

3. Examples of Letters of Congratulation

Example 1

Dear Louisa,

 Congratulations!

 I was really delighted to hear that you received the annual company award for the most outstanding salesperson of the year.

 This award is timely and well deserved. It is obviously the result of your coordinated and tireless sales effort.

 We look forward to your continuing success.

Yours sincerely,

Example 2

Dear Michael,

Please accept our heartiest congratulations on your achieving initial sales of 30,000 units. This impressive achievement gives us a great deal of satisfaction and fills us with confidence with regard to the future. The result more than anything demonstrates your standing in your market.

We are looking forward to your continuing success.

                                                          Yours sincerely,

Example 3

Dear Joe,

How wonderful it is to learn your new company will be open and be ready for business! Congratulations to you and all your colleagues.

With your experience and proved ability in the trade, I know your company will be a huge success. And I am sure you will make much profit in near future.

Please accept my warmest congratulations and best wishes.

                                                          Yours sincerely,

4. Writing Assignment***

Please write a letter of congratulation to Bill, your friend, on his promotion to be Production Manager.

5. Greeting Card

Example 4

To Mr. and Mrs. W. Dean

With Best Wishes

For

A Merry Christmas

And

A Happy New Year

From Mr. and Mrs. Healey

CHAPTER 18 Others

1. University Codes of Behavior — More Information

The University requires you to abide by some straightforward rules and these are enforced using the University's Disciplinary Procedure. You can find all the necessary information in detail in:

ESSENTIAL INFORMATION FOR STUDENTS, SECTIONS 19—28.

- available in print from the Undergraduate and Postgraduate Campus Offices.
- available on the web at: www.wmin.ac.uk/page-1123 (Academic Registrar's Department)

In the Code of Behaviour for Libraries and the Learning Resources Center, some of the most important things to note are below. The list is not exhaustive.

- Your mobile phone should be switched to silent mode <u>everywhere</u>. No rings, bleeps or any sounds at all, anywhere in the Library. You may only use it to make or receive calls on Floor 1 only, as long as you are not disturbing others.
- If you are using headphones no sound at all should be audible to other people.
- The Code requires quietness in the Library.
- Talking in designated silent study areas is a breach of the rules. In these areas whispering is regarded as talking and can be just as annoying for other people.
- Talking in Group Study areas is allowed. This does not mean that a high level of noise is acceptable however and the library staff have authority to judge this and enforce it.
- You may not bring any food or drink other than bottled water (nothing else). Note that the rule clearly says you may not bring these things in at all. Bringing them in and promising not to eat or drink them on the premises is not an option.
- You must produce your University ID whenever a member of staff asks you for it. Refusal will result in Security Staff being summoned and could mean that you have to leave the campus.
- Returning or renewing books late will result in sanctions and blocks on further borrowing.
- Setting off the Library's security device by taking out material which is not issued to you will also result in a formal disciplinary procedure.
- Not returning everything at the end of your course will mean that your degree certificate and your invitation to graduation are withheld until you comply.

All the library regulations are in "Essential Information" too. The less time we have to spend enforcing these rules, the more time we can spend helping you to get the best possible use out of your stay with us. We much prefer the latter!

2. Course Work

Don't!

√ work with anyone else unless you are told it's a group assignment

√ use quote from books without using quotation marks and references

√ use anyone else's facts or ideas without acknowledgement and references

√ lend your work to another student

Do!

√ check with your module leader in if doubt or you may find yourself guilty of plagiarism. Plagiarism can get you into deep trouble!

3. Tips to Keep Your Instructors Happy

Your instructors have to read and mark a lot of assignments. Please make their job as easy and pleasant as possible.

(1) Use the standard British size of paper, which is called A4. Smaller pieces of paper slip out of piles and can get lost.

(2) Skip lines—write on every second or third line. This is to give your instructor room to respond to your work. For the same reason, leave wide margins on all margins on all four sides of the sheet of paper. This amount of blank space may look wasteful, but it allows room for comments and questions from the instructor to you. Indent each new paragraph about five spaces, to show where your new idea begins.

(3) On everything you give to an instructor, write your name, their names, the course title or module code, the assignment, and the date.

(4) Photocopy assessed coursework before handing it in. That way, if it gets lost (and these things do happen), you still have a copy of your work.

(5) Word process your assignments. You will be using computers in your working life, so if you do not yet know how to use them, learn.

(6) Word processing allows you to use the automatic dictionary known as a spell-checker. However, do not trust this too much, because the computer cannot tell the difference between there and their, for example. Always proofread your work carefully for small errors.

(7) You may hand write the short weekly assignments for the instructors, although they would prefer that they were word processed or typed. If you hand write them, make sure to write very clearly. Print each letter separately.

PART TWO

ACADEMIC PAPER WRITING

学术论文写作是研究生(本科生)教学计划所规定的学习任务之一，也是学生知识与能力结合、提升理论水准的一项重要环节，学术论文写作有利于全面训练学生尤其是研究生的综合运用能力、科学研究能力和实践操作能力，有利于引导他们学会思考、发现、钻研及培养他们的创新精神。因此，学术论文不仅体现了高等教育的教学目标和要求，是高校研究生教学质量的检验方式，也是学生专业学习的总结，是必须的学术训练。

CHAPTER 1 Ways of Preparation

1. Thinking about the subject, the purpose and the readers
   A. skill: think academically
   B. product: subject
2. Thinking about what you know about the subject
   A. skill: brainstorming
   B. diagrams/notes
3. Searching for relevant books/articles
   A. skill: library/ research skills
   B. product: a reading list
4. Studying the books on your reading list
   A. reading skills: skimming & scanning
   B. product: a list of materials studied
5. Making notes and record full details of the materials you use for later reference
   A. skills: read in detail; select & note-making; paraphrase/summarize
   B. product: notes
6. Preparing a preliminary thesis statement (the controlling idea of an academic paper expressed in one sentence. It makes the claim that the paper tries to support it with evidence.)
   A. skills: extracting; condensing and organizing
   B. product: a thesis statement
7. Organizing ideas and outlining
   A. skills: planning and organizing
   B. product: an outline
8. Writing your first draft
   A. skills: writing from notes; synthesis; write paragraphs
   B. the first draft
9. Editing
   Product: the second draft

10. Proofreading your draft
    A. skills: check for spelling, punctuation, grammar, vocabulary use, style, organization, references and plagiarism etc.
    B. product: a draft with changes marked
11. Producing a final version
    A. write title/contents page
    B. product: the final draft
12. Checking everything
    A. final check
    B. product: submission

CHAPTER 2

1. Learning Objectives

To understand generic features of academic papers

To learn how to write an effective abstract

To learn how to draft an introduction

To learn how to develop the body of an academic paper

To learn how to draw a conclusion

To develop competence in using formats of referencing systems

To realize the importance to avoid plagiarism

2. General Features

Academic paper writing is a kind of formal writing, which is characterized by:

(1) little use of slang, dialectic expressions, colloquial language or informal contractions;

(2) little use of the first or second persons in order to be impersonal;

(3) use passive voice to highlight objectivity;

(4) use of precise word of scientific terminology

(5) a clear topic sentence in every paragraph with the other supporting details;

(6) avoidance of flashy and flowery prose(花里胡哨)

3. Major Sections

3-1. Title

The title should represent the central idea of the paper and facilitate the information retrieval (方便信息检索):

(1) be brief and concise (no more than 15 words)

(2) be specific

(3) avoid question titles

(4) be consistent (n. to n., ger. to ger.)

(5) be standard (avoid nonstandard abbreviation and symbol)

(6) The words used in a title are nouns, noun phrases or gerunds.

(7) Capitalize (大写) the first letter of all words except articles (the/a/an), prepositions (at/on/between) and conjunctions (and/for/nor/or/but)

(8) If a short title cannot summarize the content of the article, use sub-title, with a colon (:) in between

(注:)标题是对全文重要内容的高度概括，因此用词要贴切、中肯，不能有任何随意性。为了便于检索，标题中所用的词尽量使用表达全文内容的关键词;

标题中用得最多的是名词(包括动名词)，除名词外，用得较多的是介词，有时使用形容词、冠词、连词、副词。

The Structure of a Title

1. noun/gerund phrase

   "Severe Weather and Automobile"

   "Soil Behavior and Critical Soil Mechanics"

   "High Speed Flow Sensor and Fluid Power Systems Model "

2. prep. phrase

   "On the Distribution of Sound in a Corridor"

   "On the Crushing Mechanism of Thin Walled Structures"

3. Noun/noun phrase + prep. Phrase

   "Diversity in the Future Work Force"

   " Investigation of Air Bags Deployment Forces"

4. First part : second part(sub-title)

   "Absorbable Implants in Finger Fractures: A Biomechanical and Comparative Study"

   "Impact of Cancer: Coping Process and Quality of Life"

Discussion:

Of the following titles, think whether they are Good or Poor and why.

1. "Studies on a Snake";

2. "The Thermal Ecology of a Population of Timber Rattlesnakes on Brady's Bluff, Wisconsin

1. "Studies on a Snake" (Poor. It is very general and vague, and tells the reader nothing specific.)

2. "The Thermal Ecology of a Population of Timber Rattlesnakes on Brady's Bluff, Wisconsin"(Good. The key words identify a specific behavior, the content, and the experimental position.)

Now, read the following Titles and improve the poor ones.

1. Auditory Perspectives of Different Types of Music

2. Electromagnetic Fields Have Harmful Effects on Humans

3. How to Use Water Resources for Irrigation in Semiarid Land?

4. Water Quality Can Be Protected Through the Successful Integration of Research and Education

5. The Single Community Concept: A Model for Adult Environmental Education

6. Physics and Art: Conceptual Linkages Can Be Uncovered

1. *Auditory Perspectives of Different Types of Music*

2. *Electromagnetic Fields Have Harmful Effects on Humans*
   Improved: *Harmful Effects of Electromagnetic Fields on Humans*

3. *How to Use Water Resources for Irrigation in Semiarid Land?*
   Improved: *Using Water Resources for Irrigation in Semiarid Land*

4. *Water Quality Can Be Protected Through the Successful Integration of Research and Education.*
   Improved: *Protecting Water Quality Through the Successful Integration of Research and Education.*

5. *The Single Community Concept: A Model for Adult Environmental Education.*

6. *Physics and Art: Conceptual Linkages Can Be Uncovered*
   Improved: *Physics and Art: Uncovering Conceptual Linkages*

3-2. Author

The name of a Chinese author is preferably spelt in Chinese Pin Yin, such as Zhang Minhui.

If it is a two character name, all letters of the family name are preferably capitalized so as to distinguish the given name from it, such as

  WANG Lin, CHEN Yang

The number of authors should not be over four. In case of real need, it is advisable to use "et al." after the principle authors.

The address should be written from the smaller unit to the larger ones.

3-3. Abstract and Keywords

An abstract, mostly in one paragraph, summarizes the major aspects of the entire paper. Whereas the title can only make the simplest statement about the content of your article, the abstract allows you to elaborate (详尽阐述) more on each major aspect of the paper. The abstract helps readers decide whether they want to read the rest of the paper and facilitate the information retrieval.

3-3-1. Language Tips in Expressing the Three Parts of an Abstract

3-3-1a. To state the problem/issue

"This paper attempts to simplify the usage of the Publication Manual of the American Psychological/ Association, Fifth Edition, 2010."

"The thesis is intended to explore the merging of optimization and simulation technologies."

"The overall objective of this study is to introduce a new program system used in bus fare boxes."

3-3-1b. To describe research method

"The method used in the study is known as the Hottel-Whillier-Bliss(HWB) model."

"This paper proposes to use a new method to assess performance of artificial mobility."

"The research has recorded valuable data using the newly-developed method."

3-3-1c. To indicate research result

The experimental results are summarized as follows.

"The results have been shown in Figure 6."

"In conclusion, we state that the engine using the new additive was in a better condition at the end of the tests."

"We have demonstrated in this paper that an awareness of the vocabulary signaling boundaries is part of the language user's communicative strategies."

Keywords

In the form of nouns 4-6 words from the title and/or the abstract.

The length of an abstract: 100-200 words in one paragraph.

The tense & voice in abstract: present or present perfect tense in the statement; past tense in the research method and result.

The expression: written in the 3rd person; use the standardized technical terms; concise, avoid many long and complicated sentences; avoid the "weasel words"(含糊其词) as "might, could, may, and seem".

An Example of Abstract

(Title)An Assessment of Consumers' Attitudes towards Direct Marketing Channels:
　　　　A Comparison between Unsolicited E-mail and Direct Mail

Abstract:

"The paper examines consumers' attitudes towards two major direct marketing methods, unsolicited (主动提供的) e-mail and postal direct mail. (1. the statement of the problem)

Psychological Reaction Theory was used to determine what factors might influence consumers' attitudes towards each communication method. Focus groups were conducted to discover the common themes and to identify the influential factors. (2. The research method) The results of this study indicated that in comparison, unsolicited e-mails were more problematic than postal direct mail due to the inconvenience that spam (垃圾邮件) *presented to consumers. (3. Results)"*

Keywords: *direct marketing, unsolicited e-mail spam, postal direct mail*

3-3-2. The Consistency of a Bilingual Abstract

The consistency of an abstract in Chinese and English version lies in that of the content rather than that of the format or punctuation marks due to the differences between Chinese and English.

Two kinds of inconsistency:

A. the writer deletes or adds the content at his/her own will (causes the deviation from the main theme and the confusion of the main idea of the whole thesis)

B. translating Chinese into English word for word (makes the English version lengthy and tedious or the Chinese one unnatural)

Suggestions in achieving the consistency in the bilingual abstract:

1. Follow English grammar rules and use the English expression;

2. Confirm to the standard of English terminology;

3. Use proper tense and voice.

1) The present tense is used mostly while past tense and present perfect tense are sometimes used.

   (1) The present tense is to describe the necessity of the research, state the conclusion of the research and reveal the rules governing the development of nature;

   (2) The past tense is to describe the research process and to report the results yielded by the research;

   (3) The present perfect tense is to describe the achievement of the research during a certain phase.

2) The passive voice is commonly used while active voice is increasingly used.

   (1) The passive voice gives prominence to essential information and makes the meaning salient(突出);

   (2) The active voice makes the idea concise, clear and expressive.

Writing Assignment

Write an English abstract consistent with the following Chinese.

摘要：本文以问卷调查的形式，通过描述性统计和定量分析，(随机)对任意的118名来自某大学的非英语专业新生的英语学习现状作了调查和探讨，主要发现如下：(1) 新生对中学英语教学是满意的，尽管他们对中学取得的英语成绩不太满意; (2) 他们发现在刚学习大学英语时最大的困难是词汇，而不是听力; (3) 他们在大学四年中最想掌握的是英语口语而不是阅读能力; (4) 他们知道英语学习的目的，但他们学习地非常被动。在对结果进行分析之后，文章进一步对大学英语教学提出了一些改进建议。

3-4. The Body Sections of an Academic Paper

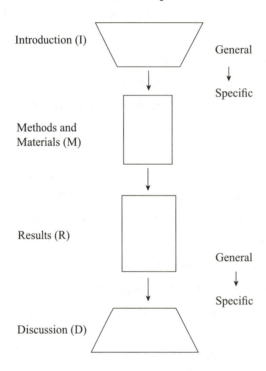

3-4-1. Introduction

An introduction fulfills the task of providing the readers with sufficient background information about the research, defining the limit of the study to direct the readers to a specific focus, and making clear its general purpose.

An introduction generally includes 3 sections:

(1) Literature review (What has been done in the field?)

(2) A statement of the existing problem (What have not been done yet?)

(3) The objective and/or significance of the present research (What am I going to do?)

3-4-1a. Language Tips

(1) To start the section with strong opening statements

　　"*Recently, there has been growing interest in…*"

　　"*The possibility of ... has generated wide interest in…*"

　　"*The development of... is a classic problem in…*"

　　"*The…has become a favorite topic for analysis…*"

"Knowledge of …has a great importance for…"
"Many recent studies have focused on…"

(2) To provide a literature review
"The previous work on…has indicated that…"
"There have been a few studies highlighting…"
"It is well known that…"
"In recent years, there has been an increased awareness of …"
"Several researches have theoretically investigated…"

(3) To highlight the existing problem(s)
"Great progress has been made in this field, but…"
"An experiment of this kind has not been made."
"Not any experiment in this area has suggested that…"
"The method we use differs greatly from those above reported…"
"The data available in literature failed to prove that…"

(4) To focus on the present research
"In this paper,… is investigated/studied/discussed/presented"
"On the basis of existing literature data, we carried out studies in an effort to…"
"The present study will therefore focus on…"
"The purpose/aim of this paper is…"
"Our primary objective in this paper is to …"
"The aim of the present paper is to give…"
"The present work extends the use of the last model by…"

3-4-1b. Function
It introduces the reader to the topic and is a preview or outline of the content and structure of the paper. It has to observe several formal rules and contains a specific set of information. Formal aspects: The introductory part should approximately make up one tenth of your entire paper.

3-4-1c. Content(s) (suggestions)
You could start the introduction of your thesis by simply pointing out your thesis statement, i.e., what issue you intend to examine in your paper and which answers/arguments you propose. This could be realized by, for example, a paragraph giving a short overview of the main argument within the criticism relevant to your topic. Questions that may be addressed

indirectly here are, among others, "Why does this approach matter in the context of this particular topic?" or "To what extent can this particular focus enrich previous models of analyzing this specific text?" Mind that you should be very clear in how you proceed to conceptualize your own findings/research

3-4-1d. The Structure
Most academic introductions follow an 'inverted pyramid' structure: they start broad and narrow down to a specific thesis or research question.
The introduction should reveal some broad knowledge of the overall topic and quickly focus on the major point of the paper.

In papers that rely on secondary research, this section would provide the necessary background or history for understanding the discussion to come. A Review-of-Literature more specifically synthesizes (明确综合) information from a variety of significant sources related to the major point of the paper.

3-4-2. Materials & Methods
Methods section can be quite variable (可调的, 可变的). In many of the social sciences, the methodology is very important and is often described in considerable detail. However, in the natural sciences and engineering and in parts of medical research, standard practices and established methods or procedures are much more widely available.

The variation (差异) across the disciplines also lies in that even the term Methods is not always used, as when authors use The Study as their section heading. In some fields, it is common to have subsections in Methods that might deal with materials, the apparatus used, definitions employed, the subjects or participants in the study, or the statistical procedures used. For example, the experiment description is very important for this section of papers of experimental nature.

In papers that rely on primary research, the Methodology section provides a detailed description of the experiment design.
In either case, this section justifies the research done by either showing that the writer has done their homework and/or has a clear understanding of research methods.

The description of an experiment is composed of the following elements:
The subjects used (plants, animals, human beings, etc.) and their pre-experiment handling and care, when and where the study or experiment was carried out.

If a field study, a description of the study site, including the physical and biological features, and precise location.

The experiment or sampling design (e.g. controls, treatments, the variables measured, how many samples were collected, etc.).

This section requires more use of the third person and passive constructions. Remember to use the past tense throughout.

Language Tips

(1) To describe measurement

"From Fig.1, it can be estimated that the melted metal will be expanded to 2.2 kg simply because large amount of compositions were added in the reaction."

(2) To describe statistics

"The proportion of university researchers surveyed relative to total academic staff as measured by HESA is largely similar across UK Regions, ranging from a lowest 12.2% for Northeast to a highest 19.5% for Southwest."

"Overall, 25% of respondents indicated that they had been involved in patenting activities at least once, with Electrical & Electronics Engineering showing the highest percentage (38%) and Mathematics and Computer Science the lowest (4 and 11%, respectively)."

(3) To describe research, means

"Four individually labeled spectrophotometer tubes were prepared using different amounts…"

"We also include the age and the academic status of the individual as explanatory variables."

"Here we examine the extent to which previous experience in research collaborations with industry has an impact on engaging in a variety of interactions."

3-4-3. Results

In the section of results, the author should boil down(make shorter)all the facts and data that have been collected. Its function is to objectively present key results in an orderly and logical sequence without interpretation.

Overall, one emerging pattern for handling a particular result looks like this:

Procedure, statement of general findings, more specific statements, example/case/commentary.

In addition, tables and figures are often inserted to make a more vivid and clearer demonstration.

Examples:

"This section is only included in papers that rely on primary research."

"This section catalogues the results of the experiment. The results should be presented in a clear and unbiased way."

"As can be seen from the Table …"

"Our experimental data are briefly summarized as follows…"

"Figure 3 shows the result obtained from studies of…"

" Table 2 indicates that people reading on internet rise by 15 times…"

As can be seen from the following Table, males are significantly more likely than females to have been reading Internet news longer. About half of men have been reading Internet news five years or more in comparison to slightly over one quarter of females. On the other hand, females...

A Comparison of Male and Female on Years Reading Internet News

1-2 Years	16	47
3-4 Years	31	26
5 Years or More	53	27
(Valid Cases)	(118)	(85)The Body Sections of an Academic Paper

As can be seen from the Table above, males are significantly more likely than females to have been reading Internet news longer. About half of men have been reading Internet news five years or more in comparison to slightly over one quarter of females. On the other hand, females are almost three times as likely to have begun reading Internet news within the past one or two years. Almost half of women have been reading Internet news for one to two years in comparison to 16 percent of men.

3-4-4. Discussion

The function of the discussion is to interpret the results in light of what was already known about the subject of the investigation, and to explain new understanding of the problem after taking the results into consideration.

The primary objective in writing this section is to show the relationship between the facts, their underlying causes, their effects, and their theoretical implications, as well as to explain the facts denoted by symbols or signs of mathematics.

3-4-4a. The discussion part includes:

(1) Analyzing the data (it's often quite extensive and the others are often quite short);

(2) Pointing out the limitations and doubts;

(3) Expressing viewpoints and how the results and interpretations agree/contrast with previously published work;

(4) Stating the theoretical implications and practical application of the study;

(5) Arriving at a conclusion.

3-4-4b. Options in Opening a Discussion

(1) It can be preceded by a statement reminding the readers of what you have done including reporting your accomplishments by highlighting major findings, relating and evaluating your data in the light of previous research, interpreting your data by making suggestions as to why your results are the way they are or anticipate and dealing with potential criticisms (if necessary).

(2) You may start your discussion with a general reorientation to the study as a whole, using "skeletal" formulations like the following:

In this paper we have investigated...

The main purpose of this paper has been to...

The survey reported on in this study has produced a wealth of data.

3-4-4c. Language Tips

(1) Use the <u>active voice</u> whenever possible in this section. <u>Forceful expressions</u> should be used to give the readers an impression of the writer's academic capability.

(2) to make general statements

"The overall results indicate…"

"In general, the experimental samples resisted…"

(3) to express limitations

"It should be noted that this study has been primarily concerned with…"

"The findings of this study are restricted to…"

"The limitations of this study are clear:…"

"We would like to point out that we have not…"

Exercise

Read the Sample of Discussion and answer the questions:

1. What are the results of the study?
2. According to the writer, what accounts for students' better performance on the writing test?
3. What limitations does the author point out?

3-4-5. Conclusion

Functions of the conclusion Include: Summing up, statement of conclusion, statement of recommendation and graceful termination. Summarizes the main arguments of the paper and adds the results of the main part.

The conclusion should reinforce the major claims or interpretation in a way that is not mere summary. The writer should try to indicate the significance of the major claim/interpretation beyond the scope of the paper but within the parameters (限度) of the field. The writer might also present complications (困难) the study illustrates or suggest further research the study indicates is necessary.

A helpful strategy to find out whether a paper is well structured is to read the introduction and then the conclusion as both should transmit (传播/送) the paper's focus, methodology as well as your results.

3-4-5a Language Tips

"From… we now conclude…"

"To sum up, we have revealed…"

"In conclusion, the results show…"

"As you can see, this essay proves the thesis that…"

"These findings of the research have led the author to the conclusion that…"

3-4-5b. Examples

Conclusion

(1) In business, sales personnel serve as the link between a company and its customers. Designing a sales force involves decisions regarding objectives, strategy, structure and compensation. Once these have been accomplished, a manager must manage its sales representatives by training supervising, motivating and evaluating the sales representatives. (summary of the main points)

(2) It has been said that in business there are two parts to every sale—the part performed by the organization and the part performed by the salesperson. Both the salesperson and the business organization must contribute proficiently(skillfully) in creating, managing, and maintaining a successful sales force. (conclusion)

4. Acknowledgement

Acknowledgement is used to show the author's gratitude.

It includes personal or institutional assistance and/or any sources of funding that supported the research.

Those who made greater contributions are followed by those who made less contributions, and individuals come first while institutions second.

Examples

"The authors would like to extend their sincere thanks to Mike Goslin, Hans Weber, Peggy Wetzel and Stump Brady. This work was supported by ARPA Contract DABT63-93-C047."

"This study was supported by a grant from the Cancer Research Society, Montreal, Canada."

"Preparation of this research was greatly aided by generous research grants from English Department, Xi'an Jiaotong University as well as from Centers for Chinese Studies in University of Michigan."

"Our special appreciation goes to all those involved, who were dedicated to working with us generously and devoting all their energy to complete the project."

"The author wishes to express his/her sincere appreciation to Professor Wang Lan for reading the manuscript and giving valuable advice."

"The author is indebted to Professor Wang Lan for reading the manuscript and giving valuable advice."

"We have also benefited from researchers who gave us the most advanced grounding in economics, management and philosophy of science."

5. Reference/Bibliography

Some General Remarks:

Whatever you write about, a critical re-evaluation as well as accurate documentation of your sources are essential to an academic paper. Your paper should be based on a consistent line of argumentation that constitutes your own approach. You need to Document(记录) your sources to <u>avoid plagiarism (剽窃)!</u>

Plagiarism is the most severe crime in academia. You plagiarize when you use someone else's formulations directly but also when you display someone else's ideas, trains of thoughts, or line of argumentation as your own without acknowledging the sources. If found out, you will not receive credit and you will not be given the opportunity to write an alternative paper for the course. If you plagiarize, you severely damage your academic reputation. And remember that your instructors have discovered the internet as well!

5-1 Documentation of Sources (Reference)

(1) The careful documentation of sources is crucial to good scholarly writing. Whenever you draw on the work of another person or institution, you must document your source by indicating what you borrowed—whether fact, opinions, or quotation—and where you borrowed it from. Whether you quote from another text directly, paraphrase it, or take from it an idea which you express entirely in your own words, you must properly document that source.

(2) The last page of your paper must be a statement by which you guarantee that you have not used any unacknowledged (未被承认的)sources.

(3) Follow the citation or reference style the professor indicates is appropriate or that is most common in your discipline.

(4) A reference list includes only the works that have been cited in the paper;

5-2 Documentation of Sources (Bibliography)

A bibliography, apart from the above, may also include other books and articles that have been important sources of information in the preparation of the paper.

5-3 Referencing Systems

APA (the American Psychological Association) Style is primarily used in the social sciences and in many of the physical sciences.

MLA (the Modern Language Association) Style is mainly used in the humanities.

MLA and APA styles, both in the alphabetical listing, can cover most fields.

5-4 Quotations

Citation can be divided into two types: direct quotations and indirect quotations.

5-4-1 Direct quotations

Quotation marks (" ") are used to indicate the directly cited fragment. The author's last name and the page number altogether appear within parentheses ( ) at the end of the sentence.

E.g. It is said that "little difference has been observed between the technological integrated classroom and the traditional classroom" (Zhong 43).

5-4-2 Indirect quotations

Compared with the direct quotations, the only difference is <u>no quotations marks</u> here.

In APA Style, the authors' last name and the date of publication appear in the sentence (APA Style)

Example

Fisher, Dwyer and Yocam (1996) detailed the Apple Classrooms of Tomorrow (ACOT) project.

More examples:

Ancient writers attributed the invention of the monochord (单弦琴)to Pythagoras (毕达哥拉斯), who lived in the sixth century BC (Marcuse 197).

Marcuse reports that ancient writers attributed the invention of the monochord to Pythagoras who lived in the sixth century BC (197).

MLA Style	Heading
Works Cited Craner, Paul M. "New Tool for an Ancient Art: The Computer and Music." Computer and the Humanities 25 (1991):303-313.	**The basic format for an online periodical:** Author's last name, First name. "Title of the work." Name of the periodical Volume number Date of publication. Date of access <network address>. Author's last name, First name, "Title of the article." Name of the periodical Volume number (Date of publication): Page ranges.
Thompson, Smith. The Folktale. New York: Dryden, 1946.	**The basic format for a book:** Author's last name, First name. Title of the book. Publisher's location: Name of publisher, Date of publication.
Tully, R. Brent, et al. " Global Extinction in Spiral Galaxies." Astronomical Journal 115.6 (1998).27 June 1998 <http://www.journals.uchicago.edu/AJ/journal/issues/v115n6/980002/980002.html>.	**The basic format for an online periodical:** Author's last name, First name. "Title of the work." Name of the periodical Volume number Date of publication. Date of access <network address>.

PART THREE

BUSINESS LETTERS

CHAPTER 1 Sales Promotion

1. The Purpose of Writing "Sales Letters"

To extend business, to persuade the reader—the buyer to buy what the sellers are able to supply.

When writing a sales letter, the seller should try to present the offer from the point of view of the buyer, not the seller so as to promote sales of the goods.

2. How to Write a Good Sales Letter ?

A good sales letter consists of four essential elements, it must

(1) arouse interest

(2) create desire

(3) carry conviction

(4) induce action

3. Examples of Sales Letters

Example 1

Informing of New Oven into the Market

Dear Sirs,

We have pleasure in telling you that we have just introduced our electronic oven to the market, and are enclosing sales promotional literature to give you full details. No doubt your customers will appreciate the opportunity to purchase this fine product and with this in mind we are enclosing an order form for you to complete and please return to us without delay.

You will receive a special introductory discount of 10% which we can maintain until October 10.

Yours faithfully,

(注: sales promotional literature 促销说明书; order form 订货单; enclose 附寄)

Example 2

Recommending the Best Selling Product

Dear Sirs,

　　You will be interested to hear that we have recently developed our new product, which is selling very strongly on the home market.

　　Because of its success in this country, we thought there might be a sales potential abroad, and we would welcome your advice as to whether, in your opinion, there is a market in your district.

　　If you agree we shall be glad to supply you with our samples for you to show to the potential customers. You will find enclosed an order form in case you wish to make an immediate order.

Yours faithfully,

(**注**: a sales potential 销售潜力; potential customers 潜在客户)

Example 3

Promoting Sales for Plastic Handbag

Dear Sirs,

　　We are taking the liberty of sending you with this letter a copy of our current price list for plastic handbags. The high quality of our products is well known and universally acknowledged and we are confident that a trial order would convince you that, at the prices quoted, the goods we are offering are excellent value for money.

　　From all list prices we allow a trade discount of 35% and a further special discount of 5%, making 40% in all, on orders received on or before 31st May. Under pressure of rising costs we shall not find it possible to extend these favourable terms beyond that date, so why not take advantage of them now and send us an immediate order?

　　We are offering you goods of the very high quality on unusually generous terms and would welcome the opportunity to serve you.

Yours faithfully,

(**译文**: 今冒昧随函附寄一份我方塑料手提包价目表。我方产品质量已被普遍承认。我们认为，以所报价格试订，你方会认识到，该种产品确值此价。对5月31日前收到的订单，我们将给予35%的交易折扣及5%的特别折扣，其总数为40%。因受价格上涨压力，我方不能将此优惠条件往后延期，敬请速下订单。我方以极优惠条件向你方提供高质量商品，并愿借此机会为贵方服务。)

4. Useful Sentences on Sales Promotion

(1) We have pleasure in sending you our catalogue and price list, which will give you full information about our various new products.

(2) We are able to quote you very advantageous terms and assure you that all your orders will receive our immediate and most careful attention.

(3) We hope to be favored with your orders, in the execution of which we will neglect nothing that can contribute towards giving you entire satisfaction.

(Note: be favored with your orders 敬请订购; neglect nothing 尽全力)

(4) To acquaint you with the Light Industrial Goods we handle, we are sending you, under separate cover by airmail, a commodity list and several samples for your reference.

(Note: to acquaint sb. with sth. 使……了解……)

(5) We have learned that there is a good demand for... in your market, and we would like to take this opportunity of enclosing our quotation No.... for your consideration. We would thank you in advance for your pushing the sale of our products.

(6) We note with regret that our earlier offers in respect of.... have not interested you, but we take the liberty of enclosing an offer of our new product and hope that you will be ready to consider it.

(7) We believe that you will carefully consider our offer and expect to have favorable news from you shortly. You may be aware that these goods have been shipped to various markets where they have been favorably received. It would be to your advantage to try out a shipment.

(Note: to sb's advantage 对某人有利; try out a shipment 试订)

(8) We hope you received our catalogue safely. Not hearing from you gives us cause to wonder if it has gone astray in the post. If on the other hand you have received it, we should deem it a favour if you would write us saying on which point you are hesitating.

(Note: we should deem it a favour if... 如能……我们不胜感激)

(9) The price offered is already very reasonable, but in order to encourage business between us, we are prepared to allow you a discount of 2%.

(10) As we are willing to expand the trade relations with you, we have quoted you very low prices. When our present stock is exhausted, we shall be unable to repeat them.

(Note: When our present stock is exhausted, we shall be unable to repeat them. 一旦现货售完,我方便无法以此价格供货。)

(11) As far as the quality is concerned, you may rest assured that our products compare favorably with those of other origins supplied at the same price level.

(12) You will note that our packing has been greatly improved, with the result that our recent shipments have all turned out to the satisfaction of our clients.

(Note: with the result that our recent shipments have all turned out to the satisfaction of our clients. 因而顾客对我们近期的装船十分满意。)

CHAPTER 2 Ordering

1. What's an Order ?

When ordering, an order is needed. An order is a request to supply a specified quantity of goods, which may result from an offer or an enquiry with subsequent quotations.

2. The Quality of an Order/an Order-Letter

Accuracy and clarity are the essential qualities of an order or an order-letter, which should:

(1) include full details of description of the goods, such as quantities, prices and article numbers;

(2) state the mode of packing, the port of destination and the time of shipment;

(3) confirm the terms of payment as agreed upon in preliminary negotiations.

(Note: preliminary negotiations 初期洽谈)

"First" orders, the orders from new customers, should most certainly be acknowledged by a letter, which should:

(1) express pleaure at receiving the order;

(2) add a favorable comment on the goods ordered;

(3) include an assurance of prompt and careful attention;

(4) draw attention to other products likely to be of interest;

(5) hope for further orders.

3. Examples of Ordering

Example 1

Making a Trial Order

Dear Sirs,

　　Thank you for your letter of × ×. Having studied your illustrated catalogue and price list, we have chosen six models among them, for which we'd like to enclose our order.

We would like to stress the fact that this is a trial order. If we are satisfied with both the quality of goods and shipment, you can expect our regular repeated orders. In order to avoid any difficulties with the customs authorities here, please make sure that our shipping instructions are carefully observed.

For our financial and credit standing, we refer you to the Chamber of Commerce in your country.

Yours faithfully,

(Note: financial and credit standing 财务及信誉状况; refer... to... 向……打听, 查询; the Chamber of Commerce 商会)

Example 2

Acknowledgement of Order No. 5

Dear Sirs,

Re: Your Order No. 5

We have booked you Order No.5 for ×× and are sending you here with our Sales Confirmation No. AP-111 in duplicate. Please sign and return one copy to us for file.

It is understood that a letter of credit in our favour covering the above-mentioned goods will be established immediately. We wish to point out that the stipulations in the relevant credit should strictly conform to the terms stated in our Sales Comfirmation in order to avoid subsequent amendments. You may rest assured that we shall effect shipment with the least possible delay upon receipt of the credit.

We appreciate your cooperation and look forward to receiving your further orders.

Yours faithfully,

Example 3

Confirming the Order

Dear Sirs,

We are very pleased to receive your order and confirm that all the items required are in stock. It is a pleasure to have the opportunity of supplying you and we are sure that you will be satisfied with the quality of our goods.

Your method of payment, a draft at sight under L/C, is quite acceptable to us. On receiving your credit from the bank we will make up your order and will make shipping advice as soon as the shipment is completed. We assure you that this order and further orders shall have our immediate attention.

Yours faithfully,

4. Useful Sentences on Ordering

(1) We have pleasure to enclose here with our contract No. 110 in two originals for your counter-signature. Please send us one copy back at your earliest convenience.

(Note: for your counter-signature 给您会签)

(2) Enclosed please find our clients' order for..., but it should be noted that this order is placed on your guarantee for their quality as stated in your letter of...

(3) We hereby confirm our acceptance of your order and are enclosing here with our sales confirmation in two originals, one of which please sign and return to us for our file.

(Note: for our file 供我们存档)

(4) We regret to inform you that owing to our heavy commitments, we are unable to entertain any fresh order for... However, we are keeping your enquiry before us and, as soon as we are in a position to accept new orders, we will contact you by cable.

(Note: heavy commitments 过量订单; unable to entertain any fresh order 不能接受任何新订单; keep your enquiry before us 留意你方询盘/要求)

(5) If the quality of your... is satisfactory and the prices are right, we expect to place regular orders for fairly large numbers with you.

(Note: place regular orders for fairly large numbers with you 定期向你方大量订购)

(6) We have been informed that an L/C covering the above-mentioned goods will be established immediately. You may rest assured that we will arrange for dispatch by the first available steamer without any delay upon receipt of your L/C.

(Note: rest assured 放心; dispatch 分派)

(7) Please pay your attention to the fact that the stipulations in this relevant credit should strictly conform to the terms as stated in our S/C so as to avoid subsequent amendments.

(**译文**: 请注意，信用证条款必须与我方销售确认书条款完全相符，以免日后修改。)

(8) Your order No. × for... has been booked. Please inform us the color assortment immediately and open the covering L/C in our favor according to the terms contracted.

(**译文**: 我方已接受你方订购××的第×号订单。请即告花色品种，并按合同规定条款开立以我方为受益人的有关信用证。)

(9) We regret to inform you that there is no market for the high-priced goods at this end. Please offer only the goods of the medium price range.

(**译文**: 今歉告，本地市场没有高价商品的销路，敬请提供中等价格的商品。)

(10) Having studied your catalogue and price list, we find that the price you offered is about 5% higher than the level workable to us, and we refrain from making a counteroffer.

(**译文**: 研究你方目录及价目表后，我方发现，你方所报价格比我方所能接受价格高出5%，故我方无法做出还盘。)

CHAPTER 3 Urging, Examining and Amending L/C

1. Urging the Establishment of L / C

When the buyer fails to establish L /C, or it does not reach the seller in time, the seller should send a letter, a fax, a telex or a cable to the buyer to urge him to expedite the L /C. or to ascertain its whereabouts. When writing the first urging letter, the tone should be polite, while the second one will show disappointment and surprise though still restrained.

(Note: urging, examing and amending L /C 催证、审证和改证; expedite 加速开立; whereabouts 下落)

1.1 Examples of Urging Letters

Example 1

Dear Sirs,

<u>Our Sales Confirmation No. TE123</u>

With reference to the 4,000 dozen shirts under our Sales Confirmation No.TE123, we wish to draw your attention to the fact that the date of delivery is approaching , but up to the present we have not received the covering Letter of Credit. Please do your utmost to expedite its establishment, so that we may execute the order within the prescribed time.

In order to avoid subsequent amendments, please see to it that the L/C stipulations are in exact accordance with the terms of the contract.

We look forward to receiving your favorable response at an early date.

Yours faithfully,

Example 2

Gentlemen,

    Re: <u>Order No. 234</u>

    With reference to your Order No.234 for..., we want to invite your attention to the fact that the covering L/C hasn't reached us in spite of our repeated requests by letters and telexes.

    Your Purchase Order stipulates shipment to be made during October and L/C to reach here by the end of September. Today it is already October 17, yet we don't appear to have received your L/C. In order to book the shipping space at an earlier date, you are requested once again to have the L/C established immediately by cable.

    If your L/C fails to reach here by the end of this month, we'll have to cancel your order.

    We await your immediate attention to this matter.

Yours truly,

1.2 Useful Sentences on Urging L/C

(1) An irrevocable L/C covering this order for $40,000 in your favor has been opened available until...

(**译文**：以你方为受益人、金额为40,000美元的此笔订单的不可撤销信用证业已开出,有效期至……月……日止。)

(2) More than two months have passed since the date of the signing of the above mentioned contract, but the relevant L/C has not yet reached us. Please expedite the L/C as soon as possible.

(3) As stipulate in our Sales Confirmation No..., the covering L/C should reach us not later than...We should request you to expedite the establishment of the L/C so that we may effect shipment by the direct steamer scheduled to arrive here about...

(Note: effect shipment 装船)

(4) As the goods against your Order No.... have been ready for shipment for quite some time, it is imperative that you take immediate action to have the covering L/C established at your earliest convenience.

(Note: the goods against your Order No.... have been ready for shipment 你方第……号订单货物已备妥,待装船。)

(5) With reference to your indent No...., we have not yet received the relative L/C up to now. As this order has been outstanding for considerable time, we would ask you to give this matter your immediate attention.

(Note: with reference to 关于; indent 订单; outstanding 未解决的,未履行的)

2. Examining and Amending L/C

When the seller finds that there are some discrepancies or some unforeseen special clauses to which he does not agree in the L/C, the seller should send an advice to the buyer, asking him to make amendment.

(Note: discrepancy 差异; unforeseen 无法预料的)

2.1　Examples

Example 1　Asking for Amendment to L/C

Dear Sirs,

　　We would like to explain the matter of L/C amendment.

　　According to the L/C we received, the payment was to be made at 120 d/s. But we want it to be made at sight. This was agreed on by you and expressly mentioned in your order sheet. Therefore please amend it as stated. The goods will be shipped by 20th of this month. We should be obliged for your immediate amendment of the L/C as requested by us.

　　Please reply by cable.

Yours faithfully,

Example 2　Amending L/C to Allow Partial Shipment and Transshipment

Dear Sirs,

　　Letters of Credit No. 567 issued by the Bank of New South Wales has duly arrived. On perusal, we find that transshipment and partial shipment are not allowed.

　　As direct steamers to your port are few and far between, we have to ship via Hong Kong more often than not. As to partial shipment, it would be to our mutual benefit if we could ship immediately whatever is ready instead of waiting for the whole shipment to be completed. Therefore, we have cabled you this morning, asking you to amend your L/C to read "Partshipment and Transshipment Allowed."

　　We hope you will see to it that the amendment is cabled without delay.

Yours faithfully,

(Note: on perusal 经详阅/细读; via 经过; more often than not 时常)

Example 3 Asking for Extension of L/C

Dear Sirs,

　　We have cabled you today asking for a 2-week extension of the L/C covering your order No. 129 for 1000 units of our _____. The cable read:

　　the L/C came in yesterday but we regret to find that our supplier cannot get the shipment out here before the expiration of the shipping time april 30 please extend L/C 2 weeks more.

　　Please note that on shipment of anything coming from the South, we need lots of time for shipment—particularly in the summer time when the transportation conditions are worse.

　　Your prompt attention to this matter would be much appreciated.

Yours faithfully,

(Note: extension 延长; expiration 到期)

2.2 Useful Sentences on Amending L/C

(1) Since there is no direct steamer sailing for your port, we would have to request you to amend your L/C to allow transshipment.

(2) Kindly ask the bank to amend Credit No.... to read: "Joint Bills of Lading with Credit No.... acceptable."

(译文：请要求银行将第……号信用证修改为："接受第……号信用证项下联运提单。")

(3) Please delete from the L/C the clause: "All bank commission and charges are for beneficiary's account." Such should be paid by the exporting party only.

(译文：请将信用证中"所有银行佣金和费用均由受益人支付"之条款删去。因这些费用应由出口方承担。)

(4) Your L/C stipulates 60 days sight, whereas our contract shows 30 days sight. So you are requested to make necessary amendment to the L/C and advise us by telex before...

(Note: 60 days sight 60天期票)

(5) Please amend L/C No.... as follows:

Amount is to be increased by RMB ￥506;

The words "12 dozen per carton" are to be replaced by "20 dozen per carton."

(Note: carton 纸箱)

2.3 An Example of Advice of Amendment

| 受益人
Beneficiary
_____ | 澳门南通银行
NAN TUNG BANK LTD.,
MACAU | 年　月　日
Dated |

修改通知书

Advise of Amendment

用航邮通知/电报证实书　　　　　　　通知银行
By Air Mail/Cable Confirmation　　　　Advising Bank _____

　　　　　关于　我行信用证第　号　　金额
　　　　　Re: Our L/C No.　　　Amount: _____

敬启者, 兹应申请人:　　之要求特将上述信用证之条款作下列修改:

Upon request of the grantor: the above mentioned L/C is to be amended as follows:

其他条款不变, 即希洽照为荷。

while other terms and conditions remain unchanged which please take note.

澳门南通银行

NAN TUNG BANK LTD., MACAU

CHAPTER 4 Complaints, Disputes and Claims

1. Why Do the Complaints Arise?

The complaints generally arise from one of the following situations:

(1) The wrong goods may have been sent.

(2) The quality may not be satisfactory.

(3) The goods may have been delivered damaged or late.

(4) The prices charged may be excessive, or not as agreed.

2. How to Write a Complaint or Claim Letter ?

A complaint or claim letter usually follows the under mentioned outlines:

(1) Begin by regretting the need to complain.

(2) Mention the date of the order, the date of delivery and the goods complained about.

(3) State your reasons for being dissatisfied and ask for an explanation.

(4) Refer to the inconvenience caused.

(5) Suggest how the matter should be put right.

3. How to Write Letters Concerning Disputes ?

Letters concerning disputes should be written tactfully and reasonable. They must be confined to a statement of facts and insist on the absolute truth.

4. Examples of Correspondence (Letters of Complaints, Disputes and Claims)

Example 1A   Complaining about Delay in Shipment

Dear Sirs,

We enclose here with the figures of sales in your product during the past six months, from which you will see that our sales of the special line are quite disappointing.

Because the end-users here are in urgent need of the goods, we requested your prompt shipment of them, which you accepted. However, five weeks went by before the goods arrived instead of three weeks, and we lost a wonderful opportunity of sales.

On enquiry we found that the goods were not shipped until four weeks after the date of dispatch. We have been put to considerable inconvenience through long delay and have to ask you to make us allowance corresponding to our loss.

Yours faithfully,

Example 1B   Apologizing for the Delay of Shipment

Dear Sirs,

We have received your letter complaining our delay of shipment, and we are very sorry that we have not been able to deliver your order on time. The delay was caused by the belated arrival of some of the new materials.

It is on account of the reasons entirely beyond our control. We are glad, however, that your order will be ready for shipment next week, and we hope that they will arrive in time for the season. Please accept our apologies to you for the delay and the inconvenience it has caused you.

Yours faithfully,

Example 2A   Claim for Inferior Quality and Short Weight

Dear Sirs,

<u>**Re: Contract No. 1111 × × ×**</u>

With reference to the newly arrived shipment ex S.S. "Great Wall" under the captioned contract, we regret to state that we have found upon inspection that × × × content is only 97.12%, which is obviously inferior to the quality stipulated in the contract. We have also discovered that 11 drums are short of weight, each from 10 to 12 kilos, totaling 124 kilos.

Please let us know how you are going to settle this case with us. Your prompt reply will be appreciated.

Yours faithfully,

Example 2B Acknowledging Receipt of a Claim

Dear Sirs,

　　We acknowledge receipt of your letter of... complaining about the quality and the shortage in weight in connection with our shipment of ×××per S.S. "Great Wall". We shall immediately make a thorough investigation which, however, will take a little time, and shall advise you of the result upon the conclusion of our enquiry.

　　Nevertheless, we regret the inconvenience you have experienced, and wish to thank you for having brought the matter to our attention.

Yours faithfully,

Example 2C Rejecting a Complaint

Dear Sirs,

<u>Re: Your Complaint about Quality and Weight of ×××</u>
<u>Ex S.S. "Great Wall"</u>

　　Referring to your letter of... on the above subject, we wish to inform you that the shipment in question was carefully examined by our experts at the time of shipment and was found to be in strict conformity with the provision in the contract as regards both quality and weight.

　　Under such circumstances we regret that we are not in a position to entertain your claim, and trust that you will see your way clear to treat the matter properly.

Yours faithfully,

Example 3A Proposing Settlement by Arbitration

Dear Sirs,

　　We are surprised to note from your letter dated..., that you are not prepared to consider our offer of a 15% discount to compensate you for the defects in the goods supplied according to S/C No.115.

　　Though we consider our offer adequate, and even very generous, we are prepared to admit that our views may not be all justified. At the same time, we regard with disfavor your threat to suspend business connection if we do not entertain your claim. We suggest that the dispute be settled by arbitration.

> We shall be pleased to discuss with you where and how the arbitration is to take place.
>
> Yours faithfully,

(Note: proposing settlement by arbitration 建议提交仲裁解决; S/C 销售合同; we regard with disfavor your threat to suspend business connection if we do not entertain your claim. 我们不赞成你们以若不同意索赔就中断业务往来相威胁的做法。)

Example 3B   On Award of Arbitration

> Dear Sirs,
>
> We are pleased to see that, concerning our disputes under Contract No...., both of us are satisfied with the fair and reasonable arbitration award which was rendered by the Foreign Economic and Trade Arbitration Commission of CCPIT after they had thoroughly examined every aspect of this case. The award is being carried out by both sides. What pleases us most is that our friendly relationship has not been marred by the disputes which had to be resolved by arbitration. On the other hand, this case has deepened the mutual understanding and confidence between us.
>
> We highly appreciate your cooperation and expect further development of business between us.
>
> Yours faithfully,

(Note: award 裁决; the Foreign Economic and Trade Arbitration Commission of CCPIT 中国国际贸易促进委员会对外经济贸易仲裁委员会; mar 损害)

5. Useful Sentences on Complaints, Disputes and Claims

(1) The goods arrived 12M/T short, so the buyers lodged a claim on this shipment for US $1,200 for short weight.
(Note: M/T 公吨)

(2) As long as the shipping company is found to be responsible for the damage, the seller shouldn't be held liable.

(3) We agree to withdraw our claim on condition that you make us an offer for an equal quantity at a price 10% lower.
(Note: at a price 10% lower 以低10%的价格。)

(4) We will compensate you in one way or another with your next order provided you

withdraw your claim.

(5) We regret to inform you that the goods arrived in a damaged condition.

(6) Shippers require a survey report so that they may know the extent of the damage.

(7) We are sending you some samples drawn at random from your shipment in order that you can see yourselves the degree of the damage.

(8) We have to make a claim on you for compensation as your shipment is inferior to the sample.

(9) You can file a claim against the People's Insurance Company of China for $8,800 for the damage of the goods in transit.

(10) Disputes may be submitted for arbitration in case no settlement can be reached through negotiation between both parties.

6. Some Terms Used in Complaints, Disputes and Claims

Discharge of a debt; discharge of liability; discharge one's debt 清偿债务

Claim against sb 向……索赔

Claim arising from a breach of the contract 违约所引起的赔偿要求

Claim arising on a bill of lading 有关提单所引起的索赔

Claim arising from a defect of the goods 货物瑕疵所引起的索赔

Claim barred by reason of limitation 时效受限制的索赔

Claim based on lack of conformity of the goods 货物不符产生的索赔

Claim based on physical loss damage 货物灭失所产生的索赔

Claim for compensation of damage 损害赔偿的诉权

Claim for contribution in general average 要求分摊共同海损

Claim for damage 由于损坏而索赔

Claim for financial loss 关于经济损失的诉权

Claim for general average 共同海损分担的诉权

Claim for inferior quality 由于品质低劣而索赔

Claim for payment 要求赔偿货款

Claim for reimbursement 要求偿还，索偿

Claim for short delivery 由于短装而索赔

Accept / Entertain a claim 受理索赔

Dismiss a claim 驳回索赔

Reject a claim 拒绝索赔

Relinquish / Withdraw a claim 撤回索赔

Settle a claim 解决索赔

Admit a claim 同意索赔

Waive a claim 放弃索赔

Have recourse to 向……行使追索权

With recourse 有追索权

Without recourse 无追索权

Faulty goods 有毛病的货物

Faulty packing 有缺陷的包装

Short-weight 短重

Short delivery 短交

Short shipment; Short-shipped 短装

Short-calculated 少算

Short-invoiced 发票少开

Short-landed 短卸

Short-paid 少付

Survey Report on Examination of Damage or Shortage 检验残损或短缺证明书

Survey Report on Inspection of Tank Hold 船舱鉴定证明书

Survey Report on Quality 品质鉴定证明书

Survey Report on Weight 重量鉴定证明书

7. Exercises

Translate the following passages on complaints or claims into Chinese.

(1) Your claim respecting the shipment under S/C No.333 based on the alleged fault that we did not abide by the contract is a great surprise to us. After going through the stipulations in the S/C, we can find nowhere have we gone wrong. It is ture that you proposed to make two amendments to the contract, but they were not agreed upon nor confirmed by us. So we emphatically reject your claim and must ask you to cancel it.

(Note: the alleged fault 所谓的过失; abide by 遵守)

(2) It is most regrettable that the numerous negotiations about your claim on quality discrepancy relating to the goods supplied under S/C No.220 have resulted in nothing. Since you still consider our proposal unacceptable, we can only agree to submit this case to arbitration as you proposed in your letter dated...

(Note: claim on quality discrepancy 质量异议索赔)

(3) We are surprised at your request for allowing you another two months to settle this claim and have to say that we are very dissatisfied with your dilatory manner in dealing with it. Under the circumstances, we are compelled to suspend new business with you.

(Note: dilatory manner 拖沓作风)

(4) As certified in our Commodity Inspection Certificate, our goods are fully up to your sample in respect of raw material used, wordmanship as well as packing. So the comments in your letter that we have passed off inferior goods as goods of good quality

are entirely groundless. Your claim is decidedly rejected.

(Note: be fully up to your sample 与你方样品完全相符; passed off inferior goods as goods of good quality 商品以次充好)

(5) The quality of the goods shipped to us last month under the Contract No.... is far below the standard quality of previous shipment. In such case, we have no choice but to make a claim on you, which we hope will receive your prompt attention.

(Note: make/lodge/file a claim on/against sb: 向……提出索赔; claim on sb. for... (compensation) 向……提出索赔; ...entitle us to ask for compensation... 使我们有权要求赔偿)

(6) Enclosed please find a duplicate copy of our statement of claim submitted to you. We trust that you will not let this claim stand in the way of further business between us and will settle it with the least delay. Your remittance in full discharge of this claim at an early date will be much appreciated.

(Note: a duplicate copy of our statement of claim 赔偿清单副本一份; with the least delay 迅速, 立即; remittance 寄/汇出; in full discharge of this claim 清偿全部索赔款项)

PART FOUR

Contractual Writing and Translation

CHAPTER 1 What's a Contract?

1. A contract shall be an agreement whereby the parties establish, change or terminate their civil relationship.
合同是当事人之间设立、变更、中止民事关系的协议。
2. Contracts referred to in this law are agreements between equal natural persons, legal persons and other organizations for the purpose of establishing, altering and terminating mutual civil rights and obligations.
合同是平等主体的自然人、法人、其他组织之间设立、变更、中止民事权利义务关系的协议。
3. 商务合同是一种契约性质的应用文。
在买方与卖方经过贸易洽谈, 双方达成协议以后, 应把双方同意的条件用文字固定下来, 所以, 这种文字产生的本身就在于郑重地表示订约人的信用, 并且用来防止当事人的利益被侵害, 因而它是负有法律责任的。
4. 商业合同由卖方制作的称为销售合同; 由买方制作的称为购货合同。现行国际贸易中采用的书面合同有两种形式：销售确认书及销售合同。
    (1) 销售确认书：适用于金额不大, 批量较少的小土特产品及轻工、服装产品。
    (2) 销售合同：也称为正式合同, 它常常在进行大宗商品或重要交易时使用。这种合同包括的内容比较全面, 项目很多, 但其基本内容可分为三大部分：合同首部; 合同本文; 合同尾部。

CHAPTER 2 The Structure of a Contract

合同由三大部分构成:

1. Preamble of a Contract: 约首
2. Body of a Contract: 约文
3. Witness Clause of a Contract: 约尾

1. Preamble of a Contract

The preamble usually includes:

title, number, date of signing, signing parties, place of signing, each party's authority, whereas clause, and so on

A Sample of Preamble

Purchase Confirmation

No. PT152   Date: March 1, 2003

Signed at: Guangzhou

Buyers: China National Produce & Animal By-Products Import & Export Corporation, Guangdong Native Produce Branch

Address: No.486, "623" Road, Guangzhou, China

Tel: Fax: E-mail:

Sellers: Datung Trading Co., Ltd.

Address: No. 165, Censa Road, Rangoon

Tel: Fax: E-mail:

The undersigned Buyers and Sellers have agreed to close the following transaction according to the terms and conditions stipulated here under:

(兹经买卖双方同意按下列条款达成如下交易。)

2. Body of a Contract

The body of a contract generally contains:

Definition clause

PART FOUR CONTRACTUAL WRITING AND TRANSLATION

General terms & conditions

Basic conditions

Duration

Termination

Assignment

Force Majeure

Governing law

Arbitration

Jurisdiction

Notice

Entire agreement clause

Amendment

And so on

2.1　The body of a contract usually involves:

(1) The type of contract and the categories and scope of the object of the contract

(2) The technical conditions, quality, standards, specification, and quantities of the object of the contract

(3) Time limit, place and method of performance

(4) The price terms, amount to be paid, ways of payment, and various types of additional charges

(5) Whether or not the contract may be assigned or the conditions for assignment

(6) The compensation and other liabilities for breach of contract

  (违约的赔偿和其他责任)

(7) Methods for resolving disputes arising under the contract

(8) The limits of the risks to be borne by the parties in performing the object and the coverage of insurance of the object

  (明确风险责任, 约定保险范围)

(9) A period of validity for the contract and the conditions for contractual extension and contractual termination before its expiration

  (合同的有效期限, 以及可以延长合同期限和提前终止合同的条件)

2.2　Detailed items contained in the body of a contract:

√ name of commodity

√ specifications, quantity and unit price

√ total value (USD)

√ country of origin and manufacturers

√ packing

- √ shipping mark
- √ time of shipment
- √ port of shipment
- √ port of destination
- √ payment
- √ insurance
- √ documents
- √ overdue interest
- √ inspection
- √ penalty
- √ force majeure
- √ claims
- √ termination
- √ notice
- √ incoterms (international commerce terms)
- √ arbitration

3. Witness / Final Clause of a Contract

Language validity

Copies

In the presence of

Annex

Signature

Seal

Examples of Witness/Final Clause of a Contract

This Contract is made out in two originals, each copy written in Chinese and English languages, both texts being equally valid. In case of any divergence of interpretation, the Chinese text shall prevail.

(……若对其解释产生歧义,则以中文文本为准。)

The annexes as listed in Articles 19 to this Contract shall form an integral part of this Contract.

(本合同第19条列出的附件为……不可分割的组成部分。)

Any amendment and/or supplement to this Contract shall be valid only after the authorized representatives of both parties have signed written document(s), forming integral part(s) of this Contract.

(……只有当双方授权的代表在书面文件上签字后才能生效,并成为……)

This Contract shall come into force after the signatures by the authorized representatives of both parties.

4. The General Clauses Involved in a Contract Summed Up

- √ Quality Clause
- √ Quantity Clause
- √ Price Clause
- √ Packing Clause
- √ Delivery Clause
- √ Payment Clause
- √ Insurance Clause
- √ Inspection Clause
- √ Claim Clause
- √ Late Delivery and Penalty
- √ Arbitration Clause
- √ Force Majeure Clause
- √ Breach and Cancellation of Contract Clause
- √ Miscellaneous Clause (Other Terms)
- √ Remark (Supplementary Conditions)

CHAPTER 3 Letter of Credit

1. The Definition of L/C

(1) An L/C is a tool or instrument of payment, and the payment is guaranteed by a bank. It is usually called "an open letter of request", because the opening bank requests the negotiating bank to advance money or give credit to the beneficiary, and promises that he will reimburse or repay the same to the negotiating bank against a Bill of Exchange accompanied by the relative shipping documents. (信用证是一种支付工具, 付款由银行担保。通常它被称为"公开请求信", 因为开证行请求议付行向受益人垫付货款或提供信贷, 并答应凭一张跟单汇票向议付行偿付或归还这笔货款。)

(2) 信用证是一种以银行信用为保证, 凭规定的单据付款的保证文件; 信用证是由一家银行(开证行)依照客户(申请人)的要求/指示或以自身的名义, 在符合信用证条款的条件下, 凭规定的单据①向第三者(受益人)或其指定人付款, 或承兑并支付受益人出具的汇票; ②或授权另一家银行进行该项付款, 或承兑并支付该汇票; ③或授权另一家银行议付。

2. Kinds of L/Cs

1) Sight L/C (即期信用证)

(L/C available by draft at sight; L/C by sight draft): When the seller presents a sight draft together with the shipping documents as stipulated in the L/C to the negotiating bank, the latter makes payment immediately. Likewise, when the negotiating bank delivers the sight draft and the documents to the opening bank, the latter also makes reimbursement at once.

2) Time or Usance L/C (远期信用证)

When the seller presents a time draft together with the shipping documents stipulated in the L/C to the negotiating bank, the latter doesn't make payment immediately. He transmits (转递) the draft and the documents to the opening bank. The opening bank doesn't pay the money immediately either. He just accepts (承兑) the draft and returns it to the seller. He makes payment when the time draft comes due.

Three ways about the time of payment:

(1) payable at... days' sight (见票后……天付款)

(2) payable at... days after date of draft (出票后……天付款)

(3) payable at... days after issued date of B/L (提单签发日期后……天付款)。

3) Revocable L/C (可撤销信用证)

Subject to amendment or cancellation at any moment without prior notice to the beneficiary. <u>It is unlikely to be acceptable to exporters in foreign trade</u>, as it doesn't provide them with any guarantee.

A revocable L/C usually bears one of these clauses:

"This credit may be revoked at any time without prior notice."

"This credit which is subject to revocation or modification at any time without notice to you, does not convey any engagement on our part and is simply for your guidance in preparing and presenting draft and documents."

("在任何时候不经通知你方,可将本证撤销或加以修改。本证并不表明我们作了任何保证,而只是作为你方制备和提交单据时参考。")

4) Irrevocable L/C (不可撤销信用证)

An irrevocable L/C cannot be modified or withdrawn by either the opening bank or the buyer within the credit validity without the consent of the seller. As long as the shipping documents surrendered by the exporter are in conformity with the stipulations of the L/C, the opening bank will surely take the responsibility of making payment. So, in foreign trade, most of the credits belong to this kind.

An irrevocable L/C usually bears the word "Irrevocable" at the beginning of the credit and the following clause at the end of it:

"We (the opening bank) hereby agree with the drawers, endorsers and bona fide holders of drafts drawn under and in compliance with the terms of this credit that such drafts will be duly honored on presentation to the drawee."

("我行在此向汇票的出票人、背书人及合法持有人表示同意,凡根据本证规定的条件开具的汇票在提交付款人时即将照付。")

5) Transferable L/C (可转让信用证)

Under transferable L/C, the beneficiary has the right to instruct the advising bank or negotiating bank to transfer the right of issuing a draft for the total amount to another person. The transferee is called the second beneficiary. After the transfer, the second beneficiary makes shipment of the goods and receives the payment, but the first beneficiary still bears the responsibility of the seller stipulated in the Sales Contract. A transferable L/C can only be transferred once. The second beneficiary can not transfer it again.

6) Divisible L/C (可分割信用证)

Under divisible L/C, the beneficiary has the right to transfer the right of issuing drafts to two or more than two persons. A divisible L/C must be a transferable L/C, but a transferable L/C is not certainly a divisible one. A divisible L/C is for several branch offices to make shipments at different ports and receive payments separately on the basis of the above L/C.

7) L/C without Recourse and with Recourse (无追索权和有追索权信用证)

(1) L/C without Recourse: Means that once the negotiating bank pays or discounts the seller's draft, the bank or the subsequent holder of the draft has no right to claim the amount paid, should the draft not be honored by the opening bank or the buyer. It bears one of these phrases: "Draft without recourse"; "Drawers of draft under this credit are not subject to the usual recourse attached to the drawer of a bill of exchange."

(本证项下汇票的出票人免受附加于汇票出票人的通常追索权的约束。)

(2) L/C with Recourse: Means the drawer or indorser of the draft is liable in case the draft is not paid by the drawee.

("有追索权信用证"意味着一旦汇票遭到受票人拒付,出票人或背书人有义务受到追索。)

For exports, the seller usually requires payment by a confirmed, irrevocable L/C, without recourse, payable by draft at sight, as it gives full protection against risks.

8) Confirmed L/C (保兑信用证)

一家银行开出的信用证,由另一家银行加以保兑的,根据《UCP500》的规定,若信用证未注明 "Confirmed" 字样,都认为不保兑。

For exports, the seller usually requires payment by a confirmed, irrevocable L/C, without recourse, payable by draft at sight, as it gives full protection against risks.

A confirmed L/C usually bears the word "Confirmed" at the beginning of it, besides, it states its undertaking of confirmation, such as: "At the request of our correspondent, we confirm the credit and thereby undertake to honor each draft drawn and presented as above specified."

("经我们往来行的要求,我们保兑本信用证并对根据上述规定开出和提示的每一张汇票承担付款责任。")

Therefore, the exporter can get payment from the negotiating bank for the goods shipped, providing that the terms and conditions of this credit are complied with.

9) Unconfirmed L/C (不保兑信用证)

An unconfirmed L/C is an L/C advised by the advising bank, who, being unwilling to hold any liability on the documents, merely advises the beneficiary that the credit has been opened and safeguards himself by adding in the L/C some phrases such as "We have no authority from our correspondent to confirm this credit or to guarantee the acceptance or payment of drafts drawn there against."

("本行没有得到我们的往来行的授权保兑或保证承兑或支付本证项下的汇票。")

"This letter is solely an advice of the opening of the afore-said credit and conveys no engagement by us, as we have not been authorized to confirm the above-mentioned credit."

("本函只是开立上述信用证的通知,并不表明本行已作任何担保,由于我们未被授权保兑上述信用证。")

Therefore, an unconfirmed L/C does not give the exporter any protection in the event of the buyer or the opening bank being unable to pay or refusing to do so.

10) Revolving L/C (循环信用证)

If the two parties of a transaction close a contract on long term and allow partial shipments, the buyer often establishes a revolving L/C so as to simplify formalities and reduce expenses. After the total or partial amount of the L/C has been used up, it can be restored to the original amount. The L/C can be used again and again until the stipulated times of use and the stipulated total amount have been reached.

There are four kinds of revolving L/C:

(1) Automatic revolving L/C

(2) Non-Automatic revolving L/C

(3) Cumulative (累积) revolving L/C

(4) Non-Cumulative revolving L/C

循环信用证比一般信用证多了"Revolving"字样，其内容一般在信用证的特别条款中列出，如：

The total amount of drawing for any calendar month is not to exceed ×××, and unused balances are non-accumulative.

3. The Contents Involved in an L/C

1) The Relative Parties to L/C

2) Validity and Place of Expiry of L/C

3) Amount and Currency

4) Clause on Draft or Bill of Exchange

5) Description of Goods

6) Clauses on Documents (Bill of Lading; Insurance Policy)

7) Clauses on Shipment

8) Special Clauses/Conditions

9) Warranties of Issuing Bank

10) Statement on UCP

1) The Relative Parties to L/C 信用证的有关各方

(1) The opener (buyer, importer, applicant), who requests a bank to open an L/C.

(2) The issuer (the issuing, opening, establishing bank) — the bank in the importer's country issuing the L/C on request from the importer.

(3) The advising bank (notifying bank), in the exporter's country, who advises the exporter of the establishment of L/C.

(4) The drawer (seller), who sells the goods and draws a draft on the issuing bank or the buyer.

(5) The drawee (buyer)—the person, usually the buyer, on whom a draft is drawn, bears the responsibility of making payment when the draft comes due.

(6) The negotiating bank, who pays or accepts the draft presented by the exporter.

(7) The reimbursing bank, (the issuing bank itself) who repays the negotiating bank for the money

spent in advance by the latter. In some cases, it may be its reimbursing agent in a third country.

(8) The beneficiary, (the exporter) the party in whose favor the L/C is issued, i.e., the person who is entitled to draw a draft and get the payment of the shipment.

Some Expressions Concerned

At the request of... 应……的请求

At the request of and for... 应……的请求

By order of... 按……的指示

Under the instruction of 在……要求下

To issue / open / establish an L/C 开立/出信用证

In favor of... 以……为受益人

In your favor 以你方为受益人

2) Validity and Place of Expiry of L /C 信用证有效期和到期地点(的表达)

"Expiry date Oct.1,2020 in the country of the beneficiary unless otherwise."

"Documents to be presented to negotiation bank within 15 days after shipment."

This credit shall cease to be available for negotiation of beneficiary's drafts after Mar. 15, 2020.

Expiry date for negotiation:15th March, 2020

This credit holds good in China until 15th March, 2020

This credit keeps open in China until...

The letter of credit is available in China until...

The L /C is valid until...

This credit remains in force in China until...

The validity date of this L/C is...

3) Amount and Currency 金额,币制(的表达)

In amount of

For the amount of

Amounting to

To the extent of

For an amount / a sum not exceeding total of USD

Up to an aggregate amount of USD...

4) Clause on Draft or Bill of Exchange 汇票条款

Drafts <u>drawn under</u> this credit shall be presented for negotiation in Guangzhou, China on or before 25th June, 2020.

(凭本证开具的汇票须于……前(包括25日这天)在……提交议付。)

Drafts are drawn in duplicate to our order bearing the clause "Drawn under United Malayan Banking Corp. Irrevocable Letter of Credit No.... dated July 12, 2020."

(汇票一式两份，以我行为抬头，并注明根据马来亚联合银行2020年7月12日第……号不可撤销信用证项下开立。)

Available for payment / acceptance of your draft(s) at sight drawn on us.

(本证用于支付或承兑贵公司的向我行开具的即期汇票。)

Some expressions

Drawn on us (the opening bank) 向我们开具汇票

Drawn on this bank (the opening bank) 向本行开具汇票

Drawn on them (the importer) 向他们开具汇票

5) Description of Goods 货物说明

Including Name, Quality, Quantity, Unit price and Price terms etc.

Price terms

CIF (cost, insurance, freight)

CFR (cost and freight)

FOB (free on board)

4500 PCS of Stainless Steel Spade Head S821/29099, USD 9.60 per pc, according to Sales Contract No. A97DE23600256.Nov.12,2020 CIF Rotterdam (Incoterms 1990). 4500件不锈钢铲头，货号为S821/29099，根据2020年11月12日签定的A97DE23600256号合同，每件9.60美元，CIF鹿特丹(1990通则)。

6) Clauses on Documents 单据条款

常见条款有：

Documents marked "×" below: (须提交)下列注有"×"标志的单据

Accompanied by the following documents marked "×" in duplidate: 须随附下列注有"×"标志的单据一式两份

Draft(s) must be accompanied by the following documents marked "×": 汇票须随附下列注有"×"标志的单据

Documents required 需要下列单据：

...available against surrender of the following documents bearing out credit number and the full name and address of the openers. (议付时)以提交下列注明本信用证编号及开证人详细姓名、地址的各项单据为有效。

In duplicate (triplicate, quadruplicate, quintuplicate, sextuplicate, septuplicate, octuplicate, nonuplicate, decuplicate)一式两份(三、四、五、六、七、八、九、十份)

Signed commercial invoices in 6 copies签字的商业发票6份

7) Clauses on Shipment 装运条款

(1) Date of Shipment 装运期，常见条款有：

Latest date of shipment: ... 最迟装运日期：……

Shipment must be effected not later than... 货物不得迟于……装运

(2) Partial Shipment/ Transshipment 分运/转运

Transshipment is allowed provided "Through" Bills of Lading (联运提单) are presented. 如提交联运提单，允许转运。

Evidencing shipment from China to... CFR by steamer in transit Saudi Arabia not later than... of the goods specified below.

列明下面的货物按成本加运费价格用轮船不得迟于……从中国经沙特阿拉伯转运到……

8) Special Clauses/Conditions 特别条款

(1) Commission and Discount 佣金,折扣

Beneficiary's drafts are to be made out for 95% of invoice value, being 5% commission payable to credit opener. 受益人的汇票按发票金额95%开具, 5%佣金付给开证人。

(2) Charges 费用

All banking charges for seller's account. 一切银行费用由卖方负担。

(3) Negotiation and Reimbursement 议付与索偿

In reimbursement, please draw on our head office account with your London office.
偿付办法: 请从我总行在你伦敦分行的帐户内支取。

All bank charges outside U.K. are for our principals' account, but must be claimed at the time of presentation of documents. 在英国境外发生的所有银行费用, 应由开证人负担, 但须在提交单据时索取。

(4) 其他

For special instructions please see overleaf. 特别事项请看背面。

One copy of commercial invoice and packing list shall be sent to the credit openers 15 days before shipment. 商业发票和装箱单各一份须在装船前15天寄给开证人。

All documents except Bills of Exchange and B/L to be made out in name of ABC Co. Ltd. and which name is to be shown in B/L as joint notifying party with the applicant. 除汇票和提单外, 所有单据均须做成以ABC有限公司为抬头, 并以该公司和申请人作为提单的通知人。

This letter of credit is transferable in China only, in the event of a transfer, a letter from the first beneficiary must accompany the documents for negotiation.
本信用证仅在中国可转让, 如实行转让, 由第一受益人发出的书面(证明)须连同单据一起议付。

9) Warranties of Issuing Bank 开证行的保证

We hereby undertake to honor all drafts drawn in accordance with terms of this credit.
凡按本信用证所列条款开具并提示的汇票, 我行保证承兑。

We hereby engage with drawers and / or bona fide holders that draft(s) drawn and negotiated on presentation and that draft(s) accepted within the terms of this credit will be duly honored at maturity.

我行兹对出票人及/或善意持有人保证: 凡按本证条款开具及议付的汇票一经提交即予承兑; 凡依本证条款承兑的汇票, 到期即予照付。

We undertake that draft(s) drawn presented in conformity with the terms of this credit will be duly honored at maturity.
本银行保证, 凡向本银行提交符合本信用证条款规定的汇票, 届时予以付款。

10) Statement on UCP 跟单信用证统一惯例文句

Except as otherwise expressly stated herein, this credit is subject to the Uniform Customs and Practice for Documentary credits-UCP (1993 Revision) International Chamber of Commerce publication No. 500.
除非另有规定外, 本证根据国际商会1993年修订本第500号小册"跟单信用证统一惯例"办理。

PART FOUR   CONTRACTUAL WRITING AND TRANSLATION

4. Useful Sentences on L/C

(1) We are enclosing one copy of Application for Letter of Credit and shall appreciate your arranging to establish an L/C in Jardine's favor at your early convenience.

(2) We are glad to learn that you opened a letter of credit with the Commercial Bank in favor of us for the amount of $ 10,000 covering the said order available until March 17.

(3) We have pleasure in advising that a letter of credit bearing No. DSO 41 was established in your favor through the Commercial Bank on March 17th, for USD 10,000 (Ten Thousand USD only).

(4) We confirm the exchange of telegrams with you regarding the Letter of Credit for your present order for 4,000 tons of asphalt, and are glad to learn that you forwarded this on the 14th to the First National Bank in San Francisco.

(5) We request you to open Irrevocable Letter of Credit by air mail through your correspondent available by draft drawn without recourse on your correspondent by Jardine Textile Machinery Works, Ltd., 4 Pall Mall, London, W.C, 2 for account of ABC Textile Company, Ltd., at sight for any sum or sums not exceeding a total of Pounds Sterling Two Thousand and Three Hundred only accompanied by the following documents.

(6) On April 6 an irrevocable letter of credit was opened in your favor for an amount of $56,500 to cover the CIF value of this order by Bank of China through the National Provisional Bank, London.

(7) We regret that we could not ship the goods by a March vessel only because of the delay of your L/C. Please attend to this matter with all speed.

(8) From your telex of 10th July, we learn that the L/C has been arranged, but we regret to say that we have received no bank's advice yet. Please push the confirming bank in New York for their soonest action.

(9) Your Order No.224 was confirmed by our fax of September 15, subject to arrival of credit within 15 days from the date. The 15-day period having expired on October 1st without receipt of L/C, nor hearing any further advice from you, we write you today asking when the required L/C was opened.

(10) We have today instructed our Bank, the Frank Bank in London to open in your favor a confirmed, irrevocable letter of credit with partial shipment and transshipment allowed clause, available by draft at sight, against surrendering the full set of shipping documents to the negotiating bank.

(11) Please increase the cost amount by US 6,500 to US 6,000, and decrease the freight amount by US 8,000 to US 7,500, total amount unchanged.

(12) Please obtain The Bombay Trading Co.'s consent to amend the beneficiary's name to read The Tokyo Trading Co., Ltd., Tokyo.

(13) Please correct the beneficiary's address to read: Smith & James, Inc., 500 Norton Bldg., Seattle 4, Wash., USA.

(14) Please amend the price term to be on C&F basis; insurance to be effected by buycr and freight to be repaid by shipper.

(15) Please amend the price term to be on CIF basis; insurance covering war risks to be effected and freight to be repaid by shipper.

(16) Please amend this credit to be transferable and divisible.

(17) Please amend the L/C to read "Partial shipments permitted."

(18) Please extend the shipping date to May 30, expiry date unchanged.

(19) Please insert the clause "Stale bills of lading acceptable."

(20) Please delete the requirement of inspection certificate.

(21) The expiry date of the credit being June 25, we request that you will arrange with your banker to extend it up to August 10, amending the said credit.

(22) In case the above amendment of the L/C is acceptable to you, kindly confirm signing and returning to us the attached copy of this letter.

(23) In order to avoid subsequent amendments, please see to it that the L/C stipulations are exact accordance with the terms of the contract.

(24) To comply with your request, we submitted our Application for Amendment of Credit to the opening bank on May 12th, 2020, and trust you will receive from the advising bank the amendment soon.

(25) The said credit calls for shipment on or before the 31st of December. As the earliest steamer sailing for your port is s.s. "PEACE" scheduled to leave Shanghai on or about January 3, it is, therefore, impossible for us to effect shipment at the time you named. This being the case, we have to ask you to extend the date of shipment to the 15th of January, under advice to us by fax.

(26) We are sorry that owing to some delay on the part of supplier, we are unable to get the goods ready before the end of this month. So we write to you asking for an extension. We are looking forward to receiving your extension of the above L/C, thus enabling us to effect shipment of the goods in question.

(27) With reference to our faxes dated the 20th of April ands the 18th of May, requesting you to establish the L/C concerning the above mentioned order, we regret having received no news from you up to now.

(28) We wish to remind you that it was agreed, when placing the order, that you would establish the required L/C upon receipt of our Confirmation.

(29) We wish to draw your attention to the fact that the date of delivery is approaching, but up to the present we have not received the covering L/C.

(30) Please do your utmost to expedite the establishment of the L/C, so that we may execute the order within the stipulated time.

(31) We are pleased to confirm that the unused amount of US 3,500 of the credit above had been cancelled with the beneficiary's consent as instructed in your letter dated Mar. 25, 2020.

(32) The original instrument returned to us is enclosed as requested. Please acknowledge receipt of the instrument by returning to us the attached copy of this letter duly signed.

PART FOUR   CONTRACTUAL WRITING AND TRANSLATION

5. Examples of 9 Kinds of L /Cs

(1) Irrevocable Documentary Credit 不可撤销跟单保兑信用证

\multicolumn{2}{c}{**Name of Issuing Bank**}	
ABC Bank of Singapore Address:	Issued Date:
	Irrevocable documentary credit confirmed L/C No. SJ0211
Applicant International Engineering & Trading Co. (Pte) Ltd. Commercial Building Dacca, Singapore	Beneficiary Ritz Engineering Commercial Building Sinjuku, Tokyo, Japan
Advising Bank Commercial Development Bank Ref. No. JS1241 Sinjuku, Tokyo, Japan	Amount US $300,000 (Say three hundred thousand U.S. dollars only)
Expiry Date and Place This credit remains valid in Japan until _____	Partial Shipment Transshipment ☐ Allowed ☐ Allowed ☒ Not Allowed ☒ Not Allowed
	Loading on board/dispatch/taking in charge From Japan to Singapore CIF
\multicolumn{2}{l}{We hereby issue in your favor this documentary credit which is available by negotiation against presentation of the following documents: —Commercial invoice in duplicate. —Insurance policy in duplicate covering all risk, plus 10% of invoice value. —Full set clean "On Board" Ocean Bill of Lading made out to our order notify applicant and marked "Freight Prepaid." —Certificate of Inspection in triplicate. —Packing List in duplicate.}	
\multicolumn{2}{l}{Covering shipment of Tremie concrete TC—II×10,000 Barrels. Contract No. BJ890829}	
\multicolumn{2}{l}{Shipping Date Latest shipment is until 25 August, 2020}	
\multicolumn{2}{l}{This credit is subject to the Uniform Customs and Practice for Documentary Credits 1993 Revision, ICC Publication No. 500.}	
\multicolumn{2}{l}{Special Instruction —The advising bank is requested to add their confirmation. —All banking charges are for account of beneficiary. —Documents shall be presented for negotiation within 20 days after B/L date in any event within the validity of the credit.}	

We undertake that drafts drawn and presented in conformity with the terms of this credit will be duly honored.
ABC Bank of Singapore
Signature _____
	Advising Bank's Instruction
	We have been requested to add our confirmation to this credit and we therefore undertake that any draft drawn by you in accordance with the terms of this credit will be duly paid by us.
	  Name of Advising Bank
	  Signature _____

\multicolumn{2}{c}{Countersigned by Issuing Bank _____ Advising Bank _____}	

(2) Revocable Credit 可撤销信用证

ABC BANK
Trade Plaza

London, England   Date: 20th August 20____

To: Alice Exporting Co. Ltd.   Transmitted through:
International Commercial Building   Commercial Trust Bank
Jakarta, Indonesia   Jakarta
     Indonesia

REVOCABLE LETTER OF CREDIT
NO. MISC 978-123

You are hereby authorized to draw on Iones International Trading Co., Ltd., London England for the amounts not exceeding US 64,000 (sixty four thousand U.S. dollars only) available by your draft (s) at sight drawn in duplicate accompanied by the following documents:

1. Commercial invoice in duplicate.

2. Full set of clean "On Board" ocean Bills of Lading made out to order and endorsed, blank marked "Freight Prepaid" and notify accountee.

3. Insurance policy in duplicate covering all risks plus 10% of invoice value.

Shipment from Indonesia to England not later than 10th October 20_____.

Partial shipments are allowed. Transshipments are allowed.

Covering shipment of: Materials semiductors type—III × 10 in wooden cases.

Special instructions:

1. This advice, revocable at any time without notice, is for your guidance only in preparing drafts and documents.

2. We undertake to honour your draft (s) drawn and negotiated in conformity with the terms of this credit provided such negotiation has been made prior to receipt by you of notice of cancellation.

3. Documents have to be presented within 15 days after the date of issuance of the Bill of lading or other shipping documents.

4. Draft (s) drawn must be inscribed with the number and date of this credit.

5. Draft (s) drawn under this credit must be presented for negotiation in Indonesia on or before 5th November 20 _____.

This credit is subject to Uniform Customs and Practice for Documentary Credits (1993 Revision), for Documentary Credits.

                                               ABC Bank
                                   Authorized Signature and Chop_____

PART FOUR CONTRACTUAL WRITING AND TRANSLATION

(3) Seller's Usance Credit 卖方远期信用证

BDE Bank Totus Building, New Delhi, India	
Irrevocable Documentary Credit Credit No. IS 3125 , Issued Date: 15th Apr., 20 _____	
Advising Bank United Chinese Commercial Bank #0509 Singapore	Beneficiary Sea, Ocean Building Materials Co. (Pte) Ltd., #0721 Singapore

At the request of Tabowell International Building Materials Industry Co. Ltd., New Delhi, India, we establish an Irrevocable Credit (Seller's Usance Credit) in favour of Sea-Ocean Building Materials Co. (Pte) Ltd., for the amount of US $400,000 (say four hundred thousand U.S. dollars only).Expiry date & place on 15th October, 20_____ at counter of the advising bank. Available by your draft (s) drawn on applicant at 120 days after sight, discount charges, stamp duty and acceptance commission are for beneficiary' account.

Accompanied by the following documents in duplicate unless specified :

—Commercial invoice signed by general manager of Sea-Ocean Building Materials Co. (Pte)Ltd.

—Insurance policy for 110% of invoice covering all risk.

—Full set clean "On Board"ocean Bills of Lading made out to order of Tabowell International Building.

Materials Industry Co. Ltd., New Delhi, India, marked "Freight Prepaid."

Shipping date

Shipment to be effected not later than 15th May,20 _____.

Evidencing shipment of

Finishing materials & sanitary plumbing equipment

FM—50 boxes. SPE—50 boxes.

Shipment from Singapore to Calcutta. CIF

Contract No. IS 89121

Other terms

All negotiation and bank charges including advising charges under this credit are for account of the beneficiary.

Undertaking clause

We hereby engage with the drawers, endorsers and bona-fide holders of draft (s) drawn under and in compliance with the terms of the credit that such draft(s) shall be duly honoured on due presentation and delivery of documents as specified if drawn and negotiated within the validity date of this credit.

This credit is subject to the Uniform Customs and Practice for Documentary Credits 1993 Revision, ICC Publication No. 500.

Tel: 231666
Telex: CDB 266
Fax: DCDB 266

For
BDE Bank

Signature _____

(4) Irrevocable Documentary Confirmed without Recourse Letter of Credit
不可撤销跟单保兑无追索权信用证

To Wandli International Trading Co., Ltd.
10/F Commercial Centre, London, England

Date & Address of Expiry
10th November, 20×× in the country of Beneficiary.

1. At request of Tadka International Trading Co., Washington, U.S.A.

We open an irrevocable confirmed without recourse credit, L/C No.IJDK-2813 in your favour for the amount not exceeding total of US $500,000 (say U.S. dollars five hundred thousand only) available by your drafts drawn , in duplicate, with out recourse at sight on applicant , covering 100% invoice value , accompanied by the following documents.

2. Commercial invoice in duplicate , indicating contract no.

3. Full set clean "On Board" ocean Bills of Lading made out to our order notify applicant and marked "Freight Prepaid."

4. Certificate of origin in duplicate.

5. Insurance policy in duplicate covering all risks and war risk plus 100% of invoice value.

6. Packing list in duplicate.

7. Partial shipments are allowed. Shipment latest date:10th October, 20××

Transhipments are allowed.

8. Shipment from England to U.S.A. CIF.

9. Covering shipments of.

SPIx100

SOIIx50 in wooden cases.

SPIIIx50

10. Drafts at sight at sight drawn without recourse under this credit must be presented for negotiation of payment in United States on or before 31st October, 20××.

11. We have requested advising bank to add their confirmation to this credit.

12. Please endorse this credit with each payment , you may make and draw upon us at

sight for the amounts, sending us a duplicate receipt.

13. This credit is returned to us when the credit is exhausted or expired, attached to the last draft.

14. The negotiating and confirming bank have been authorized to purchase or negotiate draft (s) drawn without recourse by you. Undertaking clause:

15. We hereby engage that drafts drawn in conformity with the terms of this credit will be duly honoured on presentation.

This credit is subject to the Uniform Customs and Practice for Documentary Credits 1993 Revision, ICC Publication No.500 Union Trust Bank Washington U.S.A Signature _____	Advising Bank's Notification

	This credit bears our confirmation and we hereby engage to negotiate or purchase drafts drawn without recourse and presented in conformity with the terms of this credit on presentation to us.
	
	   Name of Advising Bank
	   Commercial Associated bank
	   London, England
	   Signature _____

Tel: 245-195 Telex: UTB—196	Date 10th, August 20xx

(5) Irrevocable Documentary Credit (Unrestricted Negotiation)

不可撤销跟单信用证(公开议付)

Commercial Development Bank	
	Telephone: 288514 Telex: 42515SC Issued Date: April 10, 20 ____
ISSUING BANK Cable: SCCB110 Commercial Development Bank Address:10th/F., International Commercial Building Colombo, Sri Lanka	Irrevocable Documentary Letter of Credit L/C NO. SHI002 Applicant
	Draft (s) drawn under this credit must be negotiated in Hong Kong on or before June15,20... after which date this credit expires.

Applicant Baodeli Communication Equiment Industry Co., Ltd. P.O. Box 2356 Colombo Sri Lanka	Beneficiary Celebrity International Trading Co. Ltd. Address:152 Lock Road , Hong Kong
Advising Bank Commercial Bank Address: Golden Commercial Building 522A Nathan Road Kowloon, Hong Kong	Amount Currency US $100,000 (one hundred thousand U. S. dollars only)
	Negotiation under the credit is unre-stricted

Dear Sir (s),
　　We hereby issue in your favor the irrevocable Document Credit which is available by negotiation of your draft(s).
Accompanied by the following documents marked "X":
☒ Commercial invoice in duplicate.
☒ Packing list in duplicate.
☒ Certificate of Original in triplicate.
☒ Full set clean "On Board" ocean Bills of Lading made out to our order notify buyer and marked "Freight Prepaid."

Covering shipments of:
　　SQE—Type II X10 Contract No. 1521 SH in wooden cases.

Shipping date:
　　Latest shipment is until 24th May 20 ＿＿＿＿
　　From Hong Kong to Colombo.

Partial shipment: ☐ Allowed　　Transshipment: ☐ Allowed
　　　　　　　☒ Not allowed

Date for presentation:

Documents must be presented for negotiation within 21 days after B/L date in any event within the validity of the credit.

Other instrutions:
　　All banking charges are for account of beneficiary.

PART FOUR   CONTRACTUAL WRITING AND TRANSLATION

Undertaking clause:

We hereby engage with the drawers, en-dorsers, and bona-fide holders of draft(s) drawn under and in compliance with the terms of the credit that such draft(s) shall be duly honoured on the presentation and delivery of documents as specified.

The amount of each draft must be endorsed on the reverse of this credit by the negotiating bank.

Except so far otherwise expressly stated, this documentary credit is subjet to the Uniform Customs and Practice for Documentary Credits 1993 Revision, ICC Publication No.500.

For Commercial Development Bank

Signature _____

NOTICE

We deliver the credit to you without any responsibility on our part.

Name of Advising Bank:

Commercial Bank

Signature _____

(6) Transferable Letter of Credit 可转让信用证

Trust Development Bank

Commercial Building

London England

Our Ref.No.1282

Data 10th May,20 _____

Issuing Bank	Expiry Data	Advising Bank
Trust Development Bank	20th August 20 in	Commercial Bank
Blue sky Building	Country of Beneficiary	Los Angeles
London England	for Negotiation	U.S.A.

To Tafu International
Trading Co.,Ltd.
Los Angeles U.S.A.

This credit is subject
to the Uniform Customs and Ptactice
for Documentary Credits 1993 Revision,
ICC Publication No.500

1. In favour of: Tafu International Trading Co. Ltd. Los Angeles U.S.A.
2. Beneficiary: Katala Electric Appliances Plant London England.
3. In accordance with instruction received from accreditors we open our Irrevocable Transferable Letter of Credit No.8902188C, in your favour as beneficiary.

4. Account of: Issuing Bank.

5. Amount of: US $ 100,000 (say one hundred thousand U.S. dollars only).

6. Accompanied by the following documents:

　　—Full set of clean On Board Ocean Bills of Lading made out to our order notify Buyer and marked "Freight Prepaid."

　　—One original signed commercial invoice and two copies.

　　—Insurance policy in duplicate (C.I.F. value plus 10 percent covering all risks.).

7. Covering shipment of MPL_11 Type 4 in wooden cases.

　　From U.S.A. to England.

8. Latest shipment date: 25th July, 20___

9. Draft (s) must indicate the number and date of this L/C.

Special instruction:

10. This credit is total transfer and this credit if transferable in U.S.A only.

11. All negotiation and transfers under this credit restricted to advising bank.

12. This credit is transferable on the express understanding that the new beneficiaries are not boycotted by the U.S.A Boycotted Office.

13. We hereby guarantee that all draft(s) drawn and negotiated in compliance with the terms and conditions of this credit shall be duly paid at maturity.

　　　　　　　　　　　　　　　　　　　　　　　　　　Trust Development Bank

Tel: 275862

E-mail Address _____　　　　　　　　　　　　　　Signature _____

Fax: TOBF 862

(7) Irrevocable Revolving Letter of Credit 不可撤销循环信用证

	Telex: BHD1142	
Opening-up Bank Blue shy Plaza, Brussels, Belgium	Telephone: 5883218 Issued Date & Place 10th February 20__ Brussels	
Revolving Credit Irrevocable	Issuing Bank Credit No. BH 0821	Advising Bank Credit No. 2108HB
Advising Bank 　Honest Bank 　Garden Plaza, Amsterdam, Holland	Applicant 　Babit Machine—Making Industry 　Co. (Ltd.) 　Bavel Building, Brussels, Belgium	

PART FOUR　CONTRACTUAL WRITING AND TRANSLATION

Beneficiary	Amount
Watat International Co., Ltd.	US $600,000
List Center Amsterdam,	(Six Hundred Thousand U.S. Dollars)
Holland	
This credit is issued subject to Uniform Customs and Practice for Documentary Credits 1993 Revision, ICC Publication NO.500	Date & Place of Expiry This credit remains valid in the country of beneficiary until 10th December 20___ (inclusive)

AUTOMATIC ACCUMULATIVE REVOLVING CREDIT
TRANSMITTED THROUGH: TRUST DEVELOPMENT BANK

Dear Sir(s),

We hereby open our Irrevocable Automatic Accumulative Revolving Documentary Credit in your favour and authorize you to draw on us at sight up to an aggregate amount of US $ 600,000 (U.S. dollars six hundred thousand only per three (3) calendar months accumulative commencing with 30th January, 20____, revolving on the first business day of each successive month and ending with 30th November, 20____.

This credit is revolving for three (3) shipments only , each shipment should be effected at three month intervals, but the amount of each shipment is not exceeding US $ 200,000 (U.S. dollars two hundred thousand only)

The unused balance of each shipment is accumulative to the following shipment.

The amount of this credit shall be restored automatically after date of negotiation.

Accompanied by the following documents:

1. Commercial invoice in duplicate copies, indicating contract no.
2. Packing list in duplicate.
3. Full set shipping clean on board bill(s) of lading marked "Freight Prepaid" to order of shipper endorsed to reconstruction bank, notifying buyers.

Conditions of shipment:

Trans-shipments are permitted.

From Rotterdam to Antwerp.

Shipment date: Shipment is to be effected not later that 10th November 20____.

Covering: List of spare parts.

Please see continuation sheet attached.

　　Special instructions:

　　Please see continuation sheet attached.

Undertaking clause: 　　We hereby agree with the drawers, endorssers and bona-fide holders of drafts drawn in compliance with the terms of credit that such drafts shall be duly honoured on presentation and paid at maturity. Yours truly. 　　pening—up Bank 　　Signature _____	Advising's Bank 　　Notification The amount of each draft negotiated, together with the date ,must be sated on the back hereof Advising Bank Signature _____

(8) Irrevocable Revolving Credit 不可撤销循环信用证

Opening-up Bank Blue shy Plaza, Brussels, Belgium	Telex: BHD1142 Telephone: 5883218 Issued Date & Place 10th February 20__ Brussels	
Revolving Credit Irrevocable	Issuing Bank Credit No. BH 0821	Advising Bank Credit No. 2108HB
Advising Bank 　　Honest Bank 　　Garden Plaza, Amsterdam, Holland	Applicant 　　Babit Machine-Making Industry Co. (Ltd) 　　Bavel Building, Brussels, Belgium	
Beneficiary 　　Watat International Co., Ltd. 　　List Center Amsterdam, 　　Holland	Amount US $600,000 (Six Hundred Thousand U.S. Dollars)	
Undertaking clause: 　　We hereby agree with the drawers, endorssers and bona-fide holders of drafts drawn in compliance with the terms of credit that such drafts shall be duly honoured on presentation and paid at maturity. 　　Yours truly. 　　Opening-up Bank 　　Signature	Advising's Bank 　　Notification The amount of each draft negotiated, together with the date, must be sated on the back hereof Advising Bank Signature _____	

This attached Sheet Forms and integral part of our Irrevocable

L/C No. BH0821

CONTINUATION SHEET (续页)

续页系本不可撤销信用证的不可分割部分

Covering: List of Spare Parts (Omit)

Special Instructions:

1. Special instructions for beneficiary

30th May 20××	Despatch the original draft and documents by first mail to the bank, which is located in the country of advising bank for unrestricted negotiation.
30th August 20××	Despatch the original draft and documents by second mail to the bank, which is located in the country of advising bank for unrestricted negotiation.
30th November 20××	Despatch the original draft and documents by third mail to the bank, which is located in the country of advising bank for unrestricted negotiation.

2. Special instruction for advising bank

Dispatch the certificate "Documents must strictly conform with the terms for this Credit" and drafts drawn at sight by the beneficiary on the Reconstruction Development Bank Brussels, Belgium, for reimburssement.

3. Remark

All drafts against this Credit must be drawn and negotiated on or before (30th May, 20××), (30th August, 20××) and (30th November 20××).

4. Charges

All banking charges are for beneficiary's account and delivery of the L/C should be withheld pending beneficiary's agreement to pay the advising bank's charges.

Signature

(9) Irrevocable Documentary Sight Credit (Drawn On Bank)

不可撤销跟单即期信用证(银行付款)

<table>
<tr><td colspan="2" align="center">Eximbank Ltd.

Malaysia
GoldenHorse Building
8th/F. Box 467101

Issuing Bank
Eximbank, Ltd.
Malaysia

Tel: 962-8815
Telex: 762517M
Issued Date and Place

June 25, 20____, Malaysia</td></tr>
<tr><td>Irrevocable Documentary Credit</td><td>Credit Number
of lssuing Bank of Advising Bank
S-01-Y-824 MS810</td></tr>
<tr><td>Advising Bank
    Development Bank, (Ltd.)
    International Trading Building
    Singapore
    P.O. Box 401015</td><td>Applicant
Dearmei Trading Co., Ltd. Malaysia
12nd/F.abc Building
Box 884666</td></tr>
<tr><td>Beneficiary
Kan Dor Bo Trading Co., Ltd.
8th/F.Forrum Building
Singapore</td><td>Expiry Date
25th August 20____
In the country of the beneficiary</td></tr>
<tr><td colspan="2">At the request of Dearmei Trading Co. Ltd., Malaysia, we open this Irrevocable Documentary Letter of Credit No. S-01-Y-824 in your favour for an amount not exceeding total of US $ 1,000,000 (one million United States dollars only) available by your drafts drawn at sight on us covering 100% invoice value accompanied by the following documents:

    1. Commercial invoice in triplicate.

    2. Insurance policy in duplicate covering all risks plus 10% of invoice value.

    3. Full set clean "On Board" ocean Bills of Lading made out to our order notify buyers and marked "Freight Prepaid."

    4. Certificate of origin in duplicate.

    5. Certificate of inspection in duplicate.</td></tr>
<tr><td colspan="2">Covering shipments of:
    ESP 20 kit
    ESPS 10 kit in crates.
    ESPSS 10 kit</td></tr>
</table>

PART FOUR　CONTRACTUAL WRITING AND TRANSLATION

Shipment from Singapore to Malaysia CIF.　　　Shipment must be effected not
Contract No. ESP 1245　　　　　　　　　　　　later than 30th July, 20 ____.

Special clause:

1. This credit is available by draft drawn on issuing bank at sight.

2. Partial shipments are prohibited.

Transshipments are prohibited.

3. Draft against this credit must be drawn and negotiated on or before August 15,20 _____.

4. The number and date of this credit must appear on draft drawn.

5. The amount of draft must be endorsed on the back hereof and this credit is to be returned to us when exhausted or expired.

We hereby guarantee that drafts drawn under and in compliance with the terms and conditions of this credit shall be accepted and paid at sight.

　　　　　　　　　　　　　　　　　　　For the Eximbank, Ltd.

Malaysia

Signature_____

6. Shipping Documents Required under L/C

1) Commercial Invoice　2) Bill of Lading　3) Insurance Policy or Certificate

4) Bill of Exchange / Draft　5) Inspection Certificate or Survey Report

6) Certificate of Origin(Co)　7) Weight Memo and Packing List.　8) Shipping Advice

1) COMMERCIAL INVOICE 商业发票

(1) The definition

Commercial invoice is a document which contains identifying information about merchandise sold for which payment is to be made. All invoices should show the name and address of the debtor, terms of payment, description of items, the price per item, and the amount for which payment is to be made. Besides, the invoice should show the manner of delivery.

(2) The required invoice is stipulated in an L/C in the following ways:

Invoice is... copies, indicating Contract No.... (发票……份,注明……号合同)

Signed commercial invoice in... copies, stating Contract No.... (业经签字商业发票……份,写明……号合同)

Signed invoice in... copies, indicating Import License No.... (业经签字商业发票……份,标上……号进口许可证)

Your signed invoice in... copies in the name of the opener, certifying merchandise to be of Chinese origin. (你方出具的开证申请人名下的发票……份,证明货物的原产地为中国。)

Signed invoice in 8 folds (6 copies to accompany the original documents)业经签字发票8份

143

(6份随附正本单据)。

Examples:

√ Beneficiary's original signed commercial invoice at least in triplicate issued in the name of the buyer indicating the merchandise, country of origin and any other relevant information.

√ Signed commercial invoice in triplicate showing separately F.O.B. value, freight charge, insurance premium, C.I.F. value and country of origin.

(3) The description of the goods in the commercial invoice must correspond with the description in the credit. In all other documents the goods may be described in general terms not inconsistent with the description of the goods in the credit.

(4) Sample of Commercial Invoice

CHINA NATIONAL IMPORT & EXPORT CORPORATION

SHANGHAI BRANCH

1020 NORTH SUZHOU ROAD

SHANGHAI CHINA

TO: M/S   Invoice No. _____

S/C No. _____

INVOICE   Date................

From.................................To...

Letter of Credit No..............................Issued by....................................

Marks & Numbers	Quantities & Descriptions	Amount

CERTIFICATE OF ORIGIN:
We hereby certify that the above mentioned goods are of China Origin.

China National Import & Export Corporation

Shanghai Branch

Shanghai, China

....

2) BILL OF LADING (B/L) 海运提单

(1) 定义

Bill of Lading is a document given by a shipping company, representing both a receipt for the goods shipped and a contract for shipment between the shipping company and the shipper. It is also a document of title to the goods, giving the holder or the assignee the right to possession of the goods.

提单是轮船公司签发的单证，它既代表承运货物的收据，又代表承运人及托运人之间的运输合同。它也是代表货物所有权的证件,它给予持有人或受让人提货的权利。

《汉堡规则》第一条第七款给提单下的定义是："提单是指证明海上运输合同及货物由承运人接管或装载以及承运人保证凭以交付货物的单据。单据中关于货物应按记名人的指示或不记名人的指示交付或交付给提单持有人的规定,即是这一保证。"

(2) 海运提单的作用

海运提单的作用有以下五方面:

I. 海运提单是承运人或其代理人签发的货物收据(receipt for the goods),证明承运人已经按海运提单所列内容收到货物。

II. 海运提单是一种货物所有权的凭证 (document of title)。海运提单的合法持有人凭海运提单可在目的港向轮船公司提取货物,也可以在载货船舶到达目的港之前,通过转让海运提单而转移货物所有权,或凭以向银行办理抵押货款。

III. 海运提单是托运人与承运人之间所订立的运输契约的证明(evidence of contract of carrier),是托运人与承运人处理双方在运输中的权利并义务问题的主要依据。

IV. 海运提单可以作为收取运费的证明,以及在运输过程中办理货物的装卸、发运及交付等方面的作用。

V. 海运提单是向船舶公司或保险公司索赔的重要依据。

(3) 海运提单的种类

I. 根据货物是否装船分类

i. 已装船提单 (On Board B/L或 Shipping B/L)

已装船提单/已装运提单/装船提单是指提单上载明货物 "已由某轮装运"的字样及装运日期,指货物已确实装上即将开航的轮船后出立的提单。

ii. 备运海运提单 (Received for Shipment B/L或 Alongside Bills)

备运海运提单是指承运人在收到托运货物等待装船期间,向托运人签发的提单。待运的货物一旦装运后,在备运海运提单上加上 "已装船"字样,这样备运提单就变成 "已装船提单"。否则,"备运提单"也会被银行拒绝。

II. 根据货物表明状况有无不良批注分类

i. 清洁提单 (Clean B/L)

清洁提单是指货物交运时表面状况良好,承运人在签发提单时未加任何货损、包装不良等批注的提单。

ii. 不清洁提单 (Unclean B/L或 Foul B/L)

不清洁提单是指承运人在提单上加注货物及包装状况不良或存在缺陷等批注的提单。如 "雨淋";"两箱破裂";"一些货包破损";"唛头不清"等词句。凡提单上带有上述任何一条批注,就称为 "不清洁提单",它不能被银行接受。

III. 根据收货人抬头分类

i. 记名提单 (Straight B/L)

记名提单亦称收货人抬头提单,或不可转让提单,是指填明收货人的姓名或名称的提单。这种提单不能转让,已失去货权凭证作用,一般银行不愿意为他垫款,因此,记名提单不可议付。

ii. 不记名提单 (Blank B/L或Open B/L或Bearer B/L)

不记名提单是指记载应向提单持有人交付货物的提单。

iii. 指示提单 (Order B/L)

指示提单是指按照记名人(Named Person)的指示或非记名人(To Order)的指示交货的提单。

IV. 根据运输过程中是否转船分类

i. 直达(直运)提单 (Direct B/L)

直达(直运)提单是指货物从装运港装船后,中途不经换船而直目的港卸货,按照这种条件所签发的提单。

ii. 转船(转运)提单 (Transshipment B/L)

转船(转运)提单是指船舶从装运港装货后不直接驶往目的港而在中途的港口换船把货物输往目的港,凡按此条件所签发的包括运输全过程的提单。

iii. 联运提单 (Through B/L)

联运提单是指需经两种或两种以上的运输方式(如海陆、海河、海空或海海等)联合运输的货物,托运人在办理托运手续并交纳全程运费之后,由第一承运人所签发的包括运输全过程并能凭以在目的港提取货物的提单。

iv. 多式联运提单 (Combined Transport B/L)

多式联运提单简称,是由联运人也就是经营运输的"无船承运人"签发的提单。货物从起运地(港)到最终目的地(港)的全程运输过程中需使用陆、海、空其中两种以上运输方式,由联运人作为全程运输的总承运人签发的这种联运提单,作为对托运人的总负责人。

V. 根据海运提单内容的繁简分类

i. 全式(繁式)提单 (Long Form B/L)

全式(繁式)提单是指通常应用的、在提单背面列有承运人及托运人的权利、义务等详细条款的提单。

ii. 略式(简式)提单 (Short Form B/L)

略式(简式)提单是指仅保留全式提单正面的必要项目,例如船名、货名、标志、件数、重量或体积、装运港、托运人名称等记载,而略去提单背面全部条款的提单。

VI. 其他分类

其他还有过期提单(Stale B/L),倒签提单 (Ante Dated B/L),预借提单 (Advanced B/L),舱面提单 (On Deck B/L),集装箱提单 (Container B/L),租船提单 (Chart Party B/L)及先期提单等。

(4) 要注意的几点

I. 全套或整套提单

提单通常制成三份一套,其中两份签署,一份不签,不签的那一份保留在船长手里。除非另有说明。"全套"指那签署过的两份,议付时必须将这两份向银行提示。

Full set or complete set

The B/L is usually made out in a set of three copies, two copies being signed and one left unsigned, retained by the ship's master. "Full set" refers to the two signed copies, which shall be presented to the bank for negotiation.

II. 指示提单或不记名提单

这种提单上不填写收货人名称,收货人由托运人或开证行的指令决定,称为"空白抬头"。这一栏目的填写方式如下:

凭指定 To order

凭托运人指定 To order of shippers

凭……银行(开证行名称)指定 To order of—bank (the name of the opening bank)

凭我行(指开证行)指定 To our order (denoting the opening bank)

III. 背书

背书是指提单的托运人(出口人)在提单背面签字或作一定批注,表示把提单转让出去。

Endorsement means the shipper (exporter) of a B/L signs his name and makes certain remarks on the back of the B/L, indicating the transfer of it to another person.

i. 空白背书: 托运人只在提单背面签字, 签字后即转让, 不注明把提单转让给何人。在这种情况下, 货物的所有权转让给提单持有人。

Blank endorsement: A mere signature by the shipper on the back of the B/L with no remarks added. In this case, the title to the goods is transferred or passed on to the person holding the B/L.

ii. 特别背书: 也称直接背书或全衔背书。托运人签字并作带有 "请把货物交给 (例如)马来亚银行"的批注, 货物所有权就在法律上转让给这家银行, 因为他预先为买方垫付了货款。

Special endorsement or direct endorsement: When the shipper endorses the B/L with the remark "Please deliver to (for instance) Malayan Banking Corporation," the ownership of the goods is legally transferred to that bank, which has advanced the purchase price for the buyer.

IV. 运费

运费的支付有四种方法:

i. 运费已付或预付 Freight paid or prepaid

在装货港签发提单时,由托运人把它付给承运人或其代理人,运费须付足到目的港为止。

ii. 运费到付 Freight forward or to collect or payable at destination

也称为运费待付或运费在目的港支付。货物抵达目的港后,收货人提货时把运费付给承运人或其代理人。

iii. 运费如议 Freight as arranged

如果各方已有约定,应该预付的运费并未在装货港付给,托运人或收货人可以在以后补交,但他必须交付自应交日到实际交费日之间的一定数额的利息。

iv. 运费按租船合同交纳 Freight as per charter party

V. 通知买方

在"空白抬头"提单项下,因为没填写收货人名称,但这提单上总该写明一个人或一家公司的名称,轮船公司就可以在货物抵达目的港时通知该人。

这个栏目也可以用下述方法书写:

通知开证人	to notify the opener
通知开证申请人	to notify the applicant
通知上述汇票付款人	to notify the above-mentioned accountee
通知本行(指开证行)	to notify this bank (denoting the opening bank)

(5) Examples of B/L

Example 1

shipper		COSCO	B/L No.
consignee		中 国 远 洋 运 输 公 司	
Notify Party		CHINA OCEAN SHIPPIGN COMPANY	
Pre-carriage by	*Place of Receipt	Cable:	Telex
Ocean vessel/ Voyage NO	Port of Loading	COSCO BEIJING GUANGZHOU SHANGHAI COSCO QINGDAO TIANJIN DALIAN	22264 CPCPK CN 44080 COSCA CN 33057 COSCA CN 32037 OCSOD CN 23221 TOSCO CN 86162 DOSCO CN
Port of Discharge	*Final Destination (if goods to be transshipped at port of dis-charge)	Freight Payable at	Number of Original Bs/L
Marks & Nos.	Number & Kind of Packages	Description of Goods	Gross Weight (kgs)	Measurement (m3)
Total Packages (in words)				
Freight & Charges		SHIPPED on board the vessel named above in apparent good order and condition(unless otherwise indicated) the goods or packages specified herein and to be discharged at the above mentioned port of discharge or as near hereto as the vessel may safely get and be always afloat.		

PART FOUR   CONTRACTUAL WRITING AND TRANSLATION

	The weight, measurement, marks, numbers, quality, contents and value, being furnished by the Shipper are not checked by the Carrier on loading. The Shipper, Consignee and the Holder of this Bill of Loading hereby expressly accept and agree to all printed, written or stamped provisions, exceptions and conditions of this Bill of Loading, including those on the back hereof.
	In witness whereof, the Carrier or his Agents has signed, Bill of Loading all of this tenor and date, one of them being accomplished, the others to stand void.
	Shippers are requested to note particularly the exceptions and conditions of this Bill of Loading with reference to the validity of insurance upon their goods.
	Place and Date of Issue;
	Signed for the Carrier

(Note: Applicable only when document used as a Through Bill of Lading.)

(COSCO STANDARD FORM 06 Printed in 1989)

Example 2

S/O No..................... B/L No.........................

BILL OF LADING

DIRECT OR WITH TRANSSHIPMENT

Vessel........................Voy...................... Port of Discharge...................................

Nationality.. Port of Loading....................................

Shipper..

Consignee...or assignee..........................

Notify..

Shipped on board the vessel named above in apparent good order and condition (unless otherwise indicated) the goods or packages specified herein and to be discharged at the above mentioned port of discharge or as near thereto as the vessel may safely get and be always afloat.

The weight, measure, marks, numbers, quality, contents, and value, being particulars furnished by the Shipper, are not checked by the Carrier on loading.

The Shipper, Consignee and the Holder of this Bill of Lading hereby expressly accept and agree to all printed, written or stamped provisions, exceptions and conditions of this Bill of Lading, including those on the back hereof.

Particulars Furnished by the Shipper			
Marks & Numbers	No. of Packages	Description of Goods	Gross Weight Measurement

Total Packages (in words) (大写) _____

Freight and Charges: Shippers are requested to note particularly the exceptions
                       and conditions of this Bill of Lading with reference to the
Freight payable at _____   validity of the insurance upon their goods.
In witness whereof, the Carrier or his agents Dated.............at..
has signed Bills of Lading all of this tenor and
date, one of which being accomplished, the others............................For the Master to stand void.

3) INSURANCE POLICY OR CERTIFICATE 保险单或保险凭证

(1) 概说: 保险的种类 (Types of Insurance)

A policy must have a subject which is to be insured.

According to different subject matters of insurance, there are four kinds of insurance:

i. Life Insurance (人寿保险)

   It is a contract that, on the consideration of the premium to be paid, the insurer promises to pay the beneficiary an agreed sum of money upon the death of the person whose life is insured.

ii. Property Insurance (财产保险)

   It covers against any loss to the owner of real property which results from any damage. It includes transport insurance of international goods, for example, marine insurance, which covers damages to cargo or ship caused by "perils of the sea" and other risks listed in the policy.

iii. Liability Insurance (责任保险)

   It covers the owner or tenant of real estate against any claims for injury to persons on his premises, up to an agreed maximum amount.

iv. Security Insurance (安全保险)

   It is any person who for a consideration promises to make good for the debt or default of another person. In other words, "if you don't receive from the debtor, I will pay this debt."

(2) 本书涉及保险——财产保险(海上货物保险)

在国际货物贸易中,保险是一个不可缺少的条件及环节。保险条件的内容包括保险金额, 保险费, 保险单证及保险险别等方面。按FOB或CFR成交的货物, 卖方无义务办理保险, 但在装船后有义务通知对方, 以便买方投保。而按CIF成交的货物, 卖方有义务办理保险。

I. 保险金额 (Insurance Amount)

保险金额一般按CIF价另加10%的预期利润计算。

II. 保险费 (Insurance Premium)

保险费是为投保而向保险人支付的费用,等于保险金额乘以保险费率(Insurance Premium Rate)。

III. 保险单据 (Insurance Policy or Certificate)

保险单据主要有两种: 保险单及保险凭证。保险单 (Insurance Policy) 称为大保单, 是保险人签发给被保险人的正式凭证。保险凭证 (Insurance Certificate) 称为小保单, 是保险人签发给被保险人的简化了的凭证。小保单虽无保险条款, 但却载明按正式保单上的条款办理, 所以具有与大保单同等效力。

IV. 保险险别 (Insurance Kinds)

海洋运输货物保险主要有中国保险条款(China Insurance Clauses—C.I.C.)及伦敦学会条款(ICC), 根据1981年1月1日中国人民保险公司修改的条款, 计有i. 基本险别; ii. 一般附加险别; iii. 特别附加险。

 i. 基本险别有平安险(FPA), 水渍险(WA)及一切险(AR)

- 平安险(FPA): 即单独海损(Particular Average)不赔, 但在全损(General Average, GA)或共同海损时可以赔偿。其保险的赔偿范围比全损险大。
- 水渍险(WA): 水渍险的承保范围除全损险和平安险所担保的风险和损失外,也包括单独海损, 即指除共同海损以外的部分损失, 仅由各受损者单独负担。(is borne by the owner of this individual consignment only)
- 一切险(AR): 一切险的承保范围很广, 保费很高, 但战争、罢工、骚乱及暴动等不包括在投保范围内。

 ii. 一般附加险别是基本险别的扩充, 不能单独投保。常见的附加险有以下15种险别:

- 偷窃并提货不着险 (theft, pilferage and none-delivery, TPND)
- 淡水雨淋险 (fresh water and/or rain damage)
- 短量险 (shortage)
- 渗漏险 (leakage)
- 碰损破碎险 (clash and breakage)
- 受潮受热险 (sweat and heating)
- 包装破裂险 (breakage of packing)
- 钩损险 (hook damage)

- 锈损险 (rust)
- 串味险 (taint of odor)
- 混杂并沾污险 (intermixture and contamination)
- 转船险 (transshipment risks)
- 不计免赔险 (irrespective of percentage, I.O.P.)
- 甲板险 (jettison and/or washing over board, J.W.O.B. clause)
- 存仓火险责任扩展条款 (fire risk extension clause for storage of cargo F.R.E.C.)等

iii. 特殊附加险 (special additional risks) 有以下几种险别:

- 战争险 (war risk)
- 罢工险 (strikes risk)
- 暴动和民变险 (riots and civil commotion risk)
- 拒收险 (rejection risk)
- 交货不到险 (failure to deliver risk)
- 舱面险 (on deck)等

(3) Some Words and Expressions on Insurance

subject matter 标的(物)
perils of the sea 海上危险
on his premises 住在他楼内的人
tenant 承租人
insurable intere st 保险利益/可保权益
recovery 追偿,弥补
enforceable 可执行的
underwriter 承保人
claim 索赔
proposal form 投保单
insurer 保险人
policy 保险单
indemnify and reimburse 赔偿及偿付
designate 指明

consideration 对价
liability insurance 责任保险
make good for 补偿,支付
default 违约,拖欠
take out 取得/获得(保险单)
bailee 受托人
surety insurance 担保或保证保险
broker 经纪人
insurance certificate 保险凭证
Lloyd 英国劳埃德保险公司
insured (人身保险的)被保险人
premium 保险费
coverage 承保范围/险别
cover 保险

(4) Useful Sentences on Insurance

- Please quote your lowest All Risks for shipments of TV sets to Quebec.
- Please hold us covered for the consignment referred to below.
- We should be glad if you would provide cover of $ 5,000 on... in transit from... to....
- We wish to renew the above policy for the same amount and on the same terms as before to cover.

- ✓ As requested in your letter of 3rd May, we quote below our terms for arranging cover for your consignment.
- ✓ For your information, we will arrange cover for the amount stated and on the terms requested.
- ✓ We note from your letter of... that your wish to renew open policy No. 5507 covering your goods against All Risks.
- ✓ Please inform us on what terms this insurance can be arranged.
- ✓ Please send us the necessary proposal form.
- ✓ We leave the details to you, but wish to have the consignment covered against All Risks.
- ✓ The consignment is covered by our open policy No. 55087 and we shall be glad to receive your certificate of insurance.
- ✓ The policy is being prepared and should reach you by the end of next month. In the meantime we are holding you covered.
- ✓ We undertake all classes of insurance and would welcome the opportunity to transact further business with you.
- ✓ I regret to report the loss of our goods insured with you under the above policy.
- ✓ I have completed and enclose the form of claim for loss of our consignment.
- ✓ Please let us know what particulars you need from us when we submit our claim.
- ✓ We have covered insurance on the 100 tons of wool for 110% of the invoice value against ALL Risks with the People's Insurance Company of China.
- ✓ The insurance is to be effected by the seller on behalf of the buyer for 110% of the invoice value against All Risks, premium to be for the buyer's account.
- ✓ Any additional premium for insurance coverage over 110% of the invoice amount, if so required, shall be borne by Buyer and be added to the invoice amount, for which the L/C shall stipulate accordingly.
- ✓ Seller shall arrange marine insurance covering W.A. plus T.P.N.D. and War Risks for 120% of the invoice value and provide for claims, if any, payable in New York City in U.S. currency.

(5) Frequent Clauses on Insurance Policy

This Policy of insurance witnesses that The People's Insurance Company of China (hereinafter called "the Company") at the request of... (hereinafter called "the Insured") and in consideration of the agreed premium paying to the Company by the Insured, undertakes to insure the under-mentioned goods in transportation subject to the conditions of this Policy as per the clauses printed over-leaf and other special clauses attached hereon.

中国人民保险公司(以下简称本公司)根据……(以下简称被保险人)的要求,由被保险人向本公司缴付约定的保险费,按照本保险单承保险别和背面所载条款与下列特款承保下述货物运输保险,特立本保险单。

(6) Exercises***

I. Fill in the Blanks based on the following definition.

Insurance Process

Mr. Smith wanted to insure his shop. He wanted ___1___ against fire and theft. He filled in the ___2___ and sent it to his ___3___ who arranged the insurance with an ___4___. Mr. Smith had to pay quite a high ___5___ each year, but it was worth it because a lot of goods were stolen. Mr. Smith put in a ___6___ for ___7___. Unfortunately, the ___8___ refused to pay him the full amount. Mr. Smith had not read the ___9___ in his ___10___ properly.

II. Definition

First, match the definition on the right with the word on the left. Then, fill in the blanks in the passage above with the words.

(1) premium   a. A person who advises on insurance

(2) underwriter   b. A document which proves you are insured

(3) insurance company c. Payment for insurance

(4) broker   d. Insurance protection

(5) claim   e. A form you fill in when you apply for insurance

(6) compensation   f. An insurer at Lloyd's of London

(7) small print   g. A limited liability company selling cover

(8) policy/insurance certificate   h. The conditions and clauses in a document of insurance, usually in small writing

(9) proposal form   i. You are paid... when your insured property is damaged

(10) cover   j. A request for payment when your insured property is damaged

(7) Example of Insurance Policy

中国人民保险公司

THE PEOPLE'S INSURANCE COMPANY OF CHINA

总公司设于北京　　一九四九年创立

Head Office: BEIJING   Established in 1949

MARIN CARGO TRANSPORTATION INSURANCE POLICY

发票号码　　　　　　　　　　　　保险单号次

Invoice No.　　　　　　　　　　　Policy No.

中国人民保险公司(以下简称公司)根据……(以下简称为被保险人)的要求由被保险人向本公司缴付约定的保险费，按照本保险单承保险别和背后所载条款与下列特款承保下述货物运输保险单。

This policy of insurance witnesses that the People's Insurance Company of China

PART FOUR CONTRACTUAL WRITING AND TRANSLATION

(hereinafter called "The Company "), at the Request of... (hereinafter called the "Insured") and in consideration of the agreed premium being paid to the company by the Insured, undertakes to insure the undermentioned goods in transportation subject to the conditions of this policy as per the clauses printed overleaf and other special clauses attached hereon.

标记 Marks & Nos.	包装及数量 Quantity	保险货物项目 Description of Goods	保险金额 Amount Insured

总保险金额：_____
Total Amount Insured

保费   费率   装载工具
Premium as arranged   Rate as Arranged   per conveyance S.S............

开航日期   自   至
Slg on or abt._____   form_____to

承保险别：
Conditions

　　所保货物，如遇风险，本公司凭本保险单及其有关证件给付赔款。

　　所保货物，如发生保险单项下负责赔偿的损失或事故，应立即通知本公司下述代理人查勘。

　　Claims, if any, payable on surrender of this policy together with other relevant document. In the event of accident whereby loss or damage may result in a claim this policy immediate notice applying for survey must be given to the Company's Agent as mentioned hereunder:

中国人民保险公司
THE PEOPLE'S INSURANCE CO. OF CHINA

赔款偿付地点
Claim payable at _____

出单公司地址   日期
Address of Issuing Office_____   Date_____

4) BILL OF EXCHANGE/DRAFT 汇票

(1) General Information

《中华人民共和国票据法》第19条对汇票作了如下定义:"汇票是出票人签发的,委托付款人在见票时或者在指定日期无条件支付确定的金额给付款人或者持票人的票据。"

(2) 汇票的当事人

i. 出票人(Drawer): 签发汇票的人, 在进出口义务中, 通常是出口人。

ii. 受票人(Drawee): 汇票的付款人(Payer), 在进出口义务中, 通常是进口人或其指定的银行。在信用证付款方式下, 若信用证没有指定付款人, 根据《UGP500》规定, 开证行即为付款人。

iii. 受款人(Payee): 汇票规定的可受领金额的人, 在进出口义务中, 若信用证没有特别指定, 受款人通常是出口人本人或其指定的银行。

(3) 汇票的种类

I. 按出票时是否附有货运单据可分为光票及跟单汇票

i. 光票(CLEAN BILL): 出具的汇票既不带发票、装运单据、物权凭证或其他类似的单证,也可不带任何为了取得付款而随附于汇票的单证。

ii. 跟单汇票(DOCUMENTARY BILL): 包括一份或一份以上的汇票,并随附在付款或承兑时所应交出的各种单证(主要包括发票、提单、装箱单、产地证、保险单等装运单证以及其他一切随附于汇票的单证)。

II. 按汇票付款时间的不同, 分为即期汇票和远期汇票

i. 即期汇票(SIGHT BILL): 指汇票上规定付款人见票后立即付款的汇票。

ii. 远期汇票(DRAFT AND TIME BILL): 指汇票上规定付款人于将来的一定日期内付款的汇票。

III. 按出票人的不同, 分为商业汇票和银行汇票

i. 商业汇票(COMMERCIAL BILL): 指汇票的出票人为商业企业的汇票。

ii. 银行汇票(BANKER'S BILL): 指汇票的出票人为银行的汇票。

IV. 按付款人的不同, 远期汇票可分为商业承兑汇票和银行承兑汇票

i. 商业承兑汇票(COMMERCIAL ACCEPTANCE BILL): 指商业企业出票而以另一商人为付款人,并经付款人承兑后的远期汇票。

ii. 银行承兑汇票(BANKER'S ACCEPTANCE BILL): 指商业企业出票而以银行为付款人,并经付款银行承兑的远期汇票。

(4) 汇票的使用程序

汇票使用一般要经过出票(ISSUE)、提示(PRESENTATIOM)、付款(PAYMENT)等程序,如是远期汇票在提示时还需承兑(ACCEPTANCE), 汇票转让时还需背书(ENDORSEMENT).

(5) 信用证汇票条款举例

"Drafts drawn under this credit shall be presented for negotiation in Guangzhou, China on or before 25th June, 2020."

凭本证开具的汇票须于……前(包括25日这天)在……提交议付。

Drafts are drawn in duplicate to our order bearing the clause "Drawn under United Malayan Banking Corp. Irrevocable Letter of Credit No.... dated July 12, 2020."

PART FOUR　CONTRACTUAL WRITING AND TRANSLATION

汇票一式两份，以我行为抬头，并注明"根据马来亚联合银行2020年7月12日第……号不可撤销信用证项下开立。

Available for payment/ acceptance of your draft(s) at sight drawn on us.
本证用于支付或承兑贵公司的向我行开具的即期汇票。

(6) Some Phrases and Expressions

Drawn on us (the opening bank) 向我们开具汇票
Drawn on this bank (the opening bank) 向本行开具汇票
Drawn on them (the importer) 向他们开具汇票
Drawn under 出票根据
Tenor 付款期限
Only 整 (用在大写金额后，防止涂改)。

(7) Examples of Bill of Exchange

Example 1

凭
Drawn under　SANWA BANK LTD OSAKA
信用证　　　第　　　号
L/C　　No.　41-1902141-003
日期　　　年　月　日
Dated　Nov. 2, 2002
按　　息　　付　　款
Payable with interest @　% per annum
号码　　　汇票金额　　　　　中国，广州　年　月　日
No... Exchange for USD 20,783,00 Guangzhou, China ......20....
见票　　　　　　日后 (本汇票之副本未付)　　　　付
At...sight of this FIRST of Exchange (Second of exchange being unpaid) pay to the order of BANK OF CHINA GUANGZHOU...
金额
the sum of U.S. DOLLARS TWENTY THOUSAND SEVEN HUNDRED EIGHTY THREE ONLY

此致
TO THE SANWA BANK LTD NEW YORK　　CHINA NATIONAL METALS AND
　　　　　　　　　　　　　　　　　　MINERALS CORP GUANGDONG
　　　　　　　　　　　　　　　　　　BRANCH
　　　　　　　　　　　　　　　　　　774 DONG FENG ROAD
　　　　　　　　　　　　　　　　　　EAST GUANGZHOU
　　　　　　　　　　　　　　　　　　THE PEOPLE'S REPUBLIC OF CHINA

Example 2

```
                    Bank's Demand Draft    即期汇票
中国银行
BANK OF CHINA
This draft is valid for one year
from the date of issue
本票自出票之日起,一年内有效        No. 300002953
                                  AMOUNT_____
                                  SHANGHAI _____ 20 ___
                                              1-326
                                               260

PAY TO _____
THE SUM OF U.S. DOLLARS _____
                              BANK OF CHINA, SHANGHAI BRANCH
TO: BANK OF CHINA, NEW YORK
    410 MADISON AVENUE
    NEW YORK NY 10017 U.S.A.
                                  _____
                                    AUTHORIZED SIGNATURE
```

5) INSPECTION CERTIFICATE OR SURVEY REPORT 商检证书或检验报告

(1) Definition

Inspection certificate or survey report is a document which shows the quality or quantity or other elements of the goods. It is issued by a commodity inspection bureau or an independent public surveyor after they inspect the goods. It performed two functions:

i. As a document of quality or quantity, it can decide whether the quality or quantity of the goods shipped by the seller is in conformity with that stipulated in the contract. It is an important proof at the time of refusing payment, lodging or settling a claim.

ii. It is one of the shipping documents used at the time of negotiating payment.

(2) The required inspection certificate or survey report is stipulated in an L/C as follows:

Inspection certificate of (for) quality, quantity, weight or origin in—copies, issued by a commodity inspection bureau. (由商品检验局签发的质量、数量、重量商检证书或产地证书……份。)

Survey report on quality, quantity, weight in—copies issued by a superintendent. 由公证行出具的质量、数量、重量检验报告……份。

Certificate of — (ex. Chinese) origin in duplicate. (原产地是……的证书一式两份。)

Certificate of origin issued by Chamber of Commerce or an Official Trade Committee stating that merchandise is of Chinese origin. (由商会或官方贸易委员会出具的注明商品的产地是中国的产地证书。)

Certificate of origin in—copies, bearing the declaration indicated in the attached Annex. (带有附录指出的声明的产地证书……份。)

(3) Example

INSPECTION CERTIFICATE OF QUALITY

DATE: July. 19, 2004
RE: L/C NO. ILCT507553
    INV.NO. 2004057WBS-5

DESCRIPT OF GOODS   MEN'S WOMEN'S SWEATERS

STYLE NO.	QUANTITY	NO. OF CTN.
22275	758 PCS	63 CTNS
22277	441 PCS	37 CTNS
22292	383 PCS	32 CTNS
22328	140 PCS	12 CTNS
22332	143 PCS	12 CTNS
52281	300 PCS	25 CTNS
52281BH	132 PCS	11 CTNS
TTL	2297 PCS	192 CTNS

THIS IS TO CERTIFICATE THAT WE HAVE INSPECTED OF CAPTIONED MERCHANDISES AND THE (CONTROL OF) QUALITY ARE IN CONFORMITY WITH S/C NO.2000CA44GMWBS11033

CERTIFIED BY:
(signature)

INSPECTOR
GUANGDONG TEXTILES
IE WOOLEN
KNITWEARS CO. LTD.
SIGNATURE:

6) CERTIFICATE OF ORIGIN (CO) 原产地证明书

(1) 产地证的作用

产地证明书是证明货物原产地和制造地的文件,也是进口国海关采取不同的国别政策和关税待遇的依据。在我国,产地证一般由商检机构或中国国际贸易促进委员会签发。

(2) 产地证的分类

    i. 普通产地证(原产地证)
    ii. 普惠制产地证
    iii. 欧洲纺织品产地证

(3) 产地证的内容

    i. 商品名称
    ii. 数量
    iii. 运输情况
    iv. 出口人对商品产地的声明
    v. 证件签发机构的证实文句

(4) 范例

1. Exporter (full name and address)		5. Certificate No.		
2. consignee (full name, address, country)		Certificate of origin of The people's Republic of China		
3. Means of transport and route		6. for certifying authority use only		
4. Destination port				
7. marks & numbers of packages	8. description of, goods, number and kind of package	9. H.S. Code	10. quantity or weight	11. number and date of invoices
1. Declaration by the exporter the undersigned hereby declares that the above details and statements are correct, that all the goods were produced in China and that they comply with the Rules of Origin of the People's Republic of China.		2. Certification It is hereby certified that the declaration by the exporter is correct.		
Place and date, signature and stamp of authorized signatory		Place and date, signature and stamp of certifying authority		

7) WEIGHT MEMO (NOTE) AND PACKING LIST 重量或装箱单

(1) The Definition

Weight memo is made out by a seller when a sale is effected in foreign trade. It is a document which indicates the net and gross weights of each package. It is used to make up the deficiency of an invoice. It enables the consignee or the customs office to check the goods.

重量单是对外贸易领域内卖方售货时出具的单据,是说明每件货物的毛重和净重的证件。它用于补充发票的不足之处,以便收货人或海关核对货物。

Packing list is also made out by a seller when a sale is effected in foreign trade. It is a document which indicates the name of the goods, the net weight, the gross weight and the complete inner packing specifications and contents of each package. It is also used to make up the deficiency of an invoice. It enables the consignee to declare the goods at customs office, distinguish and check the goods when they arrive at the port of destination.

装箱单也是贸易领域内卖方售货时出具的单据,是说明商品名称和每件货物的毛重、净重、内部包装情况及内容的证件。它也用于补充发票的不足之处,以便收货人在货物抵达目的地港时区分并核对货物及向海关申报货物。

(2) The required weight memo and packing list are stated in an L/C as follows:

Weight memo (note) or packing list in...copies, indicating gross and net weights of each package. (重量单或装箱单……份,注明每件货物的毛重和净重。)

Detailed packing list specifying net weight, gross weight and measurement of each package in metric system in duplicate required. (需要详细写明每件货物公制净重、毛重和尺码的装箱单一式两份。)

Packing list in triplicate detailing the complete inner packing specifications and contents of each package. (详细说明每件货物的内部包装情况及内容的装箱单一式三份。)

(3) Example

CHINA NATIONAL ELECTRONICS IMPORT & EXPORT CORPORATION
SHANGDONG BRANCH
PACKING LIST
ORIGINAL

TO: BBB CO..LTD   NO: 94S03
    4 BEACH ROAD   DATE: APR 12,2020
    SINGAPORE 0719   L/C: S-732-95

MARKS & NOS: QUANTITIES & DESCRIPTIONS   NEW   GW
N/W   12 FAN GEMMY BRAND
               220V 50HZ
               50% GOLD COLOR

NO. 1-200 2,000PCS		@12.5 KGS	@14.5 KGS
200CARTONS (GOLD)		25MT	29MT
NO. 201-400 2,000PCS		@12.5 KGS	@14.5 KGS
200CARTONS (WHITE)		25MT	29MT
4,000 PCS	400 CARTONS	50MT	58MT
PACKING IN CARTONS			

CHINA NATIONAL ELECTRONICS IMP.
& EXP. CORP. SHANGDONG BRANCH

8) SHIPPING ADVICE 装船通知

(1) Definition

After shipment is made, the seller writes a letter or sends a cable to the buyer, informing the latter of the name of the carrying vessel, the sailing date, the name of goods, the quantity shipped, the specifications of goods, the contract number, the L/C number, etc., so that the buyer can make preparations for taking delivery of the goods.

装船之后,卖方写信或发电报通知买方载货船只名称、开航日期、商品名称、所交数量、货物规格、合同号、信用证号等内容,这样买方就可以作提货大准备。

(2) The required shipping advise is stated in an L/C in the following ways:

A cable from sellers advising the buyers of the shipment date, the name and the quantity of goods and the name of the carrying vessel.

Your certified copy of cable dispatched to the accountee immediately after shipment, advising the name of vessel, date, quantity, weight and value of the shipment. 交货后卖方立即给汇票付款人拍发电报,通知后者船名、开航日期、货物数量、重量和价值,卖方须向本行提交加注说明文字的上述电报抄件。

Shipping details must be cabled to the buyers immediately after shipment and beneficiary's certificate to this effect is required. 交货后必须立即用电报把装船的详情通知买方,受益人须向本行提交办理上述事务的文字证明材料。

(3) Example

**CHINA NATIONAL METALS & MINERALS IMPORT & EXPORT CORP.
GUANGDONG BRANCH**
744 Dongfeng Road, Guangzhou, China
<u>**SHIPPING ADVICE**</u>

NO: 95C-379
DATE: MAR 2, 2020

PART FOUR　CONTRACTUAL WRITING AND TRANSLATION

TO: M/S JOHNSON CO
L/C NO: DB-2-875
DESCRIPTION OF GOODS: BARYTES POWDER
QUANTITY/WEIGHT: 1,200 BAGS 60M/T
SHIPPING MARKS: NEW YORK CNMMIEC IN DIOMAND
PORT OF SHIPMENT: GUANGZHOU
DATE OF SHIPMENT: MAR 2, 2020
VESSEL'S NAME: PACIFIC
PORT OF DESTINATION: NEW YORK
ESTIMATED DATE OF ARRIVAL: MAY 1, 2020

CHAPTER 4 Stylistic Features of Contractual Writing

商务合同属于法律性公文,是一种特殊的应用文体。因此,用词、写作、翻译的特点就是准确、严谨、规范。以下是合同写作的文体特征:

1. Using Archaic Words

英语中的一些古词(旧体词)在合同和其他法律文件中屡见不鲜,可以避免重复,起着承接合同条款的作用,并使行文显得正式、准确、简洁。

这些古词多数为副词,由here和there,或where作前缀加上介词组成,在句中一般作定语或状语。

here (代表this)
there (代表that)
where (代表which)

hereafter, hereby, herein, hereinafter, hereinbefore, hereof, hereto, hereunder, hereupon, herewith;

thereafter, thereby, therein, thereinafter, therefrom, thereof, thereunder, thereupon, therewith; whereas, whereby, wherein, whereof, whereon, etc.

下面较详细地解释常用的这些古词:

(1) hereby: by this means; by reason of this 特此;兹

This Contract is <u>hereby</u> made.

特签订本合同。

We <u>hereby</u> confirm having sold to you the following goods on the terms and conditions as specified below:

兹确认按下列条款售与贵公司下述商品:

The Seller <u>hereby</u> warrants that the goods meet the quality standard and are free from all defects.

……在此保证……

The undersigned <u>hereby</u> agrees that the new products whereto this trade name is more appropriate are made in China.

下述签署人同意在中国制造新产品，其品牌以此为合适。

(2) hereof: of this

The provisions hereof: the provisions of this Law.

本法规定。

Quantity set forth on the face hereof is subject to a variation of five percent (5%) plus or minus.

正面所列数量可以短装5%。

(3) hereto: to this

The Parties hereto.

本合同双方。

Appendix 4 hereto.

本协议附件4。

(4) herein: in this 此中；于此

Unfair competition mentioned herein.

本法中所称的不正当竞争。

The deposit paid by the Buyers shall not be refunded should the Buyers fail to make full payment within the time herein specified. (herein specified=specified in this contract)

如果买方在本合同规定的时间内未能全部付清货款，则买方不能领回保证金。

(5) hereinafter: later in the same Contract 在下文

This Contract is hereby made and concluded by and between _____ Co. (hereinafter referred to as Party A) and _____ Co. (hereinafter referred to as Party B) on _____ (Date), in _____ (Place), China, on the principle of equality and mutual benefit and through amicable consultation.

本合同双方，_____公司(以下称甲方)与_____公司(以下称乙方)，在平等互利基础上，通过友好协商，于___年___月___日在中国___ (地点)，特签订本合同。

(6) hereunder: under this

Each payment to be made hereunder shall be made in American currency.

以下规定的每笔款项必须以美元支付。

The principal (委托人) shall not assign or transfer any of its rights, obligations or liabilities hereunder (stipulated in this Agreement) without the express prior written consent of the General Agent.

委托人不得将本协议规定的……

(7) herewith: with this 与此；附此

A set of samples has been herewith enclosed.

(herewith=with this mail)

随信附上样品。

(8) therein: in that; in that particular context; thereon: on that

The remedying of any defects therein (=in the work).

修补工程中的缺陷。

When the Licensed Products are sold, the <u>royalty thereon</u> shall be paid within a calendar month from the date of delivery.

特许产品售出后,<u>该产品的专利权使用费</u>从交货日算起,一个日历月度内付讫。

(9) thereafter: after that今后, 此后

The commitment fee shall quarterly be paid from the date in the third month thereafter.

承诺费从其后第三个月的该日起开始按季支付。

(10) therefrom: from that由此; therefor: for that为此

"Products" means any and all agricultural products or any products derived therefrom.

……或由此衍生的……

...to bear all the legal and financial responsibilities arising therefrom.

承担因此引起的……

Before commencing the construction, the Contractor shall submit the plans and specifications therefor to the Owner for approval.

……为此编制的……

(11) whereby: by the agreement; by the following terms & conditions. etc. 凭……

A sales contract refers to a contract whereby the Seller transfers the ownership of an object to the Buyer and the Buyer pays the price for the object.

A contract shall be an agreement whereby the parties establish, change or terminate their civil relationship.

合同是当事人之间设立、变更、中止民事关系的协议。

(12) whereto: to that对于那个

The undersigned <u>hereby</u> agrees that the new products whereto this trade name is more appropriate are made in China.

下述签署人同意在中国制造新产品,其品牌以此为合适。

2. Using Capitalization

(1) The Concerned Parties to a Contract

Sellers, Buyers, the Supplier, the Purchaser, the Borrower, the Agent, the Licensee, the Licensor

(2) The Concerned Organizations in a Contract

Joint Venture Company; the Bank of China, Beijing Branch

(3) The Key Words/Phrases in a Contract

(4) The Concerned Contract and Clauses or Articles or Appendices

Party A and Party B shall make full endeavors to fulfill this Contract within the stipulated period. The schedule of various activities is attached at Appendix 3.

(5) The Concerned International Conventions, Practice, Laws, Regulations, etc.

United Nations Convention on Contracts for the International Sale of Goods

《联合国国际货物销售合同公约》

The Uniform Customs and Practice for Documentary Credits, 1993 Revision ICC Publication No.500

《跟单信用证统一惯例》(1993年修订本,国际商会第500号出版物)

International Rules for the Interpretation of Trade Terms 2000

《2000年国际贸易术语解释通则》

The Uniform Law on the Formation of Contracts for the International Sale of Goods

《国际货物买卖统一法》

The Principles of International Commercial Contracts

《国际商事合同通则》

(6) The Concerned Agreement or Documents to a Contract

3 copies of Non-negotiable Copies of Bill of Lading.

6 copies of Shipping Invoice.

6 copies of Packing List.

(7) Name of Money Used in a Country

Twenty-five percent of the Contract price shall be in Iraqi Dinar on the basis of RMB.

Seventy-five percent of the Contract price shall be paid in USD on the basis of RMB.

在以人民币计价的基础上,合同价25%用伊拉克第纳尔支付,75%用美元支付。

3. "Shall" in Legal English

"Shall"在法律文件中表示"应该""必须",决不能用"must"或"should"。

The deposit paid by the Buyers shall not be refunded should the Buyers fail to make full payment within the time herein specified.

如果买方在本合同规定的时间内未能全部付清货款,则买方不能领回保证金。

4. "Should" in Legal English

"Should"在法律文件中用作"if",只表示"如果"之意。

The board meeting shall be called and presided over by the Chairman. Should the Chairman be absent, the vice-Chairman shall, in principle, call and preside over the board meeting.

5. Using Formal Words and Phrases

Phrases often used in business contract:

(1) unless otherwise: 除非……(另有规定), 比if not/ otherwise正式

<u>Unless otherwise</u> specified in the credit, commercial invoices shall be made out in the name of the applicant for the credit.

(2) in accordance/compliance with: 比"according to"正式

Party A shall make delivery of the goods in accordance with the above-mentioned arrangement.

(3) in respect of: 比about, concerning, as regards正式

(4) be liable for sth.; be liable to sb.: be responsible in accordance with Law应负有责任

(5) in the event that; in the event of: 如果, 如果……发生

(6) in case; in (the) case of: 如果, 如果……发生, 比 when / if正式

In case of any divergence of interpretation, the Chinese text shall prevail.

(7) be deemed: 被认为, 比"be believed", "be considered" 正式

In the absence of such indication, (if a Credit is opened without the word "irrevocable"), the Credit shall be deemed to be revocable.

(在未收到这样的指示时, 信用证应被认为是可撤销的。)

(8) in witness whereof/thereof: 以此为证;兹证明

In witness thereof, this Contract shall come into effect after the Contract in question is made and signed by the Parties hereto in duplicate, and either Party will hold one copy.

(本合同由双方代表签字后生效, 一式两份, 双方各执一份。特此立据。)

In witness thereof, the parties hereto have caused this Contract to be executed in accordance with their respective law the day and year first above written.

(兹证明: 本合同由双方于上述规定的时间, 依据各自国家的法律所签订。)

(9) now these presents witness: 兹特立约为据

(10) in the presence of...: 见证人

(11) in witness whereof: 作为协议事项的证据

(12) the above-mentioned; the said; the aforesaid: 上述的/前述的

Party A shall make delivery of the goods in accordance with the above-mentioned arrangement.

Party A grants Party B an exclusive license to manufacture products by using the invention of the said letter of Patent.

The Licensee shall keep full and adequate books of account containing all particulars that may be necessary for the purpose of showing the amount of royalty payable to the Licensor. The aforesaid books of account shall be kept at the licensee's place of business.

(13) in consideration of: 考虑到;鉴于;由于

In consideration of the payments to be made by the Purchaser to the Supplier as herein mentioned, the Supplier hereby covenants with Purchaser to provide the goods and services and to remedy defects therein in conformity in all respects with the provisions to the Contract.

√ Note: 该句中供方保证履行的合同义务,是以买方支付款项为条件的。 In consideration of 体现了权利与义务的一致性,即: 一方履行某种义务完全是以另一方履行某种义务为条件或前提。

(14) to be entitled to: 有权; 应行使

The Seller shall be entitled to terminate this license in the event of failure by the Buyer to comply with any of the conditions stated in this Article.

If the Contract can not come into effect within six months after the date of signing, both parties are entitled to consider themselves absolved from the Contract.

If one or more of the following events of default shall occur and be continuing, the Agent and the Banks shall be entitled to the remedies set forth in Section 8.2.

6. Using Pairs of Synonyms

√ Each party to this Agreement shall perform and fulfill any of the obligations under this Agreement.

√ This agreement is made and entered into by and between AA Corporation and BB Company.

√ For and on behalf of sb.

√ The undersigned Buyers and Sellers have agreed to close the following transaction in accordance with the terms and conditions stipulated hereunder:

√ The shipper shall be liable for all damage caused by such goods to the ship and/or cargo on board.

√ Party A shall be unauthorized to accept any orders or to collect any account on and after September 20.

√ Our terms are cash within three months, i.e. on or before May 1.

7. Using "Include" and the Like

使用"include"或相应词如"inclusine"、"including"、"included"等，来限定含当日在内的时间。

例：本证在北京议付，有效期至1月1日。

This credit expires till January 1(inclusive) for negotiation in Beijing. (or: This credit expires till and including January 1 for negotiation in Beijing.)

(注：如果不包括1月1日在内，英译为 till and not including January 1。)

8. Using "ONLY"

为避免金额数量的差漏、伪造或涂改，英译时常用以下措施严格把关。

大写文字重复金额

英译金额须在小写之后，在括号内用大写文字重复该金额，即使原文合同中没有大写，英译时也有必要加上大写。在大写文字前加上"SAY"，意为"大写"；在最后加上"ONLY"用来限定金额。意思为"整"。必须注意：小写与大写的金额数量要一致。

例：聘方须每月付给受聘方美元500元整。

Party A shall pay Party B a monthly salary of US $ 500 (SAY FIVE HUNDRED US DOLLARS ONLY).

CHAPTER 5 About Contractual Translation

1. Specific Criteria for Contractual Translation

(1) Faithfulness and Accuracy 信实准确

(2) Expressiveness and Smoothness 达意规范 (专业)

合同翻译不仅要具备很好的外语水平,同时也要求译者具有一定的外贸专业知识,这样才能使合同翻译较好地达到其信实、准确、达意、规范的目的。

2. Confusing Synonyms

√ (1) "shipping advice" 与 "shipping instructions"
shipping advice 是"装运通知",是由出口商(卖主)发给进口商(买主)的。然而 shipping instructions 则是"装运须知",是进口商(买主)发给出口商(卖主)的。另外要注意区分 vendor (卖主)与 vendee (买主); consignor (发货人)与 consignee (收货人)。上述这三对词语在英译时极易发生笔误。

√ (2) "in" 与 "after"
当英译"多少天之后"的时间时,往往是指"多少天之后"的确切的一天, 所以必须用介词 in, 而不能用 after, 因为介词 after 指的是"多少天之后"的不确切的任何一天。

√ 例: 该货于 11 月 10 日由"东风"轮运出, 41 天后抵达鹿特丹港。
The goods shall be shipped per M.V. "Dong Feng" on November 10 and are due to arrive at Rottedam in 41 days. (M.V.= motor vessel)

√ (3) "on / upon" 与 "after"
当英译"……到后, 就……"时,用介词 on/upon, 而不用 after, 因为 after 表示"之后"的时间不明确。
例: 发票货值须货到付给。
The invoice value is to be paid on/upon arrival of the goods.

√ (4) "by" 与 "before"
当英译终止时间时,比如"在某月某日之前",如果包括所写日期时,就用介词 by 如果不包括所写日期,即指到所写日期的前一天为止,就要用介词 before。
例: 卖方须在 6 月 15 日前将货交给买方。
The vendor shall deliver the goods to the vendee by June 15. (or: before June 16, 说明含

6月15日在内。如果不含6月15日,就译为 by June 14 或者 before June 15。)

√ (5) "abide by"与"comply with"

abide by 与 comply with 都有"遵守"的意思。但是当主语是"人"时, 英译"遵守"时须用 abide by。当主语是非人称时, 则用 comply with 英译"遵守"。

例A: 双方都应遵守合同规定。

Both parties shall <u>abide by</u> the contractual stipulations.

例B: 双方的一切活动都应遵守合同规定。

All the activities of both parties shall <u>comply with</u> the contractual stipulations.

√ (6) "change A to B"与"change A into B"

英译"把 A 改为 B"用"change A to B", 英译"把 A 折合成/兑换成 B"用"change A into B", 两者不可混淆。

例: 装货期改为 8 月并将美元折合成人民币。

Both parties agree that change the time of shipment to August and change US dollar into Renminbi.

√ (7) "ex"与"per"

源自拉丁语的介词 ex 与 per 有各自不同的含义。英译由某轮船"运来"的货物时用 ex, 由某轮船"运走"的货物用 Per, 而由某轮船"承运"用 by。

例: 由"维多利亚"轮运走/运来/承运的最后一批货将于10月1日抵达伦敦。

The last batch per/ex/by S.S. "Victoria" will arrive at London on October. (S.S.=Steamship)

3. More Examples of Words with Multi-interpretations

下面列举的多义词常在合同中出现, 了解他们在不同情境及不同条款中的不同意思对读者正确理解商务合同等文件有着积极的意义。

1) DISCOUNT

(1) 折扣

The invoice shall be subject to the usual trade <u>discounts</u> allowed by the Consignor.

发票须按照发货人所给予的通常批发折扣开立(折扣是指商品在原价的基础上按百分比降价)。

You may get a 5% discount if your order is on a regular basis.

如果你方定期给我方下定单, 你方便可得到 5%的折扣。

We are prepared to grant you a <u>discount</u> of 5% on the price.

(2) 贴现

The Buyer shall lodge a 90-day note in Bank of China, Taiyuan Branch for discount.

买方将把一张90天的期票提交……<u>贴现</u>。

The Seller receives its <u>face value</u> less a deduction for certain days' interest plus the bank's commission, and thus gives this bank titles to the goods, this is "<u>discount</u>."

卖方领取扣除了若干天的利息和银行手续费后的<u>汇票(票面)金额</u>, 这样就把货物所有权交给了银行, 这就是<u>贴现</u>。

If a seller extends credit to a time draft, they have made a trade acceptance. The seller

171

can request that the bank finance the transaction by buying the draft.   The bank is said to <u>discount</u> the draft.

如卖方开出的是远期汇票，以此向买方提供信用，此时就做了一笔商业汇票承兑业务，卖方可以请银行买下商业承兑汇票，银行用这个办法对出口商融资，也就是说，银行对该汇票贴现了。

- Note: Discount (finance): a percentage deducted from the face value of a bill of exchange or promissory note when it changes hands before the due date.

2) INSTRUMENT

(1) 仪器；器械

A thermometer is an <u>instrument</u> for measuring temperature.

(2) 单据

The board of directors may authorize any agent or agents to enter into any Contract or execute and deliver any <u>instrument</u> in the name of and on behalf of the Corporation.
(董事会可授权任何代理人以公司名义并代表公司签订合同或签发单据。)

3) FREIGHT

(1) 货物

This aircraft company deals with <u>freight</u> only. It has no passenger service.

This <u>freight</u> must be carefully handled when loading.

(这种货物装载时必须小心搬运。)

1 copy of <u>Freight</u> Memo.

(……装运通知)

(2) 运费

The Ocean <u>freight</u> and transfer charges from the interior points to the port of shipment shall be paid by Buyer.

从内陆港到装运港的海运费用和中转费应由买方支付。

4) INTEREST

(1) 兴趣

I have no <u>interest</u> in politics.

The article of our immediate <u>interest</u> are your "CHUNHUI" Brand Agricultural Washing Machines.

(2) 被保险货物

The premium rates vary with differed <u>interests</u> insured and with different destinations, routes and carrying periods of insurance.

(保险费率随被保险货物的不同而变化，也随目的地、航线和保险责任有效期的不同而变化。)

(3) 利益；利息

It is to your <u>interest</u> to give up smoking.

Pay five percent <u>interest</u> on a loan.

annual <u>interest</u>.

PART FOUR　CONTRACTUAL WRITING AND TRANSLATION

5) FLOAT

(1) 浮动的

It is not surprising, then, that the world saw a return to a <u>floating</u> exchange rate system. Central banks were no longer required to support their own currencies.

After the pound was <u>floated</u>, its value went down.

(英镑对外汇率浮动后出现了贬值。)

(2) 流动的；不确定的

the <u>floating</u> population

the <u>floating</u> voters

(3) Floating policy：统保单

<u>Floating</u> policy is of great importance for export trade.

● Note: floating policy指用以承保多批次货运的一种持续性长期保险凭证。

6) CONFIRM

(1) 确认

We'd like to inform you that our counter sample will be sent to you by DHL by the end of this week and please <u>confirm</u> it ASAP so that we can start our mass production.

(……我们的回样将于本周末用特快专递给您，请尽快确认……)

(2) 保兑

Payment will be made by 100% <u>confirmed</u>, irrevocable Letter of Credit available by sight draft.

(付款方式为100%即期，保兑，不可撤消信用证。)

● Note: "保兑信用证"，即指一家银行所开的由另一家银行保证兑付的一种银行信用证。

7) NEGOTIABLE

(1) 可商议的

Part time barman required. Hours and salary <u>negotiable</u>.

The price is not <u>negotiable</u>.

(2) 可转让的

This Bill of Lading is issued in a <u>negotiable</u> form, so it shall constitute title to the goods and the holder, by endorsement of this B/L.

(所签发的提单为可<u>转让</u>的，故只要在提单上背书，便确定了货物和持票人的所有权。)

● Note: "可转让提单"经过背书后即可将所有权转让给他人。

8) ENDORSE

(1) 背书

Draft must be accompanied by full set original on board marine Bill of Lading made out to order, <u>endorsed</u> in blank (blank endorsed), marked "freight prepaid."

(汇票必须附有全套的正本海运提单，凭指示、空白背书，并写明"运费已付"。)

173

- Note: "空白背书" (blank endorsed)是"可转让提单"(negotiable B/L)的俗称, 即通过在提单背面空白处背书 (签名)而进行一次或多次转让。

  背书的方法有二:

  ① 不记名背书: 只写明背书人(endorser)而不写明特定的被背书人 endorsee);

  ② 记名背书: 既写明背书人, 又写明垫款行或议付行为被背书人, 否则银行不愿垫款议付。

(2) 推荐产品

Our products have been <u>endorsed</u> by the National Quality Inspection Association.

我们的产品为全国质量检查协会的推荐产品。

- Note: "推荐"是指用过某种产品后感到满意, 并通过媒体介绍给公众。

9) AVERAGE

(1) 平均(水平)

It's obvious that the products are below the <u>average</u> quality.

(很明显, 这批产品的品质是中下水平。)

(2) 海损

If a particular cargo is partially damaged, the damage is called particular <u>average</u>.

(如果某批货是部分受损, 我们称之为"单独海损"。)

10) CHOICE

(1) 选择

Arbitration of all questions in dispute under this Contract shall be at the <u>choice</u> of either party and shall be in accordance with the International Arbitration Rules of American Arbitration Association.

(对在合同中一切有争议的问题是否付诸仲裁将由任何一方作出选择, 并须按照美国仲裁协会的国际仲裁规则进行仲裁。)

(2) 供选择的种类

This shop has a large <u>choice</u> of hats and shoes.

(3) 上等的

Our products are manufactured from the <u>choice</u> grades of material and will satisfy you in every respect.

(我方的产品均用上等原料制成……)

11) COMMISSION

(1) 佣金

The prices quoted include a progressive <u>commission</u>, to be calculated on FOB basis, of 2% for a single order for 10 dozen or up, 3% for 30 dozen or up.

(所报价格包括累进佣金, 按FOB价为基础计算, 每订单在10打及以上时佣金为2%, 30打及以上时佣金为3%。)

(2) 委托

Party B is <u>commissioned</u> by the manufacturers to buy steel plates and this Contract shall supersede all previous commitments.

(乙方受制造厂家的委托购买钢板,因此本合同将取代以前的一切承诺。)

(3) 试运行

The Contractor shall be responsible for and shall carry out all maintenance work during <u>commissioning</u> period.

(在试运行期间,承包方应负责进行一切维修工作。)

12) DISCHARGE

(1) 卸货

The time limit for inspection and claim is 60 days after <u>discharge</u> of the cargo at the port of destination.

(2) 解除; 释放; 退役

Party B agrees that the expiration of this license shall not <u>discharge</u> party B from its obligation.

(乙方同意在许可证到期时并不免除乙方应尽的义务。)

She's been <u>discharged</u> from hospital.

(她已获允许出院。)

After my <u>discharge</u> from the army I went into business.

(我退伍后从商。)

(3) 履行(义务或诺言)

Routine duties of the Joint Venture Company are to be <u>discharged</u> by the general manager appointed by the Board of Directors.

(董事会任命的总经理,负责履行合营公司的日常职权。)

13) ADVISE

(1) 劝告,忠告

He <u>advised</u> me against giving up my job.

The lawyer <u>advised</u> us against signing the contract.

(2) 担任顾问

She <u>advises</u> on legal matters.

(3) 正式通知,告知

We wish to <u>advise</u> you that you now owe the bank $10,000.

The <u>advising</u> bank 通知行

The Sellers shall, immediately upon the completion of the loading of the goods, <u>advise</u> by cable or telex the Buyers of the Contract number, commodity, quantity, invoiced value, gross weight, name of vessel, port of shipment, port of destination and date of sailing.

14) CLAUSE

(1) (语法中的)分句, 从句

an attributive <u>clause</u>

a noun clause

an adverbial clause

(2) (合约的)条款

Definition clause

An additional clause

Special clauses

Clauses on Documents

4. Exercises

以下三个句子各有两个译文,请判断哪个正确:

√ By Irrevocable Letter of Credit available by Sellers documentary bill at sight to be valid for negotiation in China until 15 days after date of shipment, the Letter of Credit must reach the Sellers 30 days before the contracted month of shipment.

译文1 以不可取消的信用证,凭卖方即期附有单据的票据协商,有效期应为装运期15天后在中国到期,该信用证必须于合同规定的装运月份前30天到达卖方。

译文2 以不可撤销的信用证,凭卖方即期跟单汇票议付,有效期应为装运期后15天在中国到期。该信用证必须于合同规定的装运月份前30天到达卖方。

√ Three full sets of negotiable, clean on board, original ocean Bill of Lading made out to the order of shipper and blank endorsed, notifying China National Foreign Trade Transportation Corporation at the port of destination.

译文1 全套清洁海运提单正本三份,可议付的,以发运人为命令的,空白背书,通知目的港的中国对外贸易运输公司。

译文2 全套清洁海运提单正本三份,可转让,以发运人为抬头,空白背书,通知目的港的中国对外贸易运输公司。

√ Licensee will furnish to Party A copies of insurance policies and/or the endorsements.

译文1 领有许可证者将给甲方提供几份保险政策和背书。

译文2 受让方(受证人)将给甲方提供几份保险单和/或保险单上所加的变更保险范围的条款。

CHAPTER 6 Translation of the Frequent Clauses in a Contract

1–16. Clauses and Their Translations

条款是构成合同的基本单位，因此对一些常见及必要的条款应该做到熟悉并能正确翻译。

这些条款包括支付条款、质量保证条款、保险条款、不可抗力条款、包装条款、迟交与罚款条款、索赔条款、仲裁条款等等。

1. Payment

(1) In case by L/C: The Buyers, shall, upon receipt from the Sellers of the shipping advice, open an irrevocable Letter of Credit with the Bank of China, fifteen to twenty days prior to the date of delivery, in favor of the Sellers, for an amount equipment to the total value of the shipment. The Credit shall be payable against the presentation of the draft and the documents stipulated in Clause 10 hereof in the opening bank. The Letter of Credit shall be valid until the 15th day after the shipment is effected.

(2) In case by Collection: After delivery is made, the Sellers shall draw a draft and send the draft together with the documents stipulated in Clause 10 hereof from the Seller' Bank, through the Bank of China for collection from the Buyers.

√ Collection 托收

Collection is the second mode of payment in international trade. The seller issues a draft, to which the shipping documents are attached, forwards the draft to a bank in his place (i.e. the remitting bank), makes an application for collection and entrusts the remitting bank to collect the purchase price from the buyer through its correspondent bank abroad (i.e. the collecting bank)

(3) In case by M/T or T/T: Payment shall be effected within seven days after receipt of the shipping documents stipulated under Clause 10 of this Contract.

√ M/T: Mail Transfer 信汇

The buyer gives money to his local bank. The local bank issues a trust deed for payment, then sends it to a correspondent bank at the seller's end by means of mail and entrusts him to pay the money to the seller.

√ T/T: Telegraphic Transfer 电汇

At the request of the buyer, the local bank sends a trust deed for payment by cable directly to a correspondent bank at the seller's end and entrusts him to pay money to the seller.

(Note: remitting bank 受托银行; correspondent bank 往来行; entrusts 委托)

参考译文

支付条款:

(1) 如以信用证方式支付: 买方接到卖方装船通知后, 在交货期前15—20天, 由中国银行开立以卖方为受益人, 金额为货物总值的不可撤销信用证。该信用证凭汇票及合同第10条规定的各项单据在开证行付款。信用证有效期至装船后15天止。

(2) 如以托收方式支付: 交货后, 卖方应开具汇票和本合同第10条所规定的各项单据由卖方银行通过中国银行向买方收取货款。

(3) 如以信汇或电汇方式支付: 买方收到本合同第10条所规定的装船单据后于7天内付款。

√ Terms of Payment:

By Confirmed, Irrevocable, Transferable and Divisible Letter of Credit to be available by sight draft, which shall reach the Sellers before... and remain valid for negotiation through Bank of China,... until the 15th day after the aforesaid Time of Shipment.

参考译文

支付条款:

采用保兑的, 不可撤销的, 可转让的及可分割的信用证, 凭即期汇票付款; 信用证必须于___日以前达到卖方, 在中国银行议付有效期为装船后15天。

√ Terms of Payment:

L/C shall be opened within 30 days by the buyer before shipment, the seller will remit the real value differences of buying and selling to the buyer after shipment.

If the buyer makes out the bill and settles accounts of foreign currency, the buyer shall remit the total value to the seller according to the invoice/receipt value opened.

参考译文

付款条件:

由买方或买方客户于装运期前30天内将有关信用证开给卖方, 装运后由卖方将购销实际差价汇给买方。

若由买方办理制单结汇, 由买方凭卖方开具的发票/收据将货款汇给卖方。

2. Claims

√ (1) In case the Sellers are liable for the discrepancies(与……不符) and a claim has been lodged by the Buyers within the time limit of inspection and quality guarantee period as stipulated in Clause15 and 16 of this Contract, the Sellers shall settle the claim in one or any combination of the following ways.

> i. Agree to the rejection of the goods and refund(退款) to the Buyers the value of the goods so rejected in the same currency as contracted herein, and to bear all direct losses and expenses in connection therewith including interest accrued (利息自然增长), banking charges, freight, insurance premium, inspection charges, storage stevedore (码头装卸工) charges and all other necessary expenses required for the custody (保管) and protection of the rejected goods;
>
> ii. Devalue the goods according to the degree of inferiority, extent of damage and amount of losses suffered by the Buyers;
>
> iii. Replace the defective equipment party or wholly of which the replacement shall conform to the specifications, quality, and performance as stipulated in this Contract, and bear all the expenses and direct loses sustained by the Buyers. The Sellers shall, at the same time, guarantee the quality of the replacement for a further period according to Clause 15 of this Contract.

(2) The claim mentioned above shall be regarded as being accepted if the Sellers fail to reply within 30 days after the Sellers receive the Buyers' claim.

参考译文

索赔:

(1) 如果货物质量与合同规定不符, 属卖方责任, 买方在检验期和第15条规定的保证期内提出索赔, 卖方将按下列一种或几种方法解决有关索赔问题:

> i. 同意买方拒收货物, 并以合同规定货币退回拒收货物的价款, 负担一切有关费用, 包括利息、银行费用、运费、保险费、检验费、码头工人费用, 以及一切为保存拒收货物所必须支出的其他费用;
>
> ii. 根据质次的程度、损坏程度和买方遭受损失的金额, 降低货价;
>
> iii. 更换部分或全部质次货物, 换回货物的规格, 质量和性能必须符合合同规定, 并承担全部费用和买方的直接损失, 同时, 卖方须按本合同第15条延长对换回货物的质量担保期。

(2) 若卖方收到买方上述索赔要求后30天内未作出答复, 则视为卖方接受了买方的索赔要求。

√ Within 45 days after the arrival of the goods at the destination, should the quality, specifications or quantity be found not in conformity with the stipulations of the Contract except those claims for which the insurance company or the owners of the vessel are liable, the Buyers shall, have the right on the strength of the inspection certificate issued by the C.C.I.C and the relative documents to claim for compensation to the Sellers.

参考译文

索赔:

在货到目的口岸45天内如发现货物品质,规格和数量与合同不符,除属保险公司或船方责任外,买方有权凭中国商检出具的检验证书或有关文件向卖方索赔换货或赔款。

3. Late Delivery and Penalty

Should the Sellers fail to make delivery on time as stipulated in the Contract, with the exception of Force Majeure specified in Clause 18 of this Contract, the Buyers shall agree to postpone the delivery on condition that the Seller agree to pay a penalty which shall be deducted (扣除) by the paying bank from the payment under negotiation. The penalty, however, shall not exceed __% of the total value of the goods involved in the late delivery. The rate of penalty is charged at __% for every 7 days, odd days less than 7 days shall be counted as 7 days. In case the Sellers fail to make delivery 10 weeks after the time of shipment stipulated in the Contract, the Buyers shall have the right to cancel the Contract and the Sellers, in spite of the cancellation, shall still pay the aforesaid penalty to the Buyers without delay.

参考译文

迟交货与罚款:

除合同第18条不可抗力外如卖方不能按合同规定的时间交货,买方应同意在卖方支付罚款的条件下延期交货。罚款可由支付银行在议付货款时扣除。罚款率按每7天__%,不能超过迟交货物总值的__%,不足7天以7天计算。如卖方延期交货超过合同规定10周时,买方有权撤销合同。此时,卖方仍应不延迟地按上述规定向买方支付罚款。

4. Guarantee of Quality

The Sellers shall guarantee that the commodity is made of the best materials, with first-class workmanship, brand new, and unused, and complies in all respects with the quality, specifications and performance as stipulated in this Contract. The Sellers shall guarantee that the goods, when correctly mounted (安装) and properly operated and maintained, shall perform satisfactorily for a period of __ months beginning from the date on which the commodity arrives at the port of destination.

参考译文

质量保证:

卖方保证货物全新,未曾使用过,材料质优,做工一流,在质量、规格和性能等诸方面均符合本合同规定,并保证在安装,操作正确,适当维修条件下,货物正常运转期为××月,自货物到达目的港××日起计算。

5. Quality and Quantity/Weight

The contracted goods are bought on the basis of landed quality and landed quantity/weight and the certificate issued by the China Commodity Inspection Bureau shall be taken as final.

参考译文

合同中的订购货物,以上岸质量及上岸数量或重量为依据,以中国商检局颁发的检验证书为最终依据。

6. Force Majeure

√ In case of delayed shipment or non-delivery due to a generally recognized Force Majeure, the Seller must advise the buyer immediately by cable of the occurrence, and within 15 days thereafter the seller must airmail to the Buyer a certificate of the incident issued by the competent government authorities (政府主管当局) or Chamber of Commerce (商会) at the place where the incident occurred. The Seller shall not be absolved from (免除) his responsibility unless such an incident is acknowledged by the Buyer. In case conditions of Force Majeure continue to last over and above 30 days, the Buyer shall have the right to cancel the contract. The Seller's failure to obtain an export licence shall not be considered as Force Majeure.

参考译文

不可抗力:

如果由于被公认的不可抗力而导致了拖延装运或不能交货,卖方必须立即将发生的一切用电报通知买方,并在此后的15天内,必须将不可抗力发生之处的、有权威的政府机构或商会颁发的、能证明此不可抗力属实的材料,航空邮寄给买方。在买方未收到和承认关于此不可抗力的通知之前,卖方无权从责任中解脱出来。如果此不可抗力继续延续下去,并超过了30天,买方有权取消合同。出口商未能获得出口许可,不能被认为是不可抗力。

√ The sellers shall not be held responsible for the delay in shipment or non-delivery of the goods due to Force Majeure, which might occur during the process of manufacturing or in the course of loading or transit. The sellers shall advise the Buyers immediately of the occurrence mentioned above the within fourteen days there after the Sellers shall send by airmail to the Buyers for their acceptance certificate of the accident. Under such circumstances the Sellers, however, are still under the obligation to take all necessary measures to hasten the delivery of the goods.

参考译文

不可抗力:

由于人力不可抗力的原由发生在制造,装载或运输的过程中导致卖方延期交货或不能交货者,卖方可免除责任,在不可抗力发生后,卖方须立即电告买方及在14天内以空邮方式向买方提供事故发生的证明文件,在上述情况下,卖方仍须负责采取措施尽快发货。

7. Arbitration

All disputes in connection with the execution of this Contract shall be settled friendly through negotiation. In case no settlement can be reached, the case then may be submitted for arbitration to the Arbitration Commission of the China Council for the Promotion of International

Trade in accordance with the Provisional (暂定的) Rules of Procedure promulgated (公布) by the said Arbitration Commission. The Arbitration committee shall be final and binding upon both parties. and the Arbitration fee shall be borne by the losing parties.

参考译文

仲裁:

凡有关执行合同所发生的一切争议应通过友好协商解决,如协商不能解决,则将分歧提交中国国际贸易促进委员会按有关仲裁程序进行仲裁,仲裁将是终局的,双方均受其约束,仲裁费用由败诉方承担。

8. Commission

√ Party A shall pay Party B a commission of 5% on the net invoiced selling price on all orders directly obtained by Party B and accepted by Party A. No commission shall be paid until Party A receives the full payment for each order.

参考译文

佣金:

对乙方直接获取并经甲方确认接受的订单,甲方按净发票售价向乙方支付5%佣金。佣金是在甲方收到了每一笔订单的所有费用之后才支付。

√ An amount equal to 6% of the invoice value to be deducted from the amount payable to beneficiaries, this amount not to be shown on the invoice, but a separate credit note (statement) in the name of ABC CO. covering his commission to be presented.

参考译文

汇票(要求)开列94%的发票金额,另外以ABC公司的名义出具一个贷记帐单或声明,支付其所得的佣金。

9. Clauses on Bill of Lading

√ Full set of clean on board marine bills of lading, made out to order of ABC Co., marked: "freight prepaid", notify: applicant.

参考译文

海运提单:

全套清洁的已装运海运提单,作成以ABC公司为抬头,注明"运费预付",通知申请人。

√ Full set of not less than two clean on-board marine bills of lading marked "freight prepaid" and made out to order and endorsed to our order, showing ABC Co. as notifying party, short form Bills of lading are not acceptable. Bill of lading to state shipment has been effected in containers and container numbers.

参考译文

全套不少于两份清洁已装运海运提单,注明"运费预付",空白抬头并背书给开证行,通知ABC公司,不接受简式提单。提单声明集装箱运输并标明集装箱号码。

PART FOUR   CONTRACTUAL WRITING AND TRANSLATION

✓ Full set of clean shipped on board marine bills of lading, made out to our order, marked: "freight prepaid", and notify: opener, indicating L/C No. and S/C No., "received for shipment" B/L not acceptable.

参考译文

全套清洁已装运海运提单，作成以开证行为抬头，注明"运费预付"，通知开证人。标明信用证和销货合同号码，不接受"备运提单"。

10. Clauses on Insurance Policy

✓ This Policy of insurance witnesses that The People's Insurance Company of China (hereinafter called "the Company") at the request of... (hereinafter called "the Insured") and in consideration of the agreed premium (保险费) paying to the Company by the Insured, undertakes to insure the under-mentioned goods in transportation subject to the conditions of this Policy as per (按照) the clauses printed over-leaf (背面) and other special clauses attached hereon.

参考译文

保险条款：

中国人民保险公司(以下简称本公司)根据……(以下简称被保险人)的要求，由被保险人向本公司缴付约定的保险费，按照本保险单承保险别和背面所转条款与下列条款承保下述货物运输保险，特立本保险单。

✓ Insurance Policy /Certificate endorsed in blank of 110% of invoice value covering All Risks & War Risks as per CIC with claims payable at KUALA LUMPUR in the currency of draft (irrespective of percentage不计免赔率), including 60 days after discharge of the goods at port of destination (of at station of destination) subject to CIC.

参考译文

保险单或保险凭证空白背书，按发票金额的110%投保中国保险条款的一切险和战争险，按汇票所使用的货币在吉隆坡赔付(无/不计免赔率,IOP)，并根据中国保险条款，保险期限在目的港卸船(或在目的地车站卸车)后60天为止。

✓ In the event of loss or damage which may result in a claim under this Policy, immediate notice must be given to the Company Agent as mentioned hereunder. Claims, if any, one of the Original Policy which has been issued in 2 Original (s) together with the relevant documents shall be surrendered to(向……提交) the Company, if one of the Original Policy has been accomplished, the others to be void.(无效)

参考译文

所保货物，如发生本保险单项下可能引起索赔的损失或损坏，应立即通知本公司下述代理人查勘。如有索赔，应向本公司提交保险单正本(本保险单共有2份正本)及有关文件。如一份正本已用于索赔，其余正本则自动失效。

√ Insurance:

To be effected by (marked X) the Sellers for 110% of the invoice value against All Risks and War Risk in accordance with _____ (Insurance Clause).

参考译文

保险:

由卖方办理保险,按照保险条款第_____条,投保全险和战争险,投保金额为发票金额的110%。

11. Terms of Shipment

√ For CFR Terms: The Sellers shall ship the goods within the time as stipulated in Clause __ of this Contract by a direct vessel sailing from the port of loading to China Port. Transshipment en route is not allowed without the Buyers' consent.

参考译文

装船条件:

成本加运费价条款: 卖方应在本合同第___条规定之时间内,将货物由装船口岸,直接船运到中国口岸,在未经征得买方同意前,中途不得转船。

√ For FOB Terms: The shipping space for the contracted goods shall be booked by the Buyers' shipping agent, China National Chartering Corporation (Address: ...). The Sellers undertake to load the contracted goods on board the vessel nominated by the Buyers on any date notified by the Buyers, within the time of shipment stipulated in the Clause of this Contract.

参考译文

离岸价条款:

装运本合同货物的船只,由买方运输代理人中国租船公司(地址:……)租订舱位。卖方应负责将所有订货物在本合同第_____条规定的装船期限内按卖方所通知的任何日期装上买方指定的船只。

12. Inspection

It is mutually agreed that the certificates of quality and quantity or weight issued by the manufacturer shall be part of the documents to be presented to the paying bank for negotiation of payment. However, the inspection of quality and quantity or weight shall be made in accordance with the following:

In case the quality and quantity or weight of the goods be found not in conformity with those stipulated in this Contract after re-inspection by the China Commodity Inspection Bureau within 60 days after arrival of the goods at the port of destination, the Buyers shall return the goods to or lodge claims against the Sellers for compensation of losses upon the strength of Inspection Certificate issued by the said Bureau, with the exception of those claims for which the insurers or owners of the carrying vessel are liable. All expenses (including inspection fees) and losses arising from the return of the goods or claims should be borne by the Sellers. In such case, the Buyers may, if so requested, send a sample of the goods in question to the Sellers, provided that sampling is feasible.

参考译文

商品检验：

双方同意以制造厂出具之品质及数量或重量检验证明书作为卖方向付款银行议付货款单据之一。但货物的品质及数量或重量检验应按下列规定办理：

货到目的口岸60天内经中国商品检验局复验，如发现品质及数量或重量与本合同规定不相符时，除属于保险公司或船行负责外，买方凭中国商品检验局出具的检验证明书向卖方提出退货或索赔。所有因退货或索赔引起的一切费用(包括检验费)及损失均由卖方负担。在此情况下，凡货物适于抽样者，如卖方要求，买方可将样品寄交卖方。

13. Shipping Advice

Immediately after completion of goods on board the vessel the Sellers shall advise the Buyers by cable of Contract number, name of goods, quantity or weight loaded, invoice value, name of vessel, port of shipment, sailing date and port of destination.

Should the Buyers be made unable to arrange insurance in time owing to the Sellers' failure to give the above mentioned advice of shipment by cable, the Sellers shall be held responsible for any and all damage and/or loss attributable to such failure.

参考译文

装船通知：

货物装船完毕后，卖方应立即以电报通知买方合同号、货名、所装数量或重量、发票价值、船名、起运口岸、开船日期及目的口岸。如果卖方不发上述装船通知给买方而导致买方不能及时保险时，则所发生的一切损失由卖方承担。

14. Shipping Mark

On the surface of each package, the package number, measurement, gross weight, net weight and the wordings "RIGHT SIDE UP", "HANDLE WITH CARE", "KEEP DRY" and the lifting position and the following shipping mark shall be stenciled in fadeless paint.

参考译文

唛头：

卖方须在每件包装表面，用不褪色油漆清楚地标明件号、尺码、毛重、净重，以及"此端向上""小心轻放""切勿受潮"等字样，并刷印唛头。

15. Packing

To be packed in new strong wooden case (s) suitable for long distance ocean transportation and the change of climate, well protected against dampness, moisture, shock, rust and rough handling. One full set of operating instructions for each instrument or machine shall be enclosed in the package(s). The Sellers shall be liable for any rust, damage and loss attributable to inadequate or improper protective measures taken by the Sellers in regard to the packing.

参考译文

包装:

用坚固的新木箱包装, 适于长途海洋运输和天气的变化。能防潮、防湿、防震、防锈并防粗鲁装运。每件仪器或机器的包装里都要附上一整套操作说明书。若因卖方包装措施不当所产生的锈损等损害(失)由卖方负责。

16. The Shipping Documents

The Sellers shall present to the paying bank the following documents for negotiation:

(1) One negotiable copy of clean on board ocean Bill of Lading marked "FREIGHT PREPAID" indicating shipping mark, made out to order, blank endtorsed, and notifying the Buyers.

(2) 3 copies of Invoice with the insertion of Contract number and the Shipping Mark.

(3) 3 copies of Packing List showing gross and net weight for each package.

(4) 1 copy of Certificate of Quantity and Quality issued by the Manufacturers.

(5) Certified copy of cable to the Buyers, advising shipment immediately after shipment is made.

The Sellers shall, after the shipment is effected, send by airmail one set of the same copies of each of the above-mentioned documents (except Item 5) to the Buyers.

参考译文

装船单据:

(1) 一份可转让的清洁的已装运海运提单, 注明"运费预付", 标明唛头, 空白抬头, 空白背书, 并通知买方。

(2) 三份带有合同号码并唛头的发票。

(3) 三份显示每箱货物毛重和净重的装箱单。

(4) 一份由制造商出具的数量和质量证明。

(5) 一份核准的装船后立即发给买方的装船通知电报。

卖方应在装船后航邮给买方以上(第⑤项除外)文件各一份(一套)。

17. Exercises

Try to translate the following Terms into Chinese:***

√ **Payment and Terms of Payment**

(1) Currency used for the present Contract is US Dollars, Party A shall effect payment through opening irrevocable sight L/C with Bank of China. Party A must open the said L/C within fifteen days of the signing of the present Contract.

(2) As the equipment stipulated in Clause 2 of the present Contract (CIF Qingdao US $1,500,000,00). Party A is to pay 90% of the said amount to Party B after the said

shipment has reached Qingdao against clean B/L, commercial invoice and packing list, which are certified by banks of both parties to be in conformity with the size, model and quantity as stipulated by the Contract. The remaining 10% for crushing apparatus shall be paid within sixty days of receipt of documents; and the remaining mining apparatus shall be paid within twenty-one days of receipt of documents. Party A shall present a letter of guarantee by its company for the period of guarantee.

(3) As to the spare parts and repair parts stipulated in Clause 2 of the present Contract (CIF Qingdao US$78,000.00), Party A shall pay Party B once and for all after the shipment thereof has reached Qingdao against clean B/L, commercial invoice and packing list, which are certified by bank of both parties to be in conformity with what is provided in the Contract.

√ **Payment in Installments**

The total amount of payment under this Contract shall be paid in installments. The due time of payment and the sum of each installment are as follows:

(1) _____% of the total amount as advance payment, viz USD _____ (Say _____ US Dollars), shall be paid within _____ months after signing this Contract, i.e. no later than _____, 20 _____.

(2) _____% of the total amount as the first installment, viz USD _____ (Say _____ US Dollars), shall be paid within _____ months after signing this Contract. i.e. no later than _____, 20 _____.

(3) _____% of the total amount as the second installment, viz USD _____ (Say _____ US Dollars), shall be paid within _____ months after signing this Contract. i.e. no later than _____, 20 _____.

(4) _____% of the total amount as the third installment, viz USD _____ (Say _____ US Dollars), shall be paid within _____ months after signing this Contract. i.e. no later than _____, 20 _____.

√ **Ocean Marine Cargo Insurance Clauses*****

1. Scope of Cover

This insurance is classified into the following three Conditions-Free From Particular Average (F.P.A.), With Average (W.A.) and All Risks. Where the goods insured hereunder sustain loss or damage, the Company shall undertake to indemnify therefore according to the insured Conditions specified In the Policy and the Provisions of these Clauses:

1) Free From Particular Average (F.P.A.)

This insurance covers:

(1) Total or Constructive Total Losses of the whole consignment hereby insured caused in the course of transit by natural calamities—heavy weather, lightning, tsunami, earthquake and flood. In case a constructive total loss is claimed for, the Insured shall abandon to the Company the damaged goods and all his rights and title pertaining

thereto. The goods on each lighter to or from the seagoing vessel shall be deemed a complete lot.

"Constructive Total Loss" refers to the loss where an actual total loss appears to be unavoidable or the cost to be incurred in recovering or reconditioning the goods—together with the following cost to the destination named in the Policy would exceed their value on arrival.

(2) Total or Partial Loss caused by accidents—the carrying conveyance being grounded, stranded, sunk or in collision with floating ice or other objects or as fire explosion.

(3) Partial Loss of the Insured goods attributable to heavy weather, lightning and/or tsunami, where the conveyance has been grounded, stranded, sunk or burnt, irrespective of whether the event or events took place before or after such accidents.

(4) Partial or Total Loss consequent on falling of entire package or packages into sea during loading, transshipment or discharge.

(5) Reasonable cost incurred by the Insured on salvaging the goods or averting or minimizing a loss recoverable under the Policy, provided that such cost shall not exceed the sum Insured of the consignment so saved.

(6) Losses attributable to discharge of the insured goods at a port of distress following a sea peril as well as special charges arising from loading, warehousing and forwarding of the goods at an intermediate port of call or refuge.

(7) Sacrifice in and contribution to General Average and Salvage charges.

(8) Such proportion of losses sustained by the shipowners as is to be reimbursed by the Cargo Owner under the Contract of Affreightment "Both to Blame Collision" clause.

2) With Average (W.A.)

Aside from the risks covered under F.P.A. condition as above, this insurance also covers partial losses of the insured goods caused by heavy weather, lightning, tsunami, earthquake and/or flood.

3) All Risks

Aside from the risks covered under the F.P.A. and W.A. conditions as above, this insurance also covers all risks of loss of or damage to the insured goods whether partial or total, arising from external causes in the course of transit.

2. Exclusions

This insurance does not cover:

1) Loss or damage caused by the intentional act or fault of the Insured.

2) Loss or damage falling under the liability of the consignor.

3) Loss or damage arising from the inferior quality or shortage of the insured goods, prior to the attachment of this insurance.

4) Loss or damage arising from normal loss, inherent vice or nature of the insured goods, loss of market and/or delay in transit and any expenses arising therefrom.

5) Risks and liabilities covered and excluded by the ocean marine (cargo) war risks clauses and strike, riot and civil commotion clauses of This Company.

CHAPTER 7 Contracts and Agreements

1. Sales and Purchase Contracts

购销合同是国际贸易最主要的合同。其中质量、数量、包装、价格、装运和支付条款是国际贸易合同的主要条款,另外,保险、商检、不可抗力、仲裁等条款在合同中都要作出明确规定。销售合同由卖方(出口商)制作,采购合同由买方(进口商)制作。但这两种合同侧重点有所不同: 前者最注重的是能否如期收到货款,因此支付条款是销售合同的重点,此外,不可抗力条款也是出口商强调的; 而对进口方来说,他最关心的是货物的质量及数量是否与合同中所描述的一致,货物是否能如期运到等,因此,采购合同比较详细,侧重点较多,如: 质量及数量条款、装船条款、包装条款、迟交货与罚款条款、索赔条款等。在格式上,一般情况下,销售合同里卖方在前,而采购合同则买方在前。

Now read the following contracts, and try to understand and translate them.

1.1 SALES CONTRACT

No.:
Date:

The Sellers   The Buyers:
Address: Address:
Tel: Tel:
Cable Address: Cable Address:
Fax: Fax:
E-mail   E-mail

The undersigned Sellers and Buyers have agreed to close the following transaction in accordance with the terms and conditions stipulated below:

(1) Commodity and Unit Price:
Total Value CIF/CFR including __% commission.
CIF (cost, insurance, freight)
CFR (cost and freight)

(2) Packing:

(3) Time of Shipment:

From _____ to _____ during October, 2003.

(4) Loading Port & Destination:

From _____ to _____ with partial shipments and transshipment allowed.

(5) Insurance:

To be effected by the Sellers for 110% of the invoice value against All Risks and War Risk in accordance with _____ (Insurance _____ Clause).

(6) Terms of Payment:

By Confirmed, Irrevocable, Transferable and Divisible Letter of Credit to be available by sight draft, which shall reach the Sellers before... and remain valid for negotiation through Bank of China, until the 15th day after the aforesaid Time of Shipment.

(7) Shipping Mark:

The Seller's shipping mark

(8) Shipping Documents:

Certificates of quality, quantity and weight certified by the China Commodity Inspection Bureau or the Sellers, whose certificates are to be taken as final.

(9) The Sellers guarantee:

The Sellers guarantee that the commodity hereof is made of the best materials with first class workmanship, brand new and unused, and complies in all respects with the quality and specifications stipulated in this Contract.

(10) Force Majeure:

Either party shall not be held responsible for failure or delay to perform all or any part of this agreement due to flood, fire, earthquake, draught, war or any other events which could not be predicted, controlled, avoided or overcome by the relative party. However, the party affected by the event of Force Majeure shall inform the other party of its occurrence in writing as soon as possible and thereafter send a certificate of the event issued by the relevant authorities to the other party within 15 days after its occurrence.

(11) Arbitration:

All disputes arising from the performance of this agreement shall be settled through friendly negotiations. Should no settlement be reached through negotiation, the case shall then be submitted for Arbitration Commission (Beijing) and the rules of this Commission shall be applied. The award of the arbitration shall be final and binding upon both parties. The fees for the arbitration shall be borne by the losing party unless otherwise awarded.

Remarks:

5% more or less both in amount and quantity allowed at the Sellers' option.

The general Terms and Conditions of this Contract on the back page constitute an inseparable part of this Contract and shall be equally binding upon the parties hereto.

PART FOUR   CONTRACTUAL WRITING AND TRANSLATION

The Sellers: The Buyers:

(Note: Arbitration Committee 仲裁委员会; award 判决; bind 约束; remark 备注)

GENERAL TERMS AND CONDITIONS (一般条款)

1. Amendments to Letter of Credit

   The Buyers shall open Letter of Credit in accordance with the terms of this contract. If any discrepancy is found, amendments to Letter of Credit shall be made immediately by the Buyers upon receipt of the Sellers' advice, otherwise the Buyers shall be responsible for late shipment and losses thus incurred to the Sellers.

   Two originals of the Sales Contract are to be forwarded to the Buyers after all particulars have been duly filled in by the Sellers. The Buyers shall, within three days after receipt of the contracts, sign and return one of them to the Sellers and keep the other.

2. Force Majeure

   The Sellers shall not be responsible for non-delivery or late delivery of the contracted goods as a result of force majeure accident (s), such as war, flood, fire, storm, and heavy snow. In such case (s), either the time of shipment is to be duly extended, or the Sellers may cancel a part or the whole of the contract.

3. Arbitration

   All disputes in connection with or in the execution of this Contract shall be amicably settled through negotiations. In case no amicable settlement can be reached between the two parties, the case in dispute shall be submitted to arbitration, which shall be held in the country where the defendant resides. If in China, the case shall be submitted to the Foreign Trade Arbitration Commission of the China Council for the Promotion of International Trade, Beijing for arbitration in accordance with the Provisional Rules of Procedure of this Commission, and if in...(country), each of the two parties shall appoint an arbitrator and the two arbitrators thus appointed shall jointly nominate a third person as umpire to form an Arbitration Tribunal to conduct arbitration.

   The award made by the Tribunal shall be final and binding upon both parties. The fees for the arbitration shall be borne by the losing party unless otherwise awarded.

(Note: amendment 修改; forward to 寄给; tribunal 法庭)

1.2   PURCHASE CONTRACT (1)

No.:
Date:

The Buyer:
The Seller:

This Contract is made by and between the Buyers and the Sellers; whereby the Buyers agree to buy and the Sellers agree to sell the under-mentioned goods subject to the terms and conditions as stipulated hereinafter:

1. Name of Commodity & Specifications:
2. Quantity:
3. Unit Price:
4. Total Amount:
5. Country of Origin & Manufacturers:
6. Shipping Mark:

   The Sellers shall mark on each package with fadeless paint the package number, gross weight, measurement and the wordings: "KEEP AWAY FROM MOISURE", "HANDLE WITH CARE", "THIS SIDE UP", etc., and the shipping mark:

7. Time of Shipment:

   During Sep. 2002

8. Port of Loading/Shipment:
9. Port of Destination:
10. Insurance:

    To be covered by the Buyer

11. Payment:

    The Buyers shall, 20 days prior to the date of shipment, open an irrevocable Letter of Credit with the Bank of China, Guangzhou, in favor of the Sellers.

12. Documents:

    The Sellers shall present to the paying bank the following documents for negotiation:

    (1) One negotiable copy of clean on board ocean Bill of Lading marked "FREIGHT PREPAID" indicating shipping mark, made out to order, blank endorsed, and notifying the Buyers.

    (2) 3 copies of Invoice with the insertion of Contract number and the Shipping Mark.

    (3) 3 copies of Packing List showing gross and net weight for each package.

    (4) 1 copy of Certificate of Quantity and Quality issued by the Manufacturers.

    (5) Certified copy(of cable to the Buyers, advising shipment immediately after shipment is made.)

    The Sellers shall, after the shipment is effected, send by airmail one set of the same copies of each of the above-mentioned documents (except Item 5) to the Buyers.

13. Shipment:

    The Sellers shall make the shipment within the shipping time and ship the goods from the port of shipment to the port of destination. Transshipment is not allowed unless specially specified. The carrying vessel shall not fly the flag of a certain nationality unacceptable to the Buyers.

14. Shipping Advice:

    The Sellers shall, immediately upon the completion of the loading of the goods, advise by cable or telex the Buyers of the Contract number, commodity, quantity, invoiced value, gross weight, name of vessel, port of shipment, port of destination and date of sailing. In case the Buyers fail to arrange insurance in time due to the Sellers not having advised in time, all losses shall be borne by the Sellers.

15. Quality and Quantity/Weight:

    The contracted goods are bought on the basis of landed quality and landed quantity/weight and the certificate issued by the China Commodity Inspection Bureau shall be taken as final.

16. Packing:

    To be packed in strong wooden cases suitable for long distance ocean transportation and the change of climate, well protected against moisture and shocks. One full set of operating instructions for each instrument or machine shall be enclosed in the package(s). The Sellers shall be liable for any damage of the commodity and expenses incident thereto on account of improper packaging and for any rust attributable to inadequately or improperly protective measures by the Sellers in regard to the packing.

17. Late Delivery and Penalty:

    Should the Sellers fail to make delivery on time as stipulated in the Contract, with the exception of Force Majeure specified in Clause 18 of this Contract, the Buyers shall agree to postpone the delivery on condition that the Seller agree to pay a penalty which shall be deducted by the paying bank from the payment under negotiation. The penalty, however, shall not exceed ___% of the total value of the goods involved in the late delivery.

18. Force Majeure:

    In case of delayed shipment or non-delivery due to a generally recognized Force Majeure, the Seller must advise the Buyer immediately by cable of the occurrence, and within 15 days thereafter the Seller must airmail to the Buyer a certificate of the incident issued by the competent government authorities or Chamber of Commerce at the place where the incident occurred. The Seller shall not be absolved from his responsibility unless such an incident is acknowledged by the Buyer. In case conditions of Force Majeure continue to last over and above 30 days, the Buyer shall have the right to cancel the Contract. The Seller's failure to obtain an export licence shall not be considered as Force Majeure.

19. Claims:

    Within 45 days after the arrival of the goods at the destination, should the quality, Specifications or quantity be found not in conformity with the stipulations of the Contract except those claims for which the insurance company or the owners of the vessel are liable, the Buyers shall, have the right on the strength of the inspection certificate issued by the CCIB and the relative documents to claim for compensation to the Sellers.

20. Arbitration:

    All disputes in connection with this contract or the execution thereof shall be settled by way of amicable negotiation. In case no settlement can be reached, it shall be submitted for arbitration to the Foreign Trade Arbitration Commission of the China Council for the

Promotion of International Trade, Beijing, in accordance with the Provisional Rules of Procedure of the said Commission. The award by the said commission shall be deemed as final and binding upon both parties.

The Seller's Signature: _____

The Buyer's Signature: _____

(Note: operating instruction 操作说明书; attributable to 可归于……的; Chamber of Commerce 商会; absolve from 免除)

1.3　PURCHASE CONTRACT (2)

No.　GS13205

Date: Sept. 9, 2020

The Buyers: Guangdong Scientific Instruments & Materials Import & Export Corporation.

The Sellers: Walink United Co., Ltd.

This Contract is made by and between the Buyers and the Sellers, whereby the Buyers agree to buy and the Sellers agree to sell the under-mentioned commodity according to the terms and conditions stipulated below:

1. Commodity & Specifications

    13 Typewriters

    Quantity

    120 sets

    Unit　Price

    US $80.90

    (C&F Guangzhou　Packaging charges included)

    Total　Value

    US $9,708.00...

2. Country of Origin and Manufactures

    Japan

3. Packing

    To be packed in strong wooden cases suitable for long distance ocean transportation and the change of climate, well protected against moisture and shocks. One full set of operating instructions for each instrument or machine shall be enclosed in the package(s)... The Sellers shall be liable for any damage of the commodity and expenses incident thereto on account of improper packaging and for any rust attributable to inadequately or improperly protective measures by the Sellers in regard to the packing.

4. Shipping Mark

    The Sellers shall mark on each package with fadeless paint the package number, gross weight, net weight, measurement and the wordings: "KEEP AWAY FROM MOISTURE," "HANDLE WITH CARE," "THIS SIDE UP," etc., and the shipping mark:

89FL-65001CK GUANGZHOU CHINA

5. Time of Shipment

   During October, 2020

6. Port of Shipment

   Hong Kong

7. Port of Destination

   Guangzhou

8. Insurance

   To be covered by the Buyers.

9. Payment

   The Buyers shall, 20 days prior to the date of shipment, open an irrevocable Letter of Credit with the Bank of China, Guangzhou, in favor of the Sellers.

10. Documents

    The Sellers shall present to the paying bank the following documents for negotiation:

    (1) One negotiable copy of clean on board ocean Bill of Lading marked "FREIGHT PREPAID" indicating shipping mark, made out to order, blank endorsed, and notifying the Buyers.

    (2) 3 copies of Invoice with the insertion of Contract number and the Shipping Mark.

    (3) 3 copies of Packing List showing gross and net weight for each package.

    (4) 1 copy of Certificate of Quantity and Quality issued by the Manufacturers.

    (5) Certified copy of cable to the Buyers, advising shipment immediately after shipment is made.

    The Sellers shall, after the shipment is effected, send by airmail one set of the same copies of each of the above-mentioned documents (except Item 5) to the Buyers.

11. Shipment

    The Sellers shall make shipment within the shipping time and ship the goods from the port of shipment to the port of destination. Trans-shipment is not allowed unless specially specified. The carrying vessel shall not fly the flag of a certain nationality unacceptable to the Buyers.

12. Shipping Advice

    The Sellers shall, immediately upon the completion of the loading of the goods, advise by cable or telex the Buyers of the Contract number, commodity, quantity, invoiced value, gross weight, name of vessel, port of shipment, port of destination and date of sailing. In case the Buyers fail to arrange insurance in time due to the Sellers not having advised in time, all losses shall be borne by the Sellers.

13. Guarantee of Quality

    The Sellers guarantee that the commodity hereof is made of the best materials with first class workmanship, brand new and unused, and complies in all respects with the quality and specifications stipulated in this Contract. The guarantee period shall be 12 months counting from the date on which the commodity arrives at the port of destination.

14. Claims

    Within 90 days after the arrival of the goods at the port of destination, should the quality, specifications or quantity be found not in conformity with the stipulations of the Contract except those claims for which the insurance company or the owners of the vessel are liable, the Buyers shall, on the strength of the Inspection Certificate issued by the China Import and Export Commodity Inspection Bureau, have the right to claim for replacement with new goods, or for compensation, and all the expenses (such as inspection charges, freight for returning the goods and for sending the replacement, insurance premium, storage and loading and unloading charges, etc.) shall be borne by the Sellers, As regards to quality, if, within 12 months from the date of arrival of the goods at destination, damages occur in the course of operation by reason of the use of inferior materials and bad workmanship, the Buyers shall immediately notify the Sellers and put forward a claim supported by the Inspection Certificate issued by the China Import and Export Commodity Inspection Bureau. The Certificate so issued shall be accepted as the basis of a claim. The Sellers, in accordance with the Buyers' claim, shall be responsible for immediate elimination of the defect(s), or replacement of the defective portion of the shipment, or shall reduce the price according to the state of the defect(s). Where necessary, the Buyers shall be at liberty to eliminate the defect(s) themselves at the Sellers' expense. If the Sellers fail to answer the Buyers within one month after receipt of the claim, the claim shall be reckoned as having been accepted by the Sellers.

15. Arbitration

    All disputes in connection with the execution of this Contract shall be settled friendly through negotiation. In case no settlement can be reached, the case then may be submitted for arbitration to the Arbitration Commission of the China Council for the Promotion of International Trade in accordance with the Provisional Rules of Procedure promulgated by the Arbitration Commission. The decision made by the Arbitration committee shall be final and binding upon both parties and the Arbitration fee shall be borne by the losing parties.

    The Buyers: (Signature)

    _____

    The Sellers: (Signature)

    _____

(Note: moisture and shocks 潮气和震动；enclosed 被附上的；incident 易于发生的；rust 生锈；fadeless 不褪色的；freight prepad 预付款；certified copy 经核准的副本；specified: 指定的；详细说明的……；liable 有责任的；comply... with 遵守；guarantee period 保险(保修, 保用)期；on the strength of 依赖；凭借；premium 额外费用；保险费；workmanship 手艺；做工；elimination 除去；promulgated 公布）

1.4　TRADE CONTRACT

No.XS06A120003W

Date: 2020-12-16

The Sellers:

The Buyers:

This Contract is made by and between the Buyers and Sellers, whereby the Buyers agree to buy and the Sellers agree to sell the under-mentioned commodity according to the terms and conditions stipulated below:

1. Commodity & Specification	2. Unit	3. Quantity	4. Unit Price	5. Total Amount Fob Shanghai
Gloves	pair	144,720	0.21934	USD 31751.00
Total Value: Say U.S. Dollars Thirty One Thousand Seven Hundred and Fifty One Only.				

6. More or Less

   With 5% more or less both in amount & quantity.

7. Packing

   Outer paper package, the inner package is negociated between the Buyer and JiangSu WuXi HuaiZhong Gloves Company.

8. Time of Shipment

   March 30, 2021

9. Loading Port & Destination

   From SHANGHAI To HONGKONG to U.S.A. with transshipment and partial shipments allowed.

10. Insurance

    To be covered by the Buyer.

11. Terms of Payment

    Irrevocable L/C at sight issued by the Buyer in February, 2021.

12. Shipping Mark

    To be provided by the Buyer.

13. Force Majeure

    If the shipment of the Contracted goods is prevented or delayed in whole or in party by reason of war, earthquake, flood, fire, storm, heavy snow, government restrictions, or other events beyond Sellers' control, the Sellers shall not be liable for non-shipment or late shipment of the goods or non-performance of this Contract. However, the Sellers shall notify the Buyers by cable (or telex) and send by airmail the detailed information of the accident and a certificate issued by the competent government authorities of the place where the accident occurs. The Buyers shall not claim any penalty for losses suffered therefrom, and the Buyers must accept the delivery made within a reasonable time after the termination of the aforesaid cause, or at the Sellers' option accept the termination of all or any part of the Contract.

14. Arbitration

Any dispute, controversy or claim arising out of or relating to this Contract, or the breach, termination or invalidity thereof, shall be settled amicably through negotiation. In case no settlement can be reached between the two parties, the case shall be submitted for arbitration to the CHINA INTERNATIONAL ECONOMIC AND TRADE ARBITRATION COMMISSION in accordance with its Provisional Rules of Procedure. The arbitral award shall be accepted final and binding upon both parties, neither party shall seek recourse to a court or other authorities for revising the decision. The arbitration fee shall be borne by the losing party.

15. Document Requirement

Triplicate of Invoice, Packing list and B/L.

THE SELLERS   THE BUYERS
(Signature)   (Signature)

1.5 SALES CONFIRMATION

XIAMEN SEZ DAFENG GROUP CO.

ADDRESS: 167 AHONG SHAN ROAD, XIAMEN, CHINA

TEL: 2133506   CABLE: 4103   FAX: 2223725   E-mail: _____

SALES CONFIRMATION   No. _____

                                             Date: _____

                                             Place: _____

Buyers: _____

Address: _____   Tel: _____

Cable: _____   E-mail: _____

The undersigned Sellers and Buyers have agreed to close the following transactions according to the terms and conditions stipulated below:

No.	Description	Total Quantity	Unit Price	Total Amount	Remarks

Total Value
_____

Packing:

Time of Shipment: From Xiamen, China to _____ during _____ with transshipment and partial shipment allowed.

Insurance: To be effected by Sellers covering All Risks and War Risk (excluding S.R.C.C.罢工险)as per The Ocean Marine Cargo Clauses of The People's Insurance Company of China, for _____% of invoice value.

Terms of Payment: By Confirmed Irrevocable, Transferable and Divisible Letter of Credit to be available by sight draft to reach the Sellers before _____ and to remain valid for negotiation in Xiamen, China until the day after the aforesaid Time of Shipment.

Shipping Mark: Sellers' shipping marks.

Quality, quantity and weight certified by the China Commodity Inspection Bureau or the Sellers as per the former's Inspection Certificate or the latter's certificate, are to be taken as final.

Remarks(备注): (1) 5% more or less both in amount and quantity allowed at the Sellers' option

(2) Please indicate this S/C number on your L /C.

(3) We hereby confirm your cable/letter dated. (本确认书根据你方_日函/电确认)

(4) Please sign and return one copy of this S/C for our file.

THE SELLERS_____   THE BUYERS_____

2. Sales Agency Agreement

代理是指代理人 (AGENT) 按照委托人 (PRINCIPAL) 的授权代表委托人同第三者订立合同或其他法律行为。代理可分为总代理(GENERAL AGENCY)、独家代理 (EXCLUSIVE AGENCY OR SOLE AGENCY) 及佣金代理 (COMMMISSION AGENCY)。总代理即委托人的全权代表；独家代理是指在某一规定时间、某一规定区域只委托一个代理人。佣金代理又称一般代理, 是指在同一代理地区、时间及期限内, 同时有几个代理人代表委托人行为的代理。

代理协议是明确双方委托人与代理人之间权利与义务的法律文件, 其主要内容有:

(1) 协议双方的名称及地点

(2) 代理商品的名称

(3) 代理区域

(4) 代理的权利

(5) 协议有效期

(6) 代理人佣金

(7) 非竞争条款

(8) 最低成交额条款

(9) 市场情报、广告宣传条款

Now read the following agreements, and try to understand and translate them.

2.1 SALES AGENCY AGREEMENT

No:

Date:

This Agreement is entered into between the parties concerned on the basis of equality and mutual benefit to develop business on terms and conditions mutually agreed upon as follows:

1. Contrating Parties

   Supplier: (hereinafter called "party A")

   Agent: (hereinafter called "party B")

   Party A hereby appoints Party B to act as his selling agent to sell the commodity mentioned below.

2. Commodity and Quantity or Amount

   It is mutually agreed that Party B shall undertake to sell not less than… of the aforesaid commodity in the duration of this Agreement.

3. Territory

   In... only.

4. Confirmation of Orders

   The quantities, prices and shipments of the commodities stated in this Agreement shall be confirmed in each transaction, the particulars of which are to be specified in the Sales Confirmation signed by the two parties hereto.

5. Payment

   After confirmation of the order, Party B shall arrange to open a confirmed, irrevocable L/C available by draft at sight in favor of Party A within the time stipulated in the relevant S/C. Party B shall also notify Party A immediately after L/C is opened so that Party A can get prepared for delivery.

6. Commission

   Upon the expiration of the Agreement and Party B's fullfilment of the total turnover mentioned in Article 2, Party A shall pay to Party B...% commission on the basis of the aggregate amount of the invoice value against the shipment effected.

7. Reports on Market Conditions

   Party B shall forward once every three months to party A detailed reports on current market conditions and of consumers' comments. Meanwhile, Party B shall, from time to time, send to Party A samples of similar commodities offered by other suppliers, together with their prices, sales information and advertising materials.

8. Advertising & Publicity Expenses

   Party B shall bear all expenses for advertising and publicity within the aforementioned territory in the duration of this Agreement and submit to Party A all patterns and/or drawings and description for prior approval.

9. Validity of Agreement

This Agreement, after its being signed by the parties concerned, shall remain in force for... days from... to.... If either Party wishes to extend this Agreement, he shall notice, in writing, the other party one month prior to its expiration. The matter shall be decided by the agreement and by consent of the parties hereto. Should either party fail to implement the terms and conditions herein, the other party is entitled to terminate this Agreement.

10. Arbitration

All disputes arising from the execution of this Agreement shall be settled through friendly consultations. In case no settlement can be reached, the case in dispute shall then be submitted to the Foreign Trade Arbitration Commission of the China Council for the Promotion of International Trade for arbitration in accordance with its provisional rules of procedure. The dectision made by this Commission shall be regarded as final and binding upon both parties. Arbitration fees shall be borne by the losing party, unless otherwise awarded.

11. Other Terms & Conditions

(1) Party A shall not supply the contracted commodity to any other buyer (s) in the above mentioned territory. Direct enquiries, if any, will be referred to Party B. However, should any other buyers wish to deal with Party A directly, Party A may do so. But Party A shall send to Party B a copy of Sales Confirmation and give Party B...% commission on the basis of the net invoice value of the transaction(s) concluded.

(2) Should Party B fail to pass on his orders to Party A in a period of... months for a minimum of..., Party A shall not bind himself to this Agreement.

(3) For any business transacted between governments of both Parties, Party A may handle such direct dealings as authorized by Party A's government without binding himself to this Agreement. Party B shall not interfere in such direct dealings nor shall Party B bring forward any demand for compensation therefrom.

(4) This Agreement shall be subject to the terms and conditions in the Sales Confirmation signed by both parties hereto.

This Agreement is signed on... at... and is in two originals; each Party holds one.

Party A: Party B:
(Signature)   (Signature)

(Note: appoint 委托; total turnover 营业额; aggregate amount 总金额)

2.2 EXCLUSIVE AGENCY AGREEMENT

This agreement is made and entered into by and between the parties concerned on September 20, 2020 in Qingdao, China on the basis of equality and mutual benefit to develop business on terms and conditions mutually agreed upon as follows:

1. The Parties Concerned

    Party A: Qingdao Hongda Industrial Co.,Ltd.

    Add: 25 Qu tangxia Road, Qingdao,China

    Tel: (0532)2877932 Fax: (0532)2876415

    Party B: Huaxing Trading Company (Pte)Ltd.

    Add: 126 Waterloo Street, Singapore 0718

    Tel: 336 6436   Fax: 339 7862

2. Appointment

    Party A hereby appoints Party B as its Exclusive Agent to solicit orders for the commodity stipulated in Article 3 from customers in the territory stipulated in Article 4, and Party B accepts and assumes such appointment.

3. Commodity

    × × × Brand Washing Machines

4. Territory

    In Singapore only

5. Minimum Turnover

    Party B shall undertake to solicit orders for the above commodity from customers in the above territory during the effective period of this agreement for not less than USD 100,000,00.

6. Price and Payment

    The price for each individual transaction shall be fixed through negotiations between Party B and the buyer, and subject to Party A's final confirmation.

    Payment shall be made by confirmed, irrevocable L/C opened by the buyer in favor of Party A, which shall reach Party A 15 days before the date of shipment.

7. Exclusive Rights

    In consideration of the exclusive rights granted herein, party A shall not, directly or indirectly, sell or export the commodity stipulated in Article 4 to customers in Singapore through channels other than Party B; Party B shall not sell, distribute or promote the sales of any products competitive with or similar to the above commodity in Singapore and shall not solicit or accept orders for the purpose of selling them outside Singapore. Party A shall refer to Party B any enquiries or orders for the commodity in question received by Party A from other firms in Singapore during the validity of this agreement.

8. Market Report

    In order to keep Party A well informed of the prevailing market conditions, Party B should undertake to supply Party A, at least once a quarter or at any time when necessary, with market reports concerning changes of the local regulations in connection with the import and sales of the commodity covered by this agreement, local market tendency and the buyer's Comments on quality, packing, price, etc. of the goods supplied by Party A under this agreement. Party B shall also supply Party A with quotation and advertising materials on similar products of other suppliers.

9. Advertising and Expense

   Party A shall bear all expenses for advertising and publicity in connection with the commodity in question in Singapore within the validity of this agreement, and shall submit to Party A all audio and video materials intended for advertising for prior approval.

10. Commission

    Party A shall pay Party B a commission of 5% on the net invoiced selling price on all orders directly obtained by Party B and accepted by Party A. No commission shall be paid until Party A receives the full payment for each order.

11. Transactions between Governmental Bodies

    Transactions concluded between governmental bodies of Party A and Party B shall not be restricted by the terms and conditions of this agreement, nor shall the amount of such transactions be counted as part of the turnover stipulated in Article 5.

12. Industrial Property Rights

    Party B may use the trade-marks owned by Party A for the sale of the Washing Machines covered herein within the validity of this agreement, and shall acknowledge that all patents, trademarks, copy rights or any other industrial property rights used or embodied in the Washing Machines shall remain to be the sole properties of Party A... Should any infringement be found, Party B shall promptly notify and assist Party A to take steps to protect the latter's rights.

13. Validity of Agreement

    This agreement, when duly signed by the both parties concerned, shall remain in force for 12 months from October 1, 2020 to September 30, 2021, and it shall be extended for another 12 months upon expiration unless notice in writing is given to the contrary.

14. Termination

    During the validity of this agreement, if either of the two parties is found to have violated the stipulations herein, the other party has the right to terminate this agreement. However, the party affected by the event of Force Majeure shall inform the other party of its occurrence in writing as soon as possible and thereafter send a certificate of the event issued by the relevant authorities to the other party within 15 days after its occurrence.

    Party A: Party B:
    (Signature)   (Signature)

(Note: solicit 招揽; distribute 分销; prevailing 流行的; quotation 报价; enquiry 询价; infringement 侵权)

3. Consignment Agreement

寄售是寄售人 (CONSIGNOR) 将货物运交代销人 (CONSIGNEE), 由代销人在当地市场上代为销售。货物在销售以前的所有权属于寄售人, 销售所得货款由代销人扣除佣金及各项费用后汇给寄售人。

寄售协议是规定寄、售双方权利和义务的法律性契约, 是整个寄售过程运作的根据。协议内容一般包括: 货物名称、寄售期限、保险、货款汇付、佣金、仲裁等。

Now read the following agreements, and try to understand and translate them.

3.1　CONSIGNMENT AGREEMENT

No.: ＿＿＿＿＿＿＿＿

Date: ＿＿＿＿＿＿＿＿

China National Light Industrial Import and Export Corporation, Shanghai Branch (hereinafter called Party A) held talks with U.S. Forrest Gump & Co. (hereinafter called Party B) about the consignment of Gump Brand Shirts. Through friendly negotiation both parties confirm the principal points as follows:

1. Items for Consignment:

    Shirts for men, women and children, specifications of which please see the attached list.

2. Terms of Consignment:

    (1) Duration of Consignment:

    Both parties agree that sales of Gump Brand Shirts will commence on ＿＿＿＿ and terminate on ＿＿＿＿. Party A agrees to sell exclusively Gump Brand Shirts during the two years time.

    In order to facilitate Party A's work of starting the consignment sales on time, Party B shall ship the first lot of consignment goods to Shanghai before ＿＿＿.

    (2) Insurance:

    To be covered by Party B against All Risks with Warehouse to Warehouse Clause (仓到仓条款)。However, while the goods are in the warehouse at Party A's end or during the course of selling, Party A shall take the responsibility of insurance on behalf of Party B.

    (3) Party B shall submit to Party A the actual retail prices (零售价) of the aforesaid articles in Hongkong and Japanese markets for Party A's reference. Party B has no right to interfere with Party A's selling price, spot or method, but it has the right to make positive proposals. Party A is responsible to submit Party B regular reports on selling situation, problems arising in the course of selling and make proposals to improve sales. Party B should provide Party A with various arrangements which are conductive to sales (including samples free of charge, articles for trial sales, data for promoting sales, technical exchange etc.)

(4) All expenses for advertisement of these items shall be charged to Party B's account. The contents of advertisement are subject to the approval of Party A.

(5) In case of problems occurring due to quality, damage or any other matter of Party B's responsibility, Party B shall compensate (补偿) such a loss to Party A by replacement of goods or deduction of the sum in question from Party A's remittance (汇款额) to Party B against (凭着) Party A's certificate.

3. Terms of Payment:

(1) Within one month after expiration of the consignment period, Party A shall remit Party B the total sum in U.S. Dollars based on the contracted unit price for those items which have been sold. If at any time the total value of goods sold exceeds USD 250,000, Party A shall remit the total sum to Party B within one month's period of time.

(2) For those items which connot be sold, Party A should send a list of these items to Party B in order to make appropriate settlement by sending these items back or any other method.

4. Commission:

Party B agrees to pay Party A a commission of 3% (three percent) on the total value of goods sold, which shall be deducted from remittance.

5. All disputes arising in the course of the consignment period shall be settled amicably through friendly negotiation. In case no settlement can be reached through negotiation, both parties agree that the case shall be submitted for arbitration to a third country which can be accepted by both parties.

Party A   Party B
(Signature)   (Signature)

3.2 AGREEMEMT OF CONSIGNMENT***

This Agreement is entered into between ABC Co. (hereinafter referred to as the Consignor), having its registered office at _____, Shanghai, China and XYZ Co. (hereinafter referred to as the Consignee), having its registered office at _____, on the following terms and conditions:

1. The Consignor shall from time to time ship _____ (commodity) to the consignee on Consignment basis at the prevailing international market prices on CIF terms. The interval between each shipment shall be approximately ninety days.

2. The Consignee must try to sell the consignments at the best possible prices after obtaining the approval of the Consignor as to price, terms, etc.

3. Each shipment by ship at the initial stage will not exceed USD _____ and the outstanding liabilities on the Consignee shall be in the vicinity of not more than USD _____ only.

4. The Consignor shall at no time be responsible for any bad debts arising out of credit sales

to any _____ buyers. Making payments to the Consignor shall at all times be the sole responsibility of the Consignee.

5. The Consignee shall accept the Bills of Exchange drawn by the Consignor on him at 90 days' sight with interest payable at _____% per annum.

6. The Consignee shall collect the shipping documents including B/L from the Consignor's bank against Trust Receipt duly signed by the Consignee.

7. The Consignor shall absorb insurance premium and warehousing charges up to the date of delivery to customers.

8. The Consignor shall observe the regulations of the government of _____.

9. This Agreement is written in English, in two originals; each Party retains one copy.

As a token of acceptance, both parties have set their respective hands on this _____ day of _____, with understanding and knowledge of the contents stated hereinabove.

ABC Co.   XYZ Co.
(Signature)   (Signature)

4. Compensation Trade Contract

补偿贸易在西方一般称为产品回购(PRODUCT BUYBACK)，在日本称为产品分成(PRODUCTION SHARING)。在我国，补偿贸易一般是指交易的一方在对方提供信用的基础上，进口机器设备、技术或原材料，不用现汇支付，而用向对方回销上述进口设备或原料所生产的产品或其他产品，或其他劳务所得款，分期摊还。补偿贸易方式有许多，主要有回购(BUYBACK)、互购(COUNTER PURCHASE)、部分补偿(PARTIAL COMPENSATION)等。回购是指进口方用进口机器设备或技术制造的产品偿付货款。互购是指进口方不用进口设备或技术所制造的直接产品，而是以其他产品，即间接产品偿还。部分补偿是指进口的设备或技术，部分以产品偿付，部分以现汇支付。

补偿贸易合同/协议一般应包括以下内容：

(1) 设备的名称、型号、规格、性能、参数，同时应明确规定安装责任，对方应负责的技术协助，包括人员培训以及质量保证期限等。

(2) 有关信贷的条件：包括贷款金额、计价和结算货币、利率、偿还期限、偿还办法以及银行担保。

(3) 有关回购的规定：必须明确回购的产品名称，每期回购的数量；必须明确产品的作价方法；必须明确回购产品的质量标准并交货时间。

Now read the following contract, and try to understand and translate them.

COMPENSATION TRADE CONTRACT***

This Contract made on _____, at _____, China, between ABC Co. (hereinafter called Party A) with its principal office at _____, China, and PAT Co. (hereinafter called Party B) with its principal office at _____, USA.

WITNESSES

Whereas Party B has machines and equipment, which are now used in Party B's manufacturing of steel wire rope, and is willing to sell to Party A the machines and equipment; and Whereas Party B agrees to buy the products, steel wire rope, made by Party A using the machines and equipment Party B supplies, in compensation of the price of the machines and equipment; and Whereas Party A agrees to purchase from Party B the machines and equipment; and Whereas Party A agrees to sell to Party B the products, the steel wire rope, in compensation of the price of Party B's machines and equipment:

NOW THEREFORE, in consideration of the premises and convenance described hereinafter, Party A amd Party B agree as follows:

1. Purchase Arrangement

Party A agrees to purchase from Party B the following commodity under the terms and conditions set out below:

1.1 Commodity, Specificaitons and Its Capability

Commodity:

Specifications:

Capability:

1.2 Quantity

1.3 Price: On FOB _____ basis.

Unit Price: US$ _____; Total Price: US$ _____.

1.4 Payment

The price of the machines and equipment shall be compensated with the products, the steel wire rope, manufactured by Party A using the machines and equipment. The payment of the total price shall be effected three times equally in three successive years, beginning in _____.

1.5 Shipment

Time of shipment:

Port of loading:

Port of destination:

Shipping marks:

1.6 Insurance

To be effected by Party A.

1.7 Inspection

1.8 Guarantee

Party B guarantees that the machines and equipment are unused, sophisticated and of best quality, and that the machines and equipment are capable of manufacturing the steel wire rope of _____ specifications with a production of _____ meters per hour.

2. Sales Arrangement

Party A sells to Party B the steel wire rope in compensation of the price of the machines and equipment Party B sells to Party A.

   2.1 Commodity and Specifications

       Commodity: steel wire rope

       Specifications:

   2.2 Quantity

       _____ meters of steel wire rope per year, of which the price shall be US $ _____ per annum.

   2.3 Price

       The price of the steel wire rope shall be set on the basis of the prevailing price in the world market at the time when shipment is made. The price shall be based on CIF basis.

   2.4 Shipment

       Shipment shall be made twice a year, in June and in December, each for the value of _____.

       Port of loading:

       Port of destination:

       Shipping marks:

   2.5 Packing

       To be packed in wooden reels.

   2.6 Payment

       Payment shall be effected by confirmed and irrevocable letter of credit in favor of Party A, payable at sight, allowing transshipment. The letter of credit shall reach Party A 15 days before the month of shipment and shall be valid for not less than 90 days.

       The letter of credit shall be in strict accordance with the terms and conditions of the Contract. Otherwise, Party B shall be held responsible for thedelay in shipment amd Party A may lodge claims against Party B for rhe losses arising therefrom. All the expenses arising from the amendments shall be for Party B's account.

   2.7 Insurance

       To be covered by Party A for 10% of the invoice value, covering W.P.A. and War Risk.

   2.8 Inspection

       The quality certificate issued by Party A shall be regarded as final. If, on arrival of the goods at the port of destination, Party B finds the quality not up to the specifications mentioned above, Party B shall notify Party A within 45 days after arrival of the goods at the port of destination. Both Parties shall have consultations for a settlement of the matter in dispute.

   3. Force Majeure

Party A or Party B shall not be held responsible for any failure or delay in delivery of the entire lot or a portion of the goods under the Contract as a result of any force majeure accident (s).

   4. Arbitration

       All disputes arising in connection with this Contract or in the execution therof, should be settled amicably through negotiations. In case no settlement can be reached, the case in dispute shall then be submitted for arbitration in _____. The decision of the arbitration shall be accepted as final and binding upon both parties.

5. Governing Law

The formation, interpretation and performance of the Contract shall be governed by the laws of the People's Republic of China.

6. Original Text

The Contract is made, in English, in two originals, one for each party.

7. Duration

Party A: _____   Party B: _____
(Signature)   (Signature)

Appendices

APPENDIX I Reference Key to Writing Assignments

√ Chapter 1 Note

Dear Mr. Max Remington,

  As our company is purchasing a set of equipment, a lot of materials have to be translated, which is impossible to do within four months. Could you advertise for two experienced translators in the newspapers? It is urgent.

Yours truly,
Jack

√ Chapter 3 Poster

Football Match

  Under the auspices of the Student Union of our university, a friendly football match will be held between our team and the team of Chemical Engineering College on our football field on Sunday, Feb. 28th, 2021 at 4:00 p. m.

  All Are Warmly Welcome.

The Student Union
Feb. 25

√ Chapter 4 Announcement

LOST

September 4, 2021

  Due to carelessness, I lost a mobile when studying in Rm. 321 of Classroom Building No. 2 yesterday. The mobile is a present from my father for my 18th birthday, so it is very precious to me. The finder is kindly requested to send it back to Rm. 358 of Dormitory No.5.

Substantial reward for such kind returning is guaranteed*.

                                                                              Owner

                                                                              Li Mei

(注: substantial reward for such kind returning is guaranteed 定有重谢)

√ Chapter 6   Memorandum (Memo)

To: Jim Hillman, Vice President
From: Carl Johnson, President
Date: Feb. 12th
Subject: Management Development

    As we discussed earlier this week, I agree with you that we are not finding enough good people outside the organization to fill the management slots we've had to create. We need to begin developing our own managers from our sales and production staff.

    I would like you to design our own in-house management training program. After we identify those people already on board with interest and aptitude for managerial responsibilities, we can put them through our program. We could set aside one morning a week for classed. And we can use the conference room next to my office.

    Write a brief proposal(not over two pages, please) describing what you think the problem should cover. Assume the class runs four hours a week for ten weeks. Also, assume the people have no prior managerial experience or any formal course work in management. Finally, I think you should gear the program toward the activities and problems that supervisors or first-level managers are likely to face.

Chapter 9   Application

(4.1)

                                                                               Nov.12, 2021

Dear Sir,

    I have read your advertisement in yesterday's China Daily for a section manager and I think I'm a qualified one.

    I am 29 years old and have 3 years of work experience. Since I graduated from the College of Management in 1996 with Marketing as my major, I had been a salesman for one year and a half, establishing a good relationship with the customers. After that I have been the sales manager up to now, collecting various data and developing new markets, with our sales being the highest in recent 6 years.

Now I'm considering changing my job because I need new challenges to display my potentials. And I think that the position you advertised is the challenge I'm looking for.

If you want to know more about me, I am ready to provide more information, though my resume is enclosed here. I hope I can be interviewed at your convenience. You can call me at 82301191 or e-mail to me: Idw45@sina.com.cn.

Looking forward to your reply.

Sincerely yours,
Kavern Cao

(4.2)

Admission Office
New York University of Technology
New York, NY 10003

Dear Sirs,

I am graduating from Peking University of Technology next year. I wish to pursue a master degree in your Electric Engineering. Please send me your catalog and application forms for admission and financial aid.

Thank you.

Yours sincerely,
(signature)

Chapter 12 Letter of Introduction

Dear Tony,

This letter will introduce my best friend Mary Brown of whom you've often heard me mention. She is going to be in Washington D. C. next month to lecture. I want very much to have her meet you there, and this seems like an excellent chance for you to meet each other.

I think both of you will have a lot in common. So far as I know, you both are interested in modern literature. Once you meet her, you will really enjoy her company. Any kindness to her will be duly appreciated by me.

Yours affectionately,
× × ×

Chapter 15 Advertisement

Production Planner Wanted

Applicants should be college graduates with at least two years' working experience in production management. Good command of mathematics and skills in operating computers are essential. Holders of CET-4 certificates are preferred. Please send complete resume in English with one recent photo and expected salary to Post Office Box 63214, Hong Kong.

Chapter 16 Letter of Invitation

December 15

Dear Mr. Smith,

Our company has planned to hold a costume ball to mark New Year's Day, and is inviting our clients to it. Therefore, Mr. Howard would like to invite you and your clients to our costume ball with the following details:

Place: Dance Hall, 2nd Floor, Holiday Inn

Time: 8:00 p.m.

Date: December 31st, Friday

Your presence on this occasion would be our greatest honor.

We would appreciate it if you could confirm your acceptance of our invitation by telephone or letter before December 30th.

We look forward to hearing from you.

Yours Faithfully,
Mike Howard

Invitation Cards

1. For acceptance

> Mr. and Mrs. George Mailer
> Accept with pleasure
> Mr. and Mrs. Robert Smith's
> Kind invitation to dinner
> On Friday, March 26th,
> At seven o'clock.
> 17 Butter Place
> March 22nd.

2. For decline

> Mr. and Mrs. George Mailer
> Present their compliments
> To Mr. and Mrs. Robert Smith
> And regret that a previous engagement prevents them from
> Accepting the kind invitation
> To dinner on Friday, March 26th,
> At seven o'clock.
> 17 Butter Place
> March 22nd.

(注: compliment 致意; 问候)

Chapter 17 Letter of Congratulation

Dear Bill,

　　Congratulations on your recent promotion!

　　I have just heard the good news that you have been promoted to be Production Manager. Congratulations!

　　With all the hard work you have done in these years, this promotion is all you deserve. I'm sure this will not be the last promotion you get. I look forward to the day when you are in the top job.

　　Best wishes,

APPENDIX II Reference Key to Part Four, Chapter 6

3) Insurance Policy or Certificate (Part Four, Chapter 3)

(6) Exercises

I. (1—10) 1 to cover　2 proposal form　3 broker　4 underwriter　5 premium
　　　　　　6 claim　7 compensation　8 insurance company　9 small print
　　　　　　10 policy

II. (1—10) c f g a j i h b e d

17. Exercises

√ 支付与支付条件

(1) 本合同的币制采用美元结算。甲方通过中国银行开具不可撤销的即期信用证支付。甲方必须于签订合同十五日内开出信用证。

(2) 本合同第二条中的设备费,青岛到岸价150万美元,货抵青岛后,凭清洁提货单,商业发票,装箱清单,经甲乙双方银行审核与本合同规定的规格、型号、数量相符后,甲方按货价90%的金额兑现给乙方。剩余的10%破碎设备于交付单据的21天兑现。乙方必须出具本公司对保用期的保证函。

(3) 本合同第二条中的零配件费CIF青岛7.8万美元,货抵青岛后,凭清洁提货单,商业发票,装箱清单,经甲乙双方银行审核,单据无误后,一次全部兑现。

√ 分期付款

本合同项下的总金额分期支付,每期支付的时间及金额如下:

(1) 本合同签字之日起 ＿＿＿ 个月内,即不迟于20＿＿＿年＿＿＿月＿＿＿日支付本合同总金额的＿＿＿%的预付款,计＿＿＿USD(大写: ＿＿＿美元);

(2) 第一期付款为本合同签字之日起＿＿＿个月内,即不迟于20＿＿＿年＿＿＿月＿＿＿日支付本合同总金额的＿＿＿%的货款,计＿＿＿USD(大写: ＿＿＿美元);

(3) 第二期付款为本合同签字之日起＿＿＿个月内,即不迟于20＿＿＿年＿＿＿月＿＿＿日支付本合同总金额的＿＿＿%的货款,计＿＿＿USD(大写: ＿＿＿美元);

(4) 第三期付款为本合同签字之日起＿＿＿个月内,即不迟于20＿＿＿年＿＿＿月＿＿＿日支付本合同总金额的_____%的货款,计_____USD(大写:_____美元)。

√ **海洋运输保险条款**

1. 责任范围

本保险分为平安险,水渍险及一切险三种,被保险货物遭受损失时,本保险按照保险上订明承保险别的条款规定,负赔偿责任。

1) 平安险

本保险负责赔偿:

(1) 被保险货物在运输途中由于恶劣气候,雷电、海啸、地震、洪水自然灾害造成整批货物的全部损失或推定全损。当被保险人要求赔付推定全损时,须将受损货物及其权利委付给保险公司。被保险货物用驳船运往或运离海轮的,每一驳船所装的货物可视作一个整批。

推定全损是指被保险货的实际全损已经不可避免,或者恢复、修复受损货物以及运送货物到原定目的地的费用超过该目的地的货物价值。

(2) 由于运输工具遭受搁浅、触礁、沉没、互撞,与流冰或其他物体碰撞以及失火、爆炸意外事故造成货物的全部或部分损失。

(3) 在运输工具已经发生搁浅、触礁、沉没、焚毁等意外事故的情况下,货物在此前后又在海上遭受恶劣气候,雷电、海啸等自然灾害所造成的部分损失。

(4) 在装卸或转运时由于一件或数件整件货物落海造成的全部或部分损失。

(5) 被保险人对遭受承保责任内危险的货物采取抢救、防止或减少货损的措施而支付的合理费用,但以不超过该批被救货物的保险金额为限。

(6) 运输工具遭遇海难后,在避难港由于卸货所引起的损失以及在中途港、避难港由于卸货、存仓以及运送货物所产生的特别费用。

(7) 共同海损的牺牲、分摊和救助费用。

(8) 运输契约订有"船舶互撞责任"条款,根据该条款规定应由货方偿还船方的损失。

2) 水渍险

除包括上列平安险的各项责任外,本保险还负责被保险货物由于恶劣气候,雷电、海啸、地震、洪水自然灾害所造成的部分损失。

3) 一切险

除包括上列平安险和水渍险的各项责任外,本保险还负责被保险货物在运输途中由于外来原因所致的全部或部分损失。

2. 除外责任

本保险对下列损失不负赔偿责任:

1) 被保险人的故意行为或过失所造成的损失。

2) 属于发货人责任所引起的损失。

3) 在保险责任开始前,被保险货物已存在的品质不良或数量短差所造成的损失。

4) 被保险货物的自然损耗、本质缺陷、特性以及市价跌落;运输迟延所引起的损失或费用。

5) 公司海洋运输货物战争险条款和货物运输罢工险条款规定的责任范围和除外责任。

Reference Translation of Some Contracts (Part Four, Chapter 7)

✓ 3.2 寄售协议

ABC公司,注册地在中国上海××(以下简称寄售人),与XYZ公司,注册地在××(以下简称代售人),按下列条款签订本协议:

1. 寄售人将不断地把××(货物)运交给代售人代售。货物价格为市场CIF市价,约隔90天运交一次。
2. 代售人在征得寄售人对价格、条款等同意之后,必须尽力以最好价格出售寄售商品。
3. 开始阶段,每次船运货物的价格不得超过××美元,代售人未偿付的货款不能超过××美元。
4. 寄售人对赊销造成的坏帐不负任何责任,代售人在任何时候均负有支付寄售人货款的义务。
5. 代售人将接受寄售人开立的以代售人为付款人的90天远期汇票,年利×%。
6. 代售人以签字信托收据从寄售人银行换取包括提单在内的装运单据。
7. 寄售人负担货物售出之前的保险费和仓储费。
8. 寄售人必须遵守××政府的规章。
9. 本协议英文正本两份,双方各持一份。

双方确认上述内容,并于_____(时间)签字立约,以资证明。

ABC公司:_____   XYZ公司:_____
(签字)   (签字)

✓ 4. 补偿贸易合同

编号:

本合同由ABC公司,主营业所在中国××(以下称甲方),与PPT公司,主营业所在美国××(以下称乙方)于_____(时间)在中国××签订。

兹证明

鉴于乙方拥有现用于制造钢丝绳的机器设备,并愿意将机器设备卖给甲方;

鉴于乙方同意购买甲方用乙方提供的机器设备生产的钢丝绳,以补偿其机器设备的价款;

鉴于甲方同意从乙方购买该项机器设备;

鉴于甲方同意向乙方出售钢丝绳,以偿还乙方的机器设备价款;

因此,考虑到本协议所述的前提及约定,甲乙双方特此立约:

1. 购买协议

　　甲方同意从乙方按下列条款购买下述商品:

1.1　商品、规格及其生产能力

　　　商品:

　　　规格:

　　　生产能力:

1.2　数量

1.3　价格

　　　××港FOB价:

　　　单价:　　　总价:

1.4　支付

　　机器设备价款以甲方的产品——钢丝绳偿还,全部价款在连续3年内平均3次付清,自××日开始支付。

1.5　装运

　　　装运期:　　　装运港:

　　　目的港:　　　装运唛头:

1.6　保险

　　　由甲方保险

1.7　检验

1.8　保证

　　乙方保证其机器设备从未用过,性能先进,质量好,并保证该机器能生产××规格钢丝绳,产量每小时××米。

2. 销售协议

甲方以钢丝绳偿还购买乙方机器设备的价款。

2.1　商品及规格

　　　商品:钢丝绳

规格:

2.2　数量

　　钢丝绳每年××米。其价格为每年××(美元)。

2.3　价格

　　钢丝绳的价格按交货时国际市场CIF价确定。

2.4 装运

每年两次装运，一次在6月，另一次在12月，每次货价为××。

装运港：

目的港：

装运唛头：

2.5 包装

木卷轴装。

2.6 支付

凭以甲方为受益人的保兑的、不可撤销的即期信用证支付，允许转船。

信用证必须于装运日期前15天到达甲方，有效期不少于90天。信用证要与本合同完全一致。否则，乙方对迟装负责，而且甲方有权就其中的损失向乙方提出索赔。修改信用证的费用由乙方承担。

2.7 保险

甲方保险，投保水渍险和战争险，按投保金额为发票金额加10%。

2.8 检验

甲方出具的品质检验书为最后依据。若货到后乙方发现质量与上述规定不符，乙方在货到目的港后45天内通知甲方，双方协商解决有争议的问题。

3. 不可抗力

若因不可抗力事件，甲方或乙方对未交或迟交本合同项下的部分或全部货物不负责任。

4. 仲裁

有关或执行本合同的一切争议应该友好协商解决。若达不成协议，有关争议案则提交××仲裁。仲裁决定为终局的，并对双方均具有约束力。

5. 适用法律

本合同的签订，解释和履行以中华人民共和国法律为准。

6. 正本条款

本合同以英文书写，正本两份，双方各持一份。

7. 有效期

甲方： 乙方：

_____ _____

(签字) (签字)

A List of Abbreviations and Simplified Words Commonly Used in Trading Documents

a.a.	after arrival	到达以后
A.A.R.	against all risks	保一切险
Abt.	about	大约
A/C; acct.	account	账户
acc.	acceptance	承兑
A. D.	Anno Domino	公元(后)
Add.	address	地址
adv.	advance/advice	预付/通知
agrt.	agreement	协议
agt.	agent	代理
A/M	above mentioned	上述
amdt.	amendment	修改
Amt.	amount	金额
A.N.	arrival notice	到货通知
A/O	account of	由……付账
App.	appendix	附录
Approx.	approximately	大约
A.R.	all risks	一切险
Art.No.	article number	货号
A/S	at sight	见票
A.T.L.	actual total loss	实际全损
att.	attached	附
av.	average	平均海损
A/W	actual weight	实际重量, 净重

BAF	bunker adjustment factor	燃油附加费
bal.	balance	余额
B.B.Clause	both to blame collision clause	船舶互撞条款
B/C	bill for collection	托收汇票
B/D	bank draft/bill discounted	银行汇票/贴现汇票
bdle.	bundle	捆
B/E	bill of exchange/bill of entry	汇票/进口报告书
b/f	brought forward	承前页
B/G	bonded goods	保税货物
B/L	bill of lading	提单
B/O	buyer's option/branch office	买方选择/分公司
BOC	Bank of China	中国银行
B/P	bill of payable/bill purchases	付票据/出口押汇
br.	branch	分支机构
brl.	barrel	桶
BSC	bunker surcharge	燃油附加费
btl	bottle	瓶
CAF	currency adjustment factor	货币调整附加费
CAD	cash against delivery	货到付款
C. A. D.	cash against document	凭单据付款
Capt.	Captain	船长
C. B. D.	cash before delivery	付现交货
COD	cash on delivery	货到付款
cat.	catalogue; category	目录
C.C.	carbon copy	抄本
CCIB	China Commodity Inspection Bureau	中国商检局
CCPIT	China Council for the Promotion of International Trade	中国贸促会
Cert.	certificate	证明书
c/f	carried forward	续后页
CFR	cost and freight	成本加运费价
cft.	cubic feet	立方英尺
cgo.	cargo	货物
C. H.	Custom House	海关
chg.	charge	费用
CIC	China Insurance Clause	中国保险条款
CIF	cost, insurance and freight	成本、保险加运费价
C.I.O.	cash in order	订货时付款

ck.	check	支票
CNFTTC	China National Foreign Trade Transportation Corp.	中国对外贸易运输公司
C/O	certificate of origin	原产地证书
comm..	commission	佣金
COSA	China Ocean Shipping Agent	中国外轮代理公司
COSCO	China Ocean Shipping Company	中国远洋运输公司
C/P	charter party	租船合同
C/R	cargo receipt	货物承运收据
c/s	cases	箱
C.T.L.	constructive total loss	推定全损
D/A	documents against acceptance	承兑交单
D/D	demand draft	即期汇票
dd.	dated	日期
D/F	dead freight	空舱费
diam.	diametre	直径
disc.	discount	折扣
doc.	document	单证
D/O	delivery order	提货单
D/P	documents against payment	付款交单
d/s	days sight	见票……天
dup.	duplicate	副本
EEC	European Economic Community	欧洲经济共同体
E/L	export license	出口许可证
EMS	express mail service	特快专递
encl.	enclosure	附件
E.O.M.	end of the month	月底
E.O.S.	end of the season	季底
E.O.Y.	end of the year	年底
ETA	estimated time of arrival	预计到达时间
ETD	estimated time of departure	预计离港时间
ETS	estimated time of sailing	预计开航时间
Ex		1. (合同、运输上)"出自";"在……交货"; 2. (证券上)"没有";"免除"
F.A.	freight agent	货运代理行
FM	from	自

FOB	free on board	离岸价格
F.O.C	free of charge	免费
F.P.A.	free from particular average	平安险
frt.	freight	运费
F.Y.I.	for your information	供你参考
GATT	General Agreement on Tariff and Trade	关税与贸易协定
Gr. Wt.	gross weight	毛重
GSP	generalized system of preferences	普遍优惠制
H.O.	head office	总公司
ICC	International Chamber of Commerce	国际商会
ID	idem the same	同前
i.e.	id est=that is	即是
I/L	import license	进口许可证
IMF	International Monetary Fund	国际货币基金
IMP	international market price	国际市场价格
INCOTERMS	International Chamber of Commerce Terms	国际贸易术语
I.O.P.	irrespective of percentage	不计免赔率
I.Q.	import quota	进口配额
Lb.	pounds	磅
L/C	letter of credit	信用证
Max.	maximum	最高
Min.	minimum	最低
M.I.P.	marine insurance policy	海运保险单
M/S	motor ship	轮船
M/T	mail transfer/multimodal transport	信汇/多式联运
N.A., N/A	no acceptance/not applicable	拒绝承兑/不适用
N/M	no mark	无标记
O/C	outward collection	出口托收
Orig.	original	正本,原件
P.A.	particular average	单独海损
p.a.	per annum	每年
pct.	percent	百分比
P.O.D.	payment on delivery	付款交货
prem.	premium	保险费
prox.	proximo=next month	下月
ppt.	prompt	即时的
P.S.	postscript	附言

P.T.O.	please turn over	请阅后页
Q.E.F.	quod erat faciendum	这就是所要寻求的
Q.E.I.	quod etat inveniendum	这就是所要找的
Re.	with reference	关于
Rev.	revocable	可撤销的
R.F.W.D.	rain and/or fresh water damage	雨淋淡水险
S/C	sales confirmation	售货确认书
S/D	short delivery/sight draft	交货短缺／即期汇票
Sgd.	Signed	签字
shpt	shipment	装运
SINOTRANS	China National Foreign Trade Transportation Corporation	中国外贸运输公司
S/O	shipping order	装货单
spec.	specification	规格
S.R.C.C.	strike, riot and civil commotion	罢工险
Stg.	Sterling	英镑
Std.	standard	标准
tgm.	telegram	电报
T.L.O.	total loss only	全损险
T.P.N.D.	theft pilferage and non-delivery	偷窃及提货不着险
T/R	trust receipt	信托收据
T/T	telegraphic transfer	电汇
UCP	uniform customs & practice	统一惯例
U/M	under-mentioned	下述
via.	by way of	经由
viz.	namely	即是
V.V.	vice versa	反过来
W.A.	with average	水渍险
Whf.	wharf	码头
W/W	warehouse to warehouse clause	仓至仓条款
Yd (s)	yard (s)	英码
Z	zone	地区

Frequent Words and Phrases in Foreign Trade

acceptance	承兑
accountee	开证人(记入该账户下)
accreditor	开证人(委托开证人)
action	诉讼, 对……起诉
advising bank	通知行
advanced B/L	预借提单
advanced payment	预付货款
alias	别名
anti-dated B/L	倒签提单
appeal	上诉
arbitration	仲裁
assured	被保险人
available by draft at sight	凭即期汇票付款
beneficiary	受益人
by order of...	奉……之命
by parcel post	邮包装运
bona fide	真正的,真诚的
capacity	容积
carrier	承运人
caveat emptor	货物一经售出,卖主概不负责
certificate of age of vessel	船龄证明
certificate of registry	注册证明(船舶)
certificate of quantity	数量证明
certificate of origin	产地证明

claim	索赔
clean bill collection	光票托收
clean bill of lading	清洁提单
clearance of goods	结关
commercial invoice	商业发票
combined invoice	联合发票
condition	条件
confirming bank	保兑行
confirmed L/C/ unconfirmed L/C	保兑信用证/不保兑信用证
consignee	收货人
cost	成本
current price	时价
customs broker	报关行
customs duty	关税
customs invoice	海关发票
damage	赔偿损失,赔偿金
defendant	被告
description of goods	商品名称
deferred payment L/C	延付信用证
direct routing	最短航线
direct port	直达港
discharge	卸货
discount	贴现
dishonor	拒付
divisible L/C	可分割信用证
distribution center	分配(运销)中心
documents	单据
door to door	门到门(集装箱运输)
documentary L/C	跟单信用证
dockage rate	停泊费,码头费
dockmen	码头工人
drawee	受票人,付款人
drawer	出票人,收款人
draft	汇票;船的吃水
drawn on (upon)	以(某人)为付款人
drayage or cartage	(本地)运费
duly	适当地
eastbound	东向运输

effect	结果,效果,实施
endorsement	背书
endorsement in full	完全背书
endorsement in blank	空白背书
establishing bank	开证行
export duties	出口税
exceptions	溢短残损,除外
expenses	费用
for account of...	付……人帐
for the amount of USD...	金额为美元……
force majeure	不可抗力
freight forwader	运输行
fragile	易碎商品
freight	运费
free port	自由港
free trade zone	自由贸易区
free perimeter	自由过境区
freight prepaid	运费付讫
general terms and conditions	一般贸易条款
handle with care	小心轻放
hold men	舱内装卸工
holder	汇票持有人
in duplicate	一式两份
including packing charges	包括包装费
inland	内陆
inland transportation agent	内陆运输代理商
inspection certificate	检验证明
insurance	保险
insurance declaration	保险声明
inter alia	特别
in triplicate	一式三份
issuing bank	开证行
keep dry	切勿受潮
keep upright	切勿倒置
keep cool	放在阴凉处
keep on deck	甲板装运
keep in hold	装在舱内
keep flat	必须平放
leakage and breakage	漏损和破损

longshoreman	码头搬运工人
loading	装货, 装载
margin	押金, 保证金
modes of transportation	运输方式
measurement list	尺码单
more or less clause	溢短条款
most favored nation treatment	最惠国待遇
negotiation	议付
negotiation bank	议付行
no turning over	切勿倾倒
no dumping	切勿投掷
on behalf of...	代表……
on board B/L	已装船提单
on deck B/L	甲板提单
on deck risk	舱面险
opener	开证人
opening bank	开证银行
optional	可选择的
optional charge	选港费
order B/L	指示提单
origin	原产地
original B/L	正本提单
outer packing	外包装
overland transportation policy	陆运保险单
partial shipment allowed	允许分批装运
payment	支付
payee	受款人
payer	付款人
packed in case	装入箱内
parcel post risk	邮包险
parcel receipt	邮包收据
parties	当事人
paying bank	付款行
payment in advance	预付贷款
payment guarantee	付款保证书
per annum	每年
per capita	人均
per cent	每百分之
per conta	在另一方, 在对方

per diem	按日
per mensem	按月
performance guarantee	履约保证书
plaintiff	原告
prompt shipment	即装
premium	保险费
presentation	提示
prima facie	初次印象
principal	开证人, 委托开证人
proforma invoice	形式发票
proposal	申请
protest	拒付证书
proviso	附文; 限制性条款
quantity discount	数量折扣
quasi	好像; 类似的; 准的
quid pro quo	交换条件; 等同物; 赔偿; 报酬
quorum	法定人数
rebat	回佣
recourse	追索权
reimbursing bank	偿付行
restrictive endorsement	限制性背书
retail price	零售价
revocable L/C	可撤销信用证
revolving L/C	循环信用证
risk of contamination	沾污险
risk of mold (mould)	发霉险
risk of shortage	短缺险
risk of rusting	锈损险
routing	运输路线
scheduled service	定期班轮
sea-worthy packing	适合海运包装
settling agent	理赔代理人(保险)
settlement of exchange	结汇
shipper (consigner, consignor)	托运人
shipping company's certificate	船公司证明
shipping space	舱位
shipping order	装货单
sight L/C	即期信用证
usance L/C	远期信用证

specification	规格
space charter	订船
special additional risk	特别附加险
special endorsement	特别背书
special preference	优惠关税
specification list	规格明细表
spot price	现货价
supercargo	(商船)押运员
tariff	运费表, 税则
term	开庭期, 偿债期; 条款
this side up	此端向上
terminal	码头, 水陆交接点, 终点站
through B/L	联运提单
time charter	定期租轮
time drafts	远期汇票
time of delivery	交货时间
time of payment	付款期限
time of shipment	装运日期
time policy	期限保险单
tort	侵权
total value	总价
total amount	总金额
to insure	投保
transferable L/C	可转让信用证
transshipment allowed	允许转船
transshipment B/L	转船提单
transloading	交接转运
transship	转船, 转运
transit zone	自由贸易区
unscheduled service	不定期班轮
untransferable L/C	不可转让信用证
use no hooks	切勿用钩
usual practice	习惯做法
verdict	裁决
volume	容量
westbound	西向运输
wharfage	码头费
wharfage rate	码头收费率
wooden case	木箱

APPENDIX VI References

曹祖平：《国际商务写作高级教程》，北京：中国人民大学出版社，2005年7月。

陈永生、赵金仲、陈晓鹏、杨栋：《国际商务函电与合同》，北京：华语教学出版社，1999年7月。

傅伟良：《英文合同写作指要》，北京：商务印书馆，2002年1月。

郝绍伦：《英语实用文大全》，成都：电子科技大学出版社，1996年1月。

胡庚申、王春晖、申云桢：《国际商务合同起草与翻译》，北京：外文出版社，2001年3月。

胡鹏：《简历，让你脱颖而出》（第3版），北京：机械工业出版社，2011年5月。

黎海斌：《现代英语应用文写作指南》，上海：上海大学出版社，2004年1月。

李学术：《实用英语写作（非英语专业）》，北京：机械工业出版社，2005年7月。

廖瑛：《国际商务英语—商务理论、语言与实务》，长沙：中南大学出版社，2002年2月。

刘宝宏：《国际贸易单证实务全书》，北京：中国对外经济贸易出版社，1997年11月。

刘梅华：《MBA联考英语高分突破——翻译·写作》，北京：北京航天大学出版社，2002年9月。

戚云方：《合同与合同英语》，杭州：浙江大学出版社，2004年8月。

石定乐、蔡蔚：《实用商务英语写作》，北京：北京理工大学出版社，2003年8月。

宋天锡、任英：《英语应用文写作》，北京：中国书籍出版社，2002年7月。

汤平平：《商务秘书实用英语》，北京：中国建材工业出版社，2004年8月。

王宏俐、师琳：《国际学术交流英语》，西安：西安交通大学出版社，2012年5月。

王燕希：《广告英语一本通》，北京：对外经济贸易大学出版社，2004年6月。

吴林康：《国际贸易支付方式》，北京：外语教学与研究出版社，1989年10月。

夏蓓洁：《英语实用写作教程》，合肥：中国科学技术大学出版社，2012年7月。

尹小莹：《外贸英语函电》（第3版），西安：西安交通大学出版社，2004年2月。

余世明、丛凤英：《国际商务单证》，广州：暨南大学出版社，2001年7月。

张传德：《商务英语》，西安：西安交通大学出版社，2003年8月。

张青、吴定敏、齐戈等：《当代英语写作教学研究》，长春：吉林大学出版社，2012年7月。

赵培：《应用文写作模板及演练》，北京：中国宇航出版社，2005年8月。